SECURITY IN A WEB2.0+ WORLD

SECURITY IN A WEB2.0+ WORLD

A STANDARDS BASED APPROACH

C. SOLARI
and Contributors

A John Wiley and Sons, Ltd, Publication

This edition first published 2009
© 2009, John Wiley & Sons, Ltd

Registered office
John Wiley & Sons Ltd, The Atrium, Southern Gate, Chichester, West Sussex, PO19 8SQ, United
Kingdom

For details of our global editorial offices, for customer services and for information about how to
apply for permission to reuse the copyright material in this book please see our website at www.
wiley.com.

ISBN 978-0-470-74575-5

Set in 10/13 Optima by Thomson Digital
Printed in the USA by Courier Westford

About the Authors and Contributors...

Taking the challenge to write this book it was clear to me that it would need the contributions of many ideas, many hands. These ideas and concepts, and much of the actual writing are a composite of these hands and minds. Dr. Mike Schabel, Ty Sagalow, Bob Thornberry, Marco Raposo and Aleksei Resetko were contributors to Chapters 2 and 3. Mike, in particular, lent his expertise to the topic of wireless broadband communications.

Dr. Jim Kennedy wrote Chapter 4. Uma Chandrashekhar, Andrew McGee, Rao Vasireddy with others at Bell Laboratories were the developers of the Bell Labs Security Framework that became the ITU-T X.805 Recommendation. Their ideas and writings are central to this book particularly with Chapters 5 and 6.

Bob West of Echelon One with the support of Eric Green and Kirsten Francissen contributed throughout bringing the message to conclusion in Chapters 7 and 8. A special mention of Rod Beckstrom and Ty Sagalow; their contributions will open a new area of investigation to understanding the economics of cyber security.

There were a number of reviewers; John Reece in particular added great insight.

Leaving Wyatt Starnes to last is intended to single out his particular contribution. He will see his ideas throughout this book; in effect the central message of this book has been his life's work. We all owe him a great deal of gratitude for his quiet but forceful campaign to get the message through about metrics, about root of creation, about aftermarket security as an ineffective approach.

Thank you Wyatt, and thank you to all that made these important contributions.

To close, we give special acknowledgement to Dan Geer for his foreword. His prose is unmatched - we stand in awe.

—Carlos Solari

Contents

physical world begin to meld without the recognition that both need to be protected with the same vigilance.

up front in the development life cycle. It will take more than the logic of why it should be done – it will take an active role in these three domains. It starts with the buyers of technology applying the leverage of purchasing in large numbers to change a behavior already ingrained.

Foreword

Perhaps it does not need saying yet again, but security is a means, not an end. For this reason, and because technological advance is growing faster, the "means" that comprise security today are likely to be short lived, yet means short-lived-ness is not a free pass to ignore them, to put no effort into evolving them. Ends are not short lived.

Most of us who earn our keep in the security trade are well aware of the essentialness of constant adaptation. This constant adaptation is a prerequisite to getting one's job done; ironically, constant adaptation applies to both Bad Guys and Good Guys. Our problem is that the Bad Guys enjoy a structural advantage over the Good Guys: where in the physical world it is the crook who must engineer the perfect crime and the police who have all the time they need, in the digital world it is the policeman who has to be perfect and the crook who can be patient.

That the Good Guys are at a disadvantage is not a first-principles deduction by some logician – it is merely an observation. Looking back over the last decade, it is easy to observe that the amount of treasure and labor being expended on security has risen very fast indeed. At the same time, the loss of goods and control engineered by the opposition has risen. We are many. They are few. We are losing. They are winning. The reason is structural.

When you are at a structural disadvantage, the first choice might be to just get out of the game. Who wants to play baccarat against a crooked croupier? Or take a spitball when the umpire works for the other team? Better to play at another casino. Better to stand on another diamond. Sadly or not, getting out of the digital security game is not in the cards.

Something else has to happen.

We are dependent on the kind of networked cooperation made possible such a short time ago with the appearance of Mosaic (March

14, 1993, to be precise). The rate of change, even in the short retrospect of sixteen years, proves that predicting future change is an unlikely business. The one prediction that seems assured is that we may think we are dependent on networked communications today, but we ain't seen nothin' yet! Web 2.0 will see to that because, if nothing else, it is already doing so – a kind of proof-by-demonstration that William Gibson's famous bon mot embraces, "the future is already here, just unevenly distributed." If we are going to be so dependent on Web 2.0 that society literally could not survive without it, and do that in a world where the opposition has an all-but-permanent structural advantage, it really is time to get serious. As the 44th President said in his Inaugural Address, "In the words of Scripture, the time has come to set aside childish things."

This book is about setting aside childish things, such as assuming that somehow we'll muddle through. Marcus Ranum may have sounded cynical to some ears when he said: "Will the future be more secure? It'll be just as insecure as it possibly can, while still continuing to function. Just like today." But he didn't sound cynical to my ear. The difference is that the complexity of the Web 2.0 + world and our dependence on it makes the core of Ranum's remark, "while still continuing to function," the core of whatever debate there still is.

(Look,) It is entirely clear that convergence of nearly all communications-based functions in the economy and in society to Internet-based communications is inevitable if not already true. It is entirely unarguable that increasing quantities of data that make all this convenience work are held not on one's desk but on the Web itself. It is entirely predictable that the more dependent we are on something, the more its vulnerabilities matter and the more our opponents will invest in R&D aimed at it. So, Points #1 and #2: Web 2.0 is irresistible so long as it works, and the only real failure would be a loss of trust after some unignorable security shortcoming – everything else is fungible.

There is a joking restatement of the Three Laws of Thermodynamics that goes like this:

You can't win

You can't break even

You can't get out of the game

That is where we are: we cannot get out of the security game because we cannot get out of the Web 2.0 game, even if we wanted to. (Which we don't.) That we are at a structural disadvantage is just a restatement that we can't win. That we can't break even says that what we do for security will be judged as all risk management is judged: by what did not happen as much as by what did. Them's the breaks.

Behavioral psychologists will tell you that you begin to change outcome the minute you begin visibly taking data. If security is a process in its operation and a mindset otherwise, then it is time we took some data. In a structural disadvantage where success is when nothing happens, our aim is to be a less attractive target than someone else so that the things that must happen, happen to that someone else. This isn't jaded. This is Real Politik.

The authors of this book have set out to do a difficult thing, and that is to transmit what they know about how to think. In a complex world addicted to convenience, how to think often seems like an expensive hobby compared to what button to press, what exactly to do. As complexity grows, what button to press may be the only thing all but the few can do. How to think is not so quick, and it is never cut-and-dried. How to think doesn't tell you what button to press, and knowing what button to press proves nothing except that you can follow instructions. Knowing what button to press is nevertheless good enough when you don't have sentient opponents, only accidents and stray alpha particles. Knowing what button to press is useless when the opponent is sentient and is gaming you. When sentient opponents are what you are up against, you need to be able to think. You need to be able to out-think.

We all know from long experience that (1) there are never enough experts to go around, and (2) that security must be built-in rather than bolted-on. In our current world situation, it is probably fair to say that the demand for security expertise so outstrips supply that the charlatan fraction is rising. As such, some way to extend the reach of the expertise we do have would be a Very Good Thing. Because we all know that an ounce of built-in security is worth many, many pounds of field upgrades. No rational observer would argue other than that the scarce expertise absolutely must be deployed at the earliest possible stage of development, which is to say where the supply-demand imbalance is least and the leverage on what supply we do have is greatest.

Thus we come to the point of this book. By whatever precise definition you choose, Web 2.0 is the future, it is already here if unevenly distributed, and it needs security built-in, not bolted on. The best expertise we have needs to be in the front end of every Web 2.0 construction. Sure, some constructions have already been done, and, let us hope, done well. But there is a lot more to come and it needs our collective best skill if we are not to create something really bad. But how?

The answer is discipline, and discipline in the form of standards and, even, Standards. Sure, standards (or Standards) are sometimes just so much bureaucracy and self-flattery. That is not the case here. Yes, there are people who are so good at what they do that standards (or Standards) just get in the way.

There are too few of those folks to matter, and they won't live forever. If there is anything the last six months in finance have shown, it is that we humans are abundantly capable of building systems more complex than we can understand when in operation. As Mike O'Dell used to say, "Left to themselves creative engineers will deliver the most complex system they think they can debug." Given the stakes in security for Web 2.0, we have to do better, we have to get security right up front, or it is game-over.

Getting it right means using the all-too-rare skills to lay down the path of discipline, using discipline to build security in, and using built-in security to make the world safe for Web 2.0 and all it promises. That's what this book is about – taking the skill now encoded in a Standard, using that Standard to operationalize discipline, and using that discipline to build some security in.

If you have a better idea, all I can say is "Let's hear it" and, maybe, "Where have you been?"

—Daniel E. Geer, Jr., ScD

Prologue

We live in an age of great uncertainty – a period of unprecedented technical innovation that is transforming our lives. It is innovation that accelerates even as we harbor an unquiet sense of the unknown destination; where does all this new technology take us and what becomes of us in the process? Ray Kurzweil, a pre-eminent technology innovator spoke to this point of innovation acceleration at Harvard University, mindful he said of the "intertwined nature of the risks and benefits". It was February 2005. If only it could be slowed down enough that we can better understand the promise of its benefits and calculate the severity of its risks.

But innovation cannot be slowed; it runs along its own course with a gathering momentum fuelled by competitive global markets and not beholden to any other law than the one that states simply: "technology begets technology at an ever-increasing rate."

Nowhere is the uncertainty associated with accelerating innovation more pronounced than in the world of cyberspace, where information technology insinuates itself into every nook and corner and then transforms itself with blinding speed. In the world of cyberspace, we are faced with the challenge of trying to secure new territory without having entirely figured out how to protect the present – the cyber security dimension of cyberspace.

It is perhaps easiest to illustrate the challenge we face by recalling the well-known story of the frog in the cauldron of boiling water. A frog that is dropped into a cauldron of boiling water will immediately leap out to save itself. However, if this same frog is placed in a cauldron filled with tepid water that is then only gradually brought to a boil its reaction is very different. Because the increase in temperature is gradual, the frog stays put not realizing its predicament until the water reaches the boiling point and by then it is too late.

Consider in this story similarities with *Security in a Web 2.0+ World*. The present networks remain unprotected; mastery of the security paradigm remains an elusive target. So what is this ill-defined world of Web 2.0?[1] What is the risk today, and how can one address the growing risk tomorrow? The temperature is rising, yet complacency rules. It is time to sense the growing danger and make the necessary response.

There is a dilemma, however, in discussing the topic of cyber security – a problem of communication where policy makers and technologists speak, but in a language that fails to inform one to the other and fails to inject a sound understanding. Simple questions go unasked and unanswered. How serious is the problem of cyber security? Are the issues correctable, and how much time is there to take corrective measures? While risk assessments are done daily, the metrics of assessing the vulnerability of new technologies are not consistently agreed upon and not well practiced.

"We have not been able to easily discern what threats we would face, what the tools of influence would be, or who would become our opponents. The outcome has been a kind of strategic indecision that puts the United States at risk."[2]

There is general agreement on a few points, yet, these same points also illustrate why the answers are not easily forthcoming. Security is not intrinsically separate from the business functions; it is a measure of overall business risk represented in the terms of cost. What does it cost the company to lose access to the functions supported by the network and by this determination how much should be spent in security to protect against this loss? This question, addressed in Chapter 2, needs to be answered in order to better calculate business risk. Security metrics, the science of measuring security, remains undefined and so it is not well practiced. There is more to lose in financial terms and in tarnished reputations, but how much, and to what degree of impact remains a degree of conjecture.

---

[1] According to the definition available at www.wikipedia.org, "Web 2.0" describes the changing trends in the use of World Wide Web technology and web design that aim to enhance creativity, communications, secure information sharing, collaboration and functionality of the web. Note: this and other definitions obtained from the Wikipedia are licensed under the GNU Free Documentation License.

[2] *CSIS Commission on Cybersecurity for the 44th Presidency. Securing Cyberspace for the 44th Presidency.* (p. 12). Washington: Government Printing Office, 2008.

To begin to answer these questions requires putting in place the foundational constructs of technical and process metrics, the economics of loss in the era of "*cyber-value*", and to communicate the concepts of cyber security from policy to technology clearly. In the absence of these constructs, one can anticipate what is already happening: policy disconnected from reality and bureaucracy that exacerbates rather than remedies. There are many already arguing this point with Sarbanes-Oxley[3] and the California Senate Bill 1386 (SB 1386).[4] Policy without the metrics to determine its effectiveness often ends up creating a spiral of increasing costs without the intended benefits.

To better understand and communicate the issues of cyber security between policy maker and technologist requires an effort to speak to both in a manner that each can understand. With this intention, each chapter in this book begins with its own executive summary; speaking to the policy maker: the business executive, the academician, and government executive. Transitioning to the body of each chapter, the target audience shifts. It is meant not just for the security professional, but for all makers and developers of the information communications technology (ICT) systems, a term applied in this book encompassing traditional "IT" or information technology (thought of with data networks) and telecommunications systems (thought of with telephony and video systems). To embed security in the ICT systems, will require first that one begin with explaining the principles of good practice for security design to the engineers who make the products and systems.

The target audience is thus a broad population, ranging from those who need to know enough about cyber security to make effective policy decisions to the engineers who design the ICT systems. The book does not cover how to encrypt data, but where it should be considered and in what measure it should be applied. In this manner, it aims to lessen the mystery surrounding cyber security and present it as sound engineering principles that need to be applied in the right measure.

Three key points will be stated and reinforced in later chapters. The first is that there is not much time; years cannot be spent to begin the process of embedding security into current and future systems. The second is that there is a need for models that allow one to measure security in the design stage, in deployment and in production. With

---

[3] www.soxlaw.com

[4] http://info.sen.ca.gov/pub/01-02/bill/sen/sb_1351-1400/sb_1386_bill_20020926_-chaptered.html

the use of better security models, one can expect a lessening of the dependency on cyber security experts and transform the practice of security more to the science of metrics, baselines and business-rational remediation. This book proposes two models that can help make this transformation – the X.805 standard[5] and the security value life cycle. Both of these models will work toward creating greater transparency as a way to bring a more finely grained trust context into computing transactions.

The final point is that the stakes could not be higher. This will be said repeatedly: Information communications technology is embedded in the whole of technology and becoming more so with each day that we automate to improve operational efficiency and compete in the global markets.

To understand the issue of *how much time,* one needs to look no further than the *convergence* of technology and the emergence of Web 2.0 computing. *Convergence* is the move from separate infrastructures and technologies for voice, video and data to one technology platform – Internet Protocol (IP) – and toward a unified infrastructure, not separate plants.

Convergence is happening around the world – one can recognize it in the marketing speak of *triple play*[6] and IPTV,[7] as two examples. When the convergence is done, it will be too late and too expensive to redesign these systems and protect them against a hostile environment of hackers working with organized crime

There is little time to ensure that security is engineered into the systems that the wonderful benefits of convergence and Web 2.0 computing are designed to withstand the rigors of the inherent risk. As an example, "new pay-TV market data indicates that IPTV will grow by an estimated 32 percent annually over the next six years to nearly 79 million subscribers globally by the end of 2014."[8] The dependency is deep and more intertwined in everyday life.

---

[5] http://www.itu.int/rec/T-REC-X.805-200310-I/en

[6] www.wikipedia.org - tripleplay: In telecommunications, the triple play service is a marketing term for the provisioning of the two broadband services, high-speed Internet access and television, and one narrowband service, telephone, over a single broadband connection. Triple play focuses on a combined business model rather than solving technical issues or a common standard.

[7] www.wikipedia.org - IPTV is a system where a digital television service is delivered using Internet Protocol over a network infrastructure, which may include delivery by a broadband connection.

[8] Richard Grigonis, "IPTV (Telco TV) Tops Pay-TV Platform Growth at 32 Percent", http://www.tmcnet.com/channels/3g-voip-iptv-performance/articles/48691-iptv-telco-tv-tops-pay-tv-platform-growth.htm (January 14, 2009)

1

The World of Cyber Security in 2019

"The semantic Web – what is called Web 3.0[1] – is commonplace in 2019. The start of the Internet and the World Wide Web is the stuff of legacy and lore. Amid the concerns of ICT security is another dimension – the clash of virtual realities such as between the Second Life® virtual world and the physical lives. Decisions in the virtual world drive material reactions in the real world – as they are now one world with no safeguards in place."

Executive Summary

It is 2019 AD or 28 AW (after the Web), counting in years after the introduction of the World Wide Web.[2] Contrary to some predictions, ICT systems continue to be one of the primary agents of change in our lifetimes and in the history of humankind. The pace of change has been nothing short of spectacular. There have been many winners and losers as the exponential growth of technology gives rise to new and wider social divisions. This change ripples through societies, cultures and nations with unintended consequences that are too numerous to count.

---

[1] www.wikipedia.org - Web. 3.0 is one of the terms used to describe the evolutionary stage of the Web that follows Web 2.0.

[2] www.wikipedia.org - World Wide Web is a system of interlinked hypertext documents accessed via the Internet.

In hindsight, one can see where things went right and where they have gone terribly wrong. Protecting ICT systems has been one of the great challenges. With 12 years of history, Web 2.0 continues to serve, transform and interconnect the world's cultures. Nothing is left untouched by the Web 2.0 generation as worlds that were once physically and logically separate are now inextricably linked. Generation Y and Generation Z (also known as Millenials), born in the age of computers and the Internet, run the physical and virtual worlds. It is a new world, but is it "brave" or is it "foolhardy."

The threats to cyber security in 2019 are many. How did things get to this point? In hindsight, the answer is all too clear. It just happened degree by degree, like the slow-rising temperature in the cauldron. The gradual slide was something that happened even as it is clear that we could have and should have integrated security into our ICT systems. It is not that the technical know-how was missing, nor was it something that came as a surprise. It was a ripening awareness of the vulnerabilities. By the year 2009, it was understood that security had to be an integral part of system design yet by the absence of forethought, understanding and leadership, the vulnerabilities in ICT systems were left unaddressed. It is 2019 and it's time to pay the piper.

It was a sword that cut both ways; the standardization on all-IP systems is what allowed the world of data, voice and video to blend in ways that created the value of next-generation systems. Web 2.0 applications would not have achieved its broad appeal without the convergence of IP systems. It also meant that the vulnerabilities were many and were both *transmuted*[3] across the different media and infrastructure domains and replicated across the many nodes in the complexity of the Web 2.0 world. Encryption can be broken with powerful computers. Quantum computing is in our midst; even strongly encrypted national systems are at risk.

---

[3] Transmutation, is used to describe the phenomenon where as an example, a virus delivered by email to compromise computers is now re-crafted for telephony.

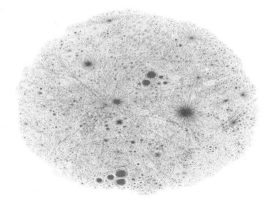

Figure 1.1   Internet Mapping

It is a situation that could have been avoided; the challenge now is to find a way to fix an installed and complex array of systems that are used for almost every type of business. Unfortunately, the complexity of system management and data stored in a dizzying range of formats cannot be remedied without starting over. Bill Cheswick's Internet mapping from 2009 shows a picture of this technology galaxy as ganglions interconnected like a constellation of stars (Figure 1.1). Today, with its accelerated growth, it looks more like a round brown blob – the number of nodes so large that one cannot see space between their connecting points.

Security in complex systems implemented after they are in production is at best a patchwork fix. However, patchwork security is ill-suited to counter the means, motive and opportunity; the deadly triad law enforcement recognizes as the source for crime. The opportunities are endless with global online access. Gone are the constraints of physical separation. The notion of nation-states means little in the global Internet; even parallel private versions of the Internet can be breached.

Vulnerabilities are so commonplace that in the period from January 1, 2007 to December 31, 2007, the IC3 (Internet Crime Complaint Center) Website received 206,884 complaint submissions.[4]

---

[4] Federal Bureau of Investigation, Bureau of Justice Assistance, The National White Collar Crime Center – "*International Crime Complaint Center 2007 Internet Crime Report*" (Washington, DC 2008), 1.

People continue to be the weakest link in the chain, the underlying fact in the social engineering schemes. Crime follows money, and with e-commerce and businesses dependent on online transactions, there is plenty of money-motivation.[5] Politics and world tensions are also motivating factors. Demonstrations have now moved online. Citizen unrest that used to make itself heard in the streets is now expressed through distributed denial of service (DDoS) attacks.[6] It is a very difficult state of affairs. The remedies available are appearing as items on a menu of poor choices dependent upon detecting and responding to a "zero-second" threat. It takes practically no time to form and launch an attack. The average password can be broken in less than ten minutes; the break-in, undetected, is only a prelude to the actual attack.[7] How does one detect and respond to "zero-second" attacks?

Thankfully, it is not the year 2019 as of this writing. 2019 is still some years in the future, and Web 2.0 is still taking shape, as are the next-generation networks that will be the underpinnings of the latest applications and services. What steps can be taken now that will yield a more positive outcome; one where security is a central part of the system design and applied in a balanced approach to the risk? How much time is there? Is there a tipping point when it becomes too late? How close is that point? Interesting questions, indeed and they need immediate answers.

A recent article in CSO Magazine *stated that, "the most risky mobile device is the laptop computer and the number one concern is the inability to properly identify and authenticate remote users."[8]*

The concern is with what can be done *now* using the methods and the technologies already available to set in place the idea that security can be *designed in* to the complex networks that are getting installed now and that will exist in 2019. Web 2.0 is still evolving and it remains

---

[5] "*International Crime Complaint Center 2007 Internet Crime Report*". In 2007 monetary losses totalling $239.09 million with a median dollar loss of $680.00 per complaint

[6] Jeremy Kirk, *Computerworld*, "Estonia recovers from massive DDoS attack", May 17, 2007.

[7] www.hackosis.com.

[8] Dr. Larry Poneman, *CSO Magazine*, "Cyber Crime: The 2009 Mega Threat", www.csoonline.com/article/print/470968 (December 16, 2008).

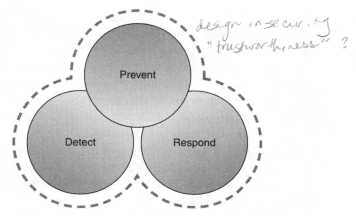

Figure 1.2 The Security Triad

the next great technology promise. There is still a chance to correct the path and *design in* a more secure destiny.

Consider another triad – the security triad of *prevent-detect-respond* as the context for all security functions (Figure 1.2). The *prevent* part of security is where the technologies around *designing in* security fit in and is the focus of this book. Prevention includes another word, overused perhaps, but still significant to this discussion. The word is *trust*. Every day people make decisions about whom they should trust. It remains to be seen whether the makers of the ICT companies will design in the security to achieve trustworthiness as a measurable attribute.

On the question of time, the point of no return after which it will be nearly impossible to achieve a positive outcome for Web 2.0 security is rapidly approaching. IPTV is already gaining a foothold and Voice over IP (VoIP) is already strongly embedded in the corporate world. Video in all its manifestations is being transmitted over IP networks. Separate infrastructures for voice, video and data are collapsing into one flat IP world.

There is also the question of risk. The paradox of Web 2.0 is that many millions of individuals are willing to incur a potential loss of privacy by opting into social networking sites in spite of the apparent risk of identity theft and other abuses that come from sharing personal information on these Web sites. Those who engage in social networking clearly believe that the benefits outweigh the potential risks

Although this book is indirectly concerned with the question of responsibility, it is directly concerned with the questions of *what* can be done and *how* to protect the new Web 2.0 environment, a set of issues that are addressed in Chapter 2. Before embarking on a path that will lead to better security, one must first discover how to measure security and then implement the systems that accomplish this measurement. This process should be based on actual measurements; and be more science than art. "There cannot be a greater mistake than that of looking superciliously upon practical applications of science. The life and soul of science is its practical application."[9] Trust can be measured, given a score, and improvements made on that score while making more informed judgments about levels of access on the basis of this score in real time. This is the value of prevention in the security triad and the point of focus.

Product developers and security professionals possess the know-how to achieve more secure environments. This book presents a set of fairly straightforward rules, and introduces a framework for security design developed in 2003 by scientists at Bell Laboratories.[10] These scientists began by asking themselves some very basic questions about how to measure, baseline and integrate security into complex ICT networks. Finding the answers unsatisfactory, the scientists decided to develop a framework to solve this problem. The framework measures security, identifies the gaps and implements remedies with consistency, rigor and practicality, focusing on such issues as "just enough" security. It is time to get started – time is of the essence.

General Review of Security Challenges

There are new security challenges each time someone invents a way to automate or integrate human activities with ICT systems. In the world of finance, this point was made clear with the scale and speed of the losses that occurred at Société Générale in 2008.[11] In ICT systems, unlike the physical world of vaults and walls, the impact can occur so much faster and reverberate with much greater damage.

---

[9] Lord Kelvin - PLA, vol. 1, "Electrical Units of Measurement", May 3, 1883.

[10] Ashok K. Gupta, Uma Chandrashekhar, Suhasini V. Sabnis, Frank A. Bastry, "Building secure products and solutions," *Bell Labs Technical Journal*,Volume 12 Issue 3, Pages: 21–38.

[11] Nicola Clark and David Jolly, "French Bank Says Rogue Trader Lost $7 Billion," *New York Times*, January 25, 2008.

Web 2.0 poses the latest of these challenges. The repercussions of loss in the cyber world are nonetheless physical; people can lose their jobs, and the public is harmed. Consider these challenges as they evolve in the services and applications of Web 2.0.

Content is king

Much attention has been paid recently to content protection. Most of this concern around content is directed at *end-user applications,* such as spreadsheets or word processing files. Content-filtering products have been primarily about "gate-checking" to make sure protected content does not leak outside the network. Still, content is found in all layers of the network and not just in a format that is recognizable to end-users. In the network infrastructure, content can take the form of account information such as billing. In services applications, it can include profile information used in target marketing. In other applications the content is the data stored in the databases and presented in application servers. Yet, no matter in what form it appears it is all content and it can all be lost, tampered with and subverted to harm people and damage systems.

Consider further the meta-data[12] content in the infrastructure and services as one example.

Target marketing makes use of business intelligence to match the right marketing information with the right target population or even the right individual. Its criminal equivalent is "spear phishing" that applies "business intelligence" gathered about wealthy people but for malicious purposes. It is still, relatively speaking, a low-level problem. What if more aggressive criminal organizations or governments were to apply these very same "business intelligence" techniques, using the meta-data content to target populations, with the purpose of keeping power, gaining power or stifling dissent? Content protection is more than just keeping business files from leaking outside the network perimeter. Consider also the background information (the meta-data) about the data, which can be as simple as the demographics of Web surfing being used for constructive or criminal purposes. Content even in the form of meta-data is king and it needs to be protected.

---

[12] Meta-data examples: "data about other data" - MP3, cookies, visited web sites, etc.

Network criminals target another form of content, the network architecture to determine detailed information about the operating systems, patching levels, and location of critical assets. By burrowing deeper into the network, the attacker can determine the access controls, break those controls and initiate the final phase of the attack. The final stage of the attack can take place in a few seconds. It may involve efforts to steal, modify, or even to encrypt the content or disrupt the service. Using database encryption as a denial of service technique an intruder can keep a business from accessing its database and disrupt its operations. This can be devastating to a business in the real-time and global online environment where even seconds of downtime can translate into millions of dollars in lost revenue.

Broadband wireless security

Fourth-generation (4G)[13] broadband wireless communications and all it promises for creating ubiquitous communications is under development. The taste of this promise is already present in 3G[14] systems. For anyone carrying a 3G wireless card, there is much to complain about, but just try to take their 3G card away and one will find that "stickiness" has already developed. The wait for 4G is filled with great anticipation. One can envision a great range of business activities that will blossom from this freedom to connect anywhere with high-capacity bandwidth that will truly enable open (non-wall gardened)[15] Web services. Has the security required for 4G systems been considered?

There is, in fact, much to consider. 4G in all its versions seems poised for success, and will undoubtedly create a demand that is only

---

[13] www.wikipedia.org - 4G is an abbreviation for Fourth-Generation, is a term used to describe the next complete evolution in wireless communications. A 4G system will be able to provide a comprehensive IP solution where voice, data and streamed multimedia can be given to users on an "Anytime, Anywhere" basis, and at higher data rates than previous generations.

[14] www.wikipedia.org - 3G is the third generation of telecommunications standards and technology for mobile networking, superseding 2.5G. It is based on the International Telecommunication Union (ITU) family of standards under the IMT-2000.

[15] Non-wall Gardened - where the network operator can act as a channel. With this model, smaller service providers, enterprises and developers can now use more advanced mobile services in a simple way to provide specific end-user services.

in the beginning stages. 4G will have to be highly available, reliable and secure to meet expected demand.

With expanded accessibility and capacity will come expanded use of personal, business and government applications, and these will gain critical mass that is far reaching. From a security perspective, tens of millions of 4G subscribers added to hundreds of millions of sensors (machine-to-machine accounts) require systems that must scale in size, in features and that must be assured. Simply put, there is an inherent degree of fragility in a highly shared, highly limited RF channel that is used for wireless communications. This fragility is not there in the same measure for wire line systems that can have high bandwidth dedicated to the subscriber at the aggregation point.

Cyber Security as the Friction and Latency of Business and Government

The value of ICT is to enable businesses to compete on the basis of agility and scale, allowing the business to adapt to market conditions faster and with greater efficiency to bring the right products or services to market at the right time. Agility is, in large measure, about a reduction in process latency and friction. Although the world is highly interconnected, the reality is that interconnectivity is still in its early stages.

As rapidly as these new capabilities that interconnect technology are entering mainstream, cybercrime is growing at an even more alarming rate.

Governments are not immune as the public demands e-government accessibility and efficiency. Yet there are numerous examples of government systems that have been compromised when sensitive data has been lost, and the trust between government and its people breached.

Web 2.0 is the next step in the maturation of the Internet, but is there sufficient understanding of the risks and the impact that can occur when systems operate without the necessary protections?

Will security incidents ultimately choke off the success to the point where outages make customers reluctant to move to more advanced online services? If not the incidents themselves, the burden of over-compliance is another form of friction; security not in the service of the business but acting as nothing more than sand in the machinery. There is a need for prudent regulatory requirements: the number of existing regulations will remain – they are not going away. Additional regulatory requirements can be anticipated in response to the public's increasing concerns that companies are not safeguarding information as they should. Many argue that cumbersome regulations, such as California's SB 1386, are already in place as regulators respond with legislative instruments and penalties for accountability.[16] Passed in 2003, SB 1386 was the first legislation that was enacted to protect against security breaches. Since then most other states in the United States have passed similar laws.

There are unintended consequences that result from passing this type of legislation, such as diminished business agility. United States businesses subject to the Sarbanes-Oxley regulation are already smarting from the high overhead costs such regulation engenders. It isn't just public companies, but virtually any company that conducts business in the United States is impacted. Many blame over-regulation on the tectonic shift of securities exchange listings from the U.S. to the exchanges of London, Singapore and other major global financial centers.

Impact also comes in the form of losses created by security incidents. This is latency and friction in its worst form. Efforts to quantify losses reveal how difficult a task it is to get companies to collect and report this information. The CSI annual cybercrime survey[17] repeatedly discusses the dilemma of too few companies willing to report cybercrime information. This is also friction – the grit that breaks down the ability to clearly express the problem to policy leaders.

Protecting Web 2.0 Data

The information flow in the Web 2.0 model has specific risks beyond the general risks with IP-based systems and the Internet discussed up to this point. These risks go hand in hand with what makes Web 2.0 a more challenging environment to protect. It's a virtual place where conventional boundaries don't always apply and where the spirit of open exchange may conflict with privacy

---

[16] http://info.sen.ca.gov/pub/01-02/bill/sen/sb_13511400/sb_1386_bill_20020926_-chaptered.html.

[17] http://www.gocsi.com/

concerns. Chapter 3 examines in some detail what makes Web 2.0 security particularly challenging. Three issues are of particular concern: control of the data, control of identity and privacy, and the value of virtual assets.

The discussion first considers content stored on public sites. These may also include software as a service (SaaS) sites that, together with consumer-driven sites, may have an implied, if not explicit, expectation for using the stores of data for target marketing. A variety of questions, issues and challenges stem from this condition of open exchange and they begin with the question of control. Data that is used in a Web 2.0 application provides a great advantage to the online service provider when it is data provided without strings attached. In some cases this data is the business. Take away this control and the business model of target marketing starts to unravel.

Who owns the data and how should control be handled? In the first point of view, it is the organization providing the service, whether it is the Web 2.0 company, a hospital, a government agency or a financial company that controls the data. The opposing view, more closely represented in European countries, is that companies storing the data can only use it in a very narrow and strictly controlled role. The end-user controls the information, and the end-user must expressly authorize any further use of the data.

Despite privacy statements provided by U.S. companies to their customers, the present balance of control tilts almost exclusively to the advantage of the company. In this instance, the end-users have given up their rights to control. Many systems are in fact designed with few, if any, opt-in end-user controls. It becomes clear after reading the fine print but few people take the time to do so.

If information is power, then there is a power base growing in the Web 2.0 + world and in every large organization that is collecting data either directly or indirectly as in the meta-data discussed earlier. The end-users have given up control. Where is the balance? Is a medical file containing an x-ray taken at a hospital safe from abuse by employees, insurance firms, hospitals and pharmaceutical companies? Should we trust that the company will protect this medical information adequately?

In the law enforcement triad, the *means* exists in the tools of the criminal world, the *motives* are many and the *opportunities* abound. The opportunities are found with the inherent vulnerabilities that exist in complex systems and the absence of a legitimate basis for trust. Until the many dimensions of the cyber security problems can be measured the problem cannot be corrected.

Information governance in an enterprise is hard enough. In the Web 2.0 + world, who safeguards the interests of the end-user when the business model is explicitly designed to support the application of information for target marketing or other similar purposes? This question is difficult to answer, because no one has clear governance over the information produced. Trust in the cyber world must be measured or it is nothing more than marketing and should not be considered a proxy for making governance decisions about finance, health or privacy.

Protecting information in the Web 2.0 + world, where it is about protecting the value of virtual presence is paramount for personal and financial risk management. A Web 2.0 company's value is not in its physical plant, but in its Web presence and infrastructure. Insuring physical assets is relatively simple. Insuring a cyber presence is radically different because it is usually more difficult to quantify. The value of an online company is almost wholly dependent upon brand value, the services offered, how well the information and its technology systems function and how well they are protected. The physical assets have, by comparison, negligible value.

When an e-commerce company has a market capitalization in the tens of billions of dollars, understanding how to protect this virtual world is exceedingly important. In the real world property is valued in terms of physical assets. In the Second Life world virtual property is sold with real money.[18] How is the physical asset to be insured? It is all about protecting Web presence, an ephemeral notion that does not fit the model of insuring physical assets and where cyber-value and cyber security is paramount.

The Present Models for Cyber Security are Broken

The current practice of cyber security is lacking in many regards, but it is not possible to address the problems until the root causes are understood. The identification of root causes starts with ICT systems

---

[18] http://secondlife.com/whatis/land.php - The Second Life® 3-D virtual world is created by its Residents. Since opening to the public in 2003, it has grown explosively and today is inhabited by millions of Residents from around the globe.

sold to a market that places the responsibility for security on the end-user. This condition is consistent no matter whether the end-user is a consumer or a company providing services that because of the size of the market makes up a part of the national infrastructure. At an individual level, consumer-owned personal computers could hardly be considered part of the national infrastructure. Taken in large numbers they are the end-tools used for all forms of online transactions and in a national emergency may even serve as the primary means to conduct government business (in a health crisis situation government employees will be expected to work from home connected to the government data centers). It is not just home PCs that have to get patched, it is also the hundreds of thousands of computers and servers in government agencies and in utility services.

Web browsers are used to perform a wide range of functions such as online transactions. At the same time that they have gained many new features Web browsers have also become more vulnerable and can be compromised by malware that steals identity and account information. The practice of cyber security must first be repaired before a wholesale move into the Web 2.0 + world can be considered, much less undertaken.

Recall the security triad. *Prevention* has been all but ignored and replaced by an almost exclusive reliance on detection and response security technologies incapable of compensating for all the inherent vulnerabilities in complex systems. The cost of security is too high, not enough results are being delivered for this investment and as the dependency on these same technology systems grows, so do the risks.

This trend is not exclusive to the business world. U.S. government agencies are rated with the Federal Information Security Management Act (FISMA) scorecard on how well they are meeting security regulations with many of them getting "green" scorecard ratings. The truth is they are a poor reflection of how well the systems and the data are secured. A simple question such as how many laptop computers are there in the inventory will stump many an agency that scores "green." If this question cannot be answered with certainty at all times, how is an agency to know what data is put on these laptops and whether the data is being protected?

"*The stolen laptop at Veterans Affairs (VA) was a failure to manage what employees do,*" *says Boots.* "*VA had a good FISMA score card, the system including the stolen laptop had been certified and accredited.*

From a FISMA standpoint, all was well." In other words, compliance doesn't always prevent breaches.[19]

The same situation exists in Europe, where reports are appearing in the press on a regular basis that detail sensitive data losses. This begs the question: do governments have the competency to protect the data its citizens have entrusted to them? Citizens are questioning whether government agencies can be trusted to protect identity information as in national identity cards or electronic voting information. There is reason to be concerned. Global spending on computer security topped US$7.5 billion in 2006.[20] Is it yielding the security that is needed?

A systemic problem

The problem does not begin with government agencies or with businesses. Consider the fundamental problems and whether the technology vendors are applying the right security controls to the systems that are sold to businesses and government agencies. What about the companies that deliver network services. Are they applying security in the right measure? A bit closer to home, are the businesses purchasing technology solutions making security a key requirement for purchase?

The answers to these questions are a mix; there are clearly positive efforts, though on the whole there is much that needs improvement. The answers discussed in the following chapters suggest that the models of cyber security are in need of repair. They also suggest that the systemic remedies start with the right models – models that can be used to guide the path of correcting significant security issues and to produce secure and reliable technology systems. Preventing security issues from happening can start yielding better results.

As the Web 2.0 + world begins to take firm hold in the business world, it is time to apply a better model based on the principles of science where measurements are paramount. To solve this problem in the long term, the integrity of systems and data must be measured and assured and this is even more urgent in a world of interconnected systems, complex supply chains and business partnerships.

---

[19] Kellie Lunney, "Cyber Security chiefs keep a low profile", *Government Executive Magazine,* September 27, 2007, http://www.govexec.com/story_page.cfm?articleid= 38145.

[20] Gartner, 2007.

2
The Costs and Impact of Cyber Security

It takes considerable knowledge just to realize the extent of your own ignorance.

—Thomas Sowell-economist

Executive Summary

There is a story often told of two men who are walking across the Steppes when they stumble across a lion that has not fed for some time. For the lion, dinner has just come knocking. The two men begin to run for their lives. The slower of the two notices that his partner is not running at full speed, keeping just one step in front and appearing rather undisturbed by the ordeal of being chased by a hungry lion. "What are you doing?" he asks his partner? "I am fast," the other partner says, "but not faster than the lion. "Still, I don't need to be faster than the lion, only faster than you, my friend."

On the surface this story serves as a convenient metaphor for the way in which security is currently practiced in the business world. It is also a cautionary tale for those charged with protecting their firm's assets. Lions, and for that matter most other predators, follow the law of the jungle preying exclusively on the weakest members of a herd, and hunting only as a means to stave off the threat of starvation and guarantee their survival.

Predators in the world of cyberspace, by contrast, follow a very different code, and their behaviour is far less predictable and far less honorable than that of the lion. For these cyber predators hunting is about conquering and destroying and rarely about survival.

probably seek weak targets

⟶ jungle metaphor does not apply in some ways: but those motivated by $ will still

15

In the cyber world, just keeping a step ahead of one's partner is not necessarily sufficient to ward off the attack of a cyber predator. The cyber predator has a different agenda, one that does indeed go after the weak and slow but also the strong and rich prize. They are motivated by more than simple survival; the cyber predator's attacks have more serious consequences with broad implications for national strategy and commercial sustainability.

Each year businesses and government agencies make significant investments to secure their systems and protect their communications networks from all manner of cyber threats. The costs expended in securing these systems are not trivial and cover a broad range of items. There is the cost to build up security infrastructure, to hire security specialists to protect technology systems, to implement security best practices, to meet compliance regulations and, where necessary, to cover the loss from incidents. And these are just some of the direct costs. There is a whole host of indirect costs to consider as well, such as litigation, lost contracts, sales and profits, as well as diminished brand equity.

This chapter evaluates the sources of expense for cyber security and provides an explanation for why the security problem grows more severe despite the ever-increasing investment in security spending. This seemingly inexplicable phenomenon is not as much a mystery as one would think. Spending more and getting increasingly less effective results is, in large part, a result of a lack of rigorous measures that could guide investment decisions.

When the budget for security comes up for review more often than not the CFO is faced with a decision to approve an expenditure for an item that has no strict measure associated with it and no guaranteed results. It is hard to imagine that a CFO would approve such a request if it were made for any other type of investment and yet in the case of security common business sense is temporarily suspended and exceptions made. It is easy to sympathize with the CFO and appreciate the predicament. On the one hand there is an unacceptable absence of rigor and on the other the spectre of potentially devastating consequences to consider. The decision is very often one that is motivated by fear not grounded in reason.

If security cannot be easily measured, how is one to determine the optimal level of spending to achieve desired results? One serious impediment is that an acceptable means for measuring the true cost of a security failure does not today exist. Chief information security officers (CISOs) may consider the cost of breaches from a purely technical perspective. While there is no doubt that this type of evaluation has merit, in the end it only yields one part of a much larger and complex picture. What it may not take into account is the effect of indirect costs that can result from a breach in security, the cost of potential litigation, for example, or the loss of customers, the loss of future business, the impact on brand equity, not to mention the cost of regulatory investigations and even the cost of fines. A true Return on Investment for security expenditures can only be achieved by ultimately quantifying the full extent of direct as well as indirect costs. To do this requires a company's leadership team to work collaboratively and examine the impact of a potential failure on the entire business. This calculation needs additional stakeholders that should be participants in the discussion including legal, compliance, communications and public relations, insurance, sales and human resources. In the case of enterprise risk management, the leadership team must also assess certain types of business risks, such as economic, credit and physical (see appendix Ch. 2, Ref.1).

Order now at:
orderpeople.com

BUSINESS REPLY MAIL

FIRST-CLASS MAIL   PERMIT NO. 22   TAMPA FL

POSTAGE WILL BE PAID BY ADDRESSEE

People®

PO BOX 62120
TAMPA FL 33663-1201

NO POSTAGE
NECESSARY
IF MAILED
IN THE
UNITED STATES

1999-2023

1999-1995

1990

1989

Muslim-1989

Code @xb0b 337y8

A historical look at the problem validates this dilemma; despite global increases in security spending, the number and the value of security breaches have not dropped but risen. "The vast majority of cases referred alleged fraud and involved a financial loss on the part of the complainant. The total dollar loss from all referred cases of fraud was $239 million with a median loss of $680 [in 2007] per complaint. This was an increase from $198.44 million in total reported losses in 2006."[1] Even the available data is suspect, as much of it remains undisclosed for fear that more harm than good can come from the disclosure of a breach.

The *"extent of our own ignorance"* in this area is significant, yet one might argue that business and government continue on the same path seemingly unable or unwilling to make a correction and change direction. It is more likely that businesses and governments are aware and are willing to make changes as evidenced by the increase in security budgets.

Rod Beckstrom, Director of the National Cyber Security Center for the U.S. Department of Homeland Security, made a presentation at the 2008 inaugural SC Magazine World Congress in New York City. He took a critical first step toward understanding the problems of cyber security from an economic perspective. He proposed a way to answer two fundamental questions: 1) What is the value of a network? and 2) What should we spend to defend it? These are not new questions, and criminals are quite skilled at determining whether they will get a satisfactory return on investment from a cyber attack. To eliminate the motivation for attack one must strengthen the defenses to a point where the cost of the attack is greater than the reward.

To answer the question of how much to spend on protecting an organization, one must answer the first question – what is the value of the network? The economics of security are then determined by subtracting the total security investments and losses (incidents) from the sum of the benefits gained from revenue the network helps the company achieve. Completing this analysis, Beckstrom made the point of different ways to achieve deterrence as the means to drive up the cost to the hacker where attacking the network is no longer lucrative. Rewarding the "good guys" to create "good code" and/or punishing the "bad guys" with "very large fines for companies with bad products" are two forms of strengthening the defenses.

Protecting Web 2.0 systems is of greater consequence when the data about millions of people is stored in databases subject to the pressures of business and government where the interests of the individual are secondary. It is high time that the technology industry resolves this conundrum and learns how to measure security so that an objective cost/benefit analysis can be realized. This way, standard business principles can be applied to how much is spent on security and to ensure that the expense is applied at the most effective points in the process from creating to deploying technology products.

Consider once again the view that treats security as a value life cycle, one where the effort to protect and harden can be measured and has tangible value. The absence of this practice can also be measured – one that removes value from this cycle. Consider also that the problem and solution start at the same place: the point of creation. Transferring these security features within the solutions, forward through the sale of technologies to the consumer, both

---

[1] *"International Crime Complaint Center 2007 Internet Crime Report"*

business and government can carry the security value to the point where technology enables the business or government to function optimally. In an ideal world, both the risks and benefits are taken into account and a balance is achieved.

For businesses, security need not imply additional cost. There are a great number of examples where the cost of security can be returned as business value, directly associated with a brand. In the automotive industry, Volvo® puts safety at the center of its strategy and uses it to differentiate itself from competitors. Similarly, security can be used to competitive advantage by enabling business partners, for example, to exchange information securely as a way of streamlining operations.

The scenario described above starts to form a process called *the Security Value Life Cycle ("SVL")*. This model is one that companies can use to better estimate true ROI from security. It is not particularly novel, but it does reveal what is wrong with the current practice. By using a structured approach to security, this value chain can be made to work with benefit to individuals, companies and governments. Security can be measured and it can be structured so that one can determine its relative value, then baseline the performance. This will allow an organization to understand its true security health over time and make improvements. This is certainly not a panacea, and achieving adequate protection of information doesn't happen overnight. However, an organization that adopts such an approach can make continuous improvements and minimize the risks to its computing environment. It may take a generation that is unwilling to tolerate incidents to effect a change, but such change must occur or the consequences for all of us will be significant.

In this chapter we evaluate the costs associated with providing security and conclude that, if there is no viable way to measure security accurately and determine its value, there is no way to determine whether industry or government can derive any positive return from it. Alternatively, trying to define a measure by considering it as the result of avoiding a negative outcome is flawed because it does not conclusively demonstrate whether the result was due to good security practice or merely the result of pure coincidence. It is also important to understand how much should be spent on deterrence. Is the status quo sustainable in the next-generation Web applications? The answer is rather fuzzy since the means to measure security remains a future task. Does this mean that the market will sort it out as an embedded cost of doing business, a risk transferred with insurance?

If we apply conventional thinking we would naturally conclude that the greater the investment in security, the smaller the risk of a security breach. As intuitive as this may appear, it is then difficult to explain why organizations find it so challenging and are plagued by so much uncertainty when trying to determine the level of spending that is required to ensure an optimal return. What makes deriving such a correlation even more difficult and makes arriving at a true measure of effectiveness next to impossible is the pace at which business functions, organizations, and technologies change from one year to the next.

The technology industry spent over $7.1 billion in 2007, a 26 percent[2] increase from the spend in 2006 for security, while estimates indicate that rather than decrease in the same period, the total losses from security breaches rose by 20 percent.[3]

With these data points in hand it is tempting to leap to the conclusion that as the cost of security breaches increases dramatically, spending for security will also increase despite no discernible corresponding decrease in the volume or loss. The most relevant conclusion to draw, however, is that there is no reliable way to determine whether a level of spending is appropriate or whether an investment is generating satisfactory returns until the technology industry figures out how to measure security more accurately.

---

[2] Gartner, 2007

[3] "*International Crime Complaint Center 2007 Internet Crime Report*"

There are some who claim that the correct way to calculate effectiveness is to consider the absence of a security breach in a given year – a mean-time-between-failure factor. It is hard to argue this point without more detailed data that would make the correlation of security practice to some given outcome possible and rule out conclusively that a security failure was due to nothing more than happenstance. Such uncertainty places the security executive in the unenviable position of having to prove that an investment is justified when there is no definitive proof that the same results could not have been achieved with no investment at all. Of course, this begs the question of what we should make of the instance where a security breach occurs in spite of significant investment in securing a computing environment, How does one justify the costs that have been incurred? This is the dilemma faced by all leaders charged with making decisions on security budgets. Clearly the breach or no breach method of measuring security is insufficient.

What if security could be measured using techniques developed by insurance companies? Following the example of the insurance industry, risk could be reduced by imposing use of a standardized practice that involves taking specific steps to harden products and solutions. Reductions in risk take many forms – reducing the frequency of the risk event, reducing the likelihood that the risk event could cause actual damage and, finally, reducing the severity of the risk event when it occurs. Viewed this way, the occurrence of a network security breach is not a "failure" in risk management parlance since it would be foolish to assume that risk management meant risk elimination. Instead, the examination of the costs of the event are reviewed, including such indirect costs as loss of customers, and these are then compared with the likely cost of the event that would have been incurred if no risk mitigation actions had been taken. When one understands that risk management can and should take place across the enterprise, the picture becomes even clearer.

Taken a step further, consider that these hardened solutions can be integrated into the operational environment and certified in that environment using a uniformly adopted standard. Finally, at the point of service delivery where process and technology combine to enable the improved efficiency of a business function or government activity, the hardening and certification yield a clear compliance measurement built from the ground up. This is a three-step process:

Step 1– at the point of creation harden the products and solutions to a given standard,

Step 2– at the point of implementation and operation to certify the solution or system,

Step 3– at the point of business enablement to validate compliance.

However, these conjectures will amount to nothing more than pipe dreams as long as the technology industry insists on treating security as a set of technologies and practices to be applied by the consumer after the fact. The unnecessary security costs in the status quo of the present environment cannot be avoided. Whether it's the cost of prevention or the cost of impact from incidents, each of these costs has many contributors to the overall number. Wouldn't it be better if the cost stemmed from effective applications of preventive measures? If the cost can be measured, then the cost resulting from having to pay penalties, lawsuits for negligence and opportunities lost because of hits on the corporate brand can be minimized.

And what of the security costs in Web 2.0 solutions? There is no doubt that the trend to implement cloud computing is gaining momentum and it will continue to grow, even if there are few methods to determine how security is applied. While systems can be outsourced, the responsibility for security and related security breaches can never be outsourced. There is not a service level agreement anywhere in force that provides for the transfer of responsibility at any price.

To aid the discussion, consider the notion of the SVL, previously defined in the executive summary, where the cost of security manifests itself at multiple points from creation to system delivery and production. A key aspect of this concept is that the life cycle does not end when the product is deployed. The SVL is a simplified representation of a complex set of market interactions, but it is useful nonetheless in illustrating that security costs continue beyond product deployment. The security patching process is evidence enough of this cost that cuts into the profits of the company that produced the product while adding cost to the company that purchased the product. The concept of an SVL is used in several chapters to aid the overall discussion on security.

Finally, the goal is to recognize that it is a life cycle. In failing to address security at the earliest point in the life cycle, the product manufacturer is creating a ripple of unintended security costs downstream in the market with some of this cost eating away at the customer's profits. While the cost of failing to secure the products and solutions occurs in many places, the total security cost may exceed any profits made from the original product sale.

The Economics of Security

Rod Beckstrom proposes that "the value of a network is equal to the sum of the net present value (NPV) to each user, calculated as the benefit value of all transactions $\sum B$ minus the sum of the costs $\sum C$ (of those transactions), from the standpoint of each user, over any time period." By this determination, the security model subtracts from the NPV with the cost of investment in security (infrastructure) $\sum SI$ and security losses such as incidents $\sum SL$. Spending on security is about finding the optimum balance between profit and loss (the intersection point between Loss and Security Investment). Improvements in deterrence are made where the cost of the transaction is reduced by the developers who provide a "good product," where the optimal expenditures to mitigate the risk of the potential loss are made through incentive and punishment: reward those that produce good quality products and punish those that produce defective products (see appendix Ch. 2, Ref.2).

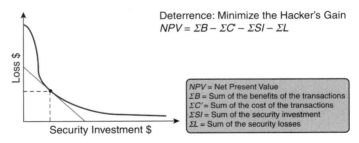

Deterrence: Minimize the Hacker's Gain
$NPV = \Sigma B - \Sigma C - \Sigma SI - \Sigma L$

NPV = Net Present Value
ΣB = Sum of the benefits of the transactions
$\Sigma C'$ = Sum of the cost of the transactions
ΣSI = Sum of the security investment
ΣL = Sum of the security losses

Figure 2.1   How much to spend on security

This analysis reveals that deterrence is the key to creating conditions where the cost is greater than the potential reward. It is deterrence that must be understood in the overall model of the network and its value; there is an optimal point for spending on deterrence.

Mr. Beckstrom's contribution to this discussion is fundamental. With this critical insight, one can start to apply the metrics of economic logic. The SVL discussion that follows is about where to apply spending on deterrence at the most effective points in the cycle of development, deployment and operation.

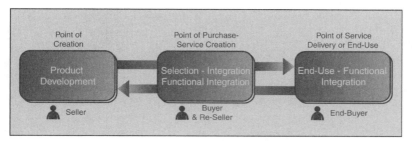

Figure 2.2 Security Value Life Cycle

The Security Value Life Cycle

As discussed, the cost of security is often framed solely in terms of security events.

These may include loss of service and productivity, loss of data, loss of good will, reputation and potential litigation. Security costs occur in other ways: responding to an incident and mitigation-prevention costs such as applying a patch to prevent further incidents. There is also the cost of the security infrastructure itself, performing risk and threat analysis, configuring and maintaining system controls, monitoring the effectiveness of the controls and auditing the security processes to ensure they are providing the level of protection the business requires. Finally, security infrastructure goes beyond just the tools and techniques used by the technology professional – there are also issues that need to be addressed by a broad group of stakeholders across the enterprise, including legal, compliance and human resources. It is easy to see that security costs vary and depend on many conditions and needs.

Security in the enterprise is not a set of standalone activities, and in order to protect critical business functions, security needs to be integrated into basic business processes. The organization needs to determine what is an acceptable level of risk, how that level of risk is most cost effectively achieved, and what, if any, risk needs to be transferred. In order to have a discussion about risk, the cost points of security need to be understood in the total.

The SVL shown in Figure 2.3 is useful in simplifying and tracking the discussion. It begins at the Point of Creation. Technical security integration should begin at the Point of Service Creation where a particular technology serves to automate a business process through the Point of Service Delivery. This chapter discusses security costs throughout the SVL. The SVL is also used to describe the benefits that the technology industry and business can derive by using a common security framework.

The top (right pointed) arrow represents the security benefits that move forward in the SVL when starting with Product Creation. Failure to integrate the requisite security features at this first point results in the removal of the top (right-pointed) arrow – there is no security to transfer forward; from this point forward, security is dependent entirely on perimeter defences to protect vulnerable internal components. Companies and governments may end up going through some form of certification such as the ISO 27000[4] or NIST 800-53,[5] but given what is known about the increasingly sophisticated threats, trying to certify unhardened systems only creates a false sense of assurance.

When security is integrated into a product at the Point of Creation, the resulting benefits can transfer forward and can accrue with the added protections made downstream in the SVL. The benefits realized depend on many factors, including the scope and effectiveness of security capabilities, how well security capabilities protect critical business assets, how well security supports certification requirements, how the security posture is implemented and maintained, compatibility of security capabilities with other technology infrastructure components, how intrinsic vulnerabilities are addressed, as well as many other factors. The security benefits represented by the top arrow must be maximized in order to support business agility and reduce costs. These benefits are further discussed in Chapters 6 and 7.

The bottom (left-pointed) arrow represents the unwanted security activities that result when needed security capabilities are not provided or are poorly implemented and configured. This arrow represents all the activities that create business friction working against business agility and increasing security costs that reduce overall profit. These

---

[4] http://www.27000.org/

[5] http://csrc.nist.gov/publications/PubsSPs.html

activities include product returns, patching, add-on security capabilities and ultimately brand damage. The lack of transparency in revealing how hardening was applied in the SVL can be a source of friction in the relationship between seller and buyer.

The three boxes represent the three transaction points and the key players in the technology creation and deployment process used to support the organization's functions.

The Point of Creation is where the technology is developed on which the components of the technology infrastructure are based and for which applications are installed downstream. Here the seller needs to consider "building in" the applicable security features during product development.

Next there is the Point of Purchase – Service Creation. This is the point at which various technologies are integrated as solutions that deliver services to either internal or external use such as an integrated solution or service to be resold with additional value to the customer. In a Web 2.0 + world, it may be the application provider, the service provider or an enterprise business that provides technology services to its own customers. For many businesses this represents a service offered to end-users and an associated revenue stream. Infrastructure components are selected, purchased, integrated and managed to provide value to users and secure payment. The ability to make sound business decisions depends on having a clear understanding of the security risks and costs. Additional decisions that need to be made include what infrastructure to use, what critical business assets to protect and at what price.

The third box represents the Point of Service to the end-user who may be a consumer, a business or government agency that is using technology to support their respective business functions. This requires functional integration into the user's unique operating environment and accommodation of devices that may include PDAs, laptops and personal computers. Security designs developed at the Point of Creation take the customer into account at the beginning of the architecture and design phase. How will personal data be protected? How will users be authenticated and authorized to ensure that they gain access only to those applications they need to do their jobs? These are some of the critical questions that need to be answered, and the earlier in the process they are considered, the more likely that security features will be delivered to customers consistently and predictably throughout the SVL.

Security Costs at the Point of Creation

Product developers must decide what security to build into the product to provide needed security capabilities for their customers. There is no hiding the fact that integrating security in the product during the development phase can result in a cost in labor, licenses and potentially capital expenses. The product developer intent on building a long-term business relationship with its customers also considers the security costs their customers will incur. Product developers must understand their customer's business, their security requirements and their certification and regulatory requirements.

Publicly traded companies in the financial services industry doing business in the United States are subject to regulations such as the Gramm-Leach-Bliley Act.[6] With this as a planning factor, there is a list of security features that drive the key considerations developed by the system designers. As an example, including non-repudiation features in the system design are particularly useful to a customer in the financial services industry. They need to pass audits to validate that information cannot be tampered with or accidentally modified. Designing for non-repudiation is important, as is identity management,

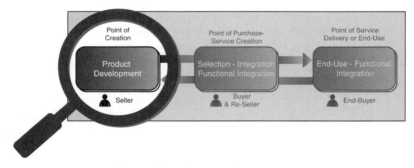

Figure 2.3   Security Value Life Cycle

---

[6] Also known as the Gramm-Leach-Bliley Financial Services Modernization Act, Pub.L. 106-102, 113 Stat. 1338, enacted November 12, 1999, is an Act of the United States Congress which repealed part of the Glass-Steagall Act of 1933, opening up competition among banks, securities companies and insurance companies. The Glass-Steagall Act prohibited a bank from offering investment, commercial banking, and insurance services.

authorization and access control. Integrating all these features into the product and solution creation phase invariably increases the cost of production. Taken individually these costs are negligible as they involve implementing standard practices or standardized common-ly-used codes or features that already exist in the operating systems. In the aggregate, however, there is a cost to integrate security at the Point of Creation. What this cost is, in actuality, is difficult to determine. Yet it is an investment cost, one that brings benefits in the sales cycle and one that is carried forward to a customer who has certification and compliance requirements to be met.

When developing solutions that are to be used in the healthcare industry specifically, the product designer needs to consider a number of other security features as personal healthcare information is sensi-tive and care needs to be taken to ensure its adequate protection. These are important considerations for a customer that must comply with the Health Insurance Portability and Accountability Act (HIPAA).[7]

These design considerations are the first cost considerations, but they may not be the last. Without the existence of a standardized practice for building security in at the beginning of the development cycle, product designers will find it difficult to avoid inefficiencies that lead to increases in the security costs that in turn directly impact the bottom line. The costs of retrofitting security are high, and this assumes that a retrofit even can be implemented. Often the underlying product architecture may not support the required security capabilities.

Companies that deliver products with vulnerabilities that are due to poor software design and missing security features can expect their customers to react negatively. As stated, the cost of maintaining a steady stream of software updates erodes both the buyers' and sellers' profits.

Many companies depend heavily on the security posture of third-party software such as operating systems, databases, and application software from partners and suppliers. It should be a basic expectation that the product creator insists that its component providers adopt a

---

[7] Was enacted by the U.S. Congress in 1996. According to the Centers for Medicare and Medicaid Services (CMS) website, Title I of HIPAA protects health insurance coverage for workers and their families when they change or lose their jobs. Title II of HIPAA, known as the Administrative Simplification (AS) provisions, requires the establishment of national standards for electronic health care transactions and national identifiers for providers, health insurance plans, and employers.

standardized method of ensuring that security is part of the fundamental design.

Consider further that all these individual products and solutions come together at some point in larger systems that themselves, in turn, become part of large, even national infrastructures. The principle of security defense in-depth[8] starts with the infrastructure itself. If the basic infrastructure itself is vulnerable, remediation that satisfies customer requirements may require overlay solutions

To limit the cost of security at the Point of Creation, security needs to be integrated into the fundamental business process. Whether it's the application development life cycle or the manufacturing process, security needs to be a component from the beginning to the end of the product development life cycle.

Security Costs at the Point of Purchase – Service Creation

It is at the second of the three points in the SVL life cycle – the Service Creator - where the security technical and functional integration takes place. It is also where the process of competitive bidding occurs that leads to selection among viable offers to meet a set of business or government security requirements.

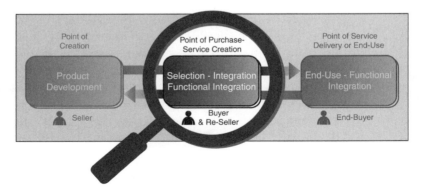

Figure 2.4 Security Value Life Cycle

---

[8] http://www.nsa.gov/snac/support/defenseindepth.pdf

There is cost in all these activities such as developing the security requirements, to make the selection and integrate the selected solution. However, the up-front investment helps the organization save money in the long term.

As an example, security requirements and integration get reinvented unnecessarily, and every time they are reinvented unnecessary costs are introduced. The production environment and the associated risks can be defined up front for the different vertical markets and passed to the technology creators (Point 1 in the SVL).

Unfortunately, the present situation is that security integration with individual products that are part of an overall solution takes place where it is least suited (Point 2 in the SVL) and arguably is an impossible task. The right level of security integration at the solution level is only practical at the point of the product and solution development – not point two in the three-point process, but at point one. Unless security is integrated at the beginning of the SVL, unnecessary costs are added, and integrating security after the fact is of only marginal value. In the aggregate this cost robs funding from other areas of security where its need is greater and it is better applied.

Airbags are a good example. They cannot be added and be expected to perform effectively after an automobile rolls off the assembly line. Imagine the absurd situation of having a front-end car crash, then having to push a button to make the airbags work. In today's complex technology environment, it is amazing that an aftermarket approach to security is precisely what is attempted.

Typically, security integration is not attempted at all. The customer (the buyer – reseller in this case) may only get whatever level of inconsistent security was provided by the different components, an inadequate implementation in the overall solution. This increases the potential that the customer will operate the technology with unnecessary risk and may lead to further financial loss and decreased customer confidence.

As stated earlier, there are at least three types of costs: security incidents, meeting compliance requirements and the costs of building a security infrastructure. If security is built into the product, the cost of doing business will be lower.

Incidents includes costs of business outages, loss of productivity, penalties incurred from lapses in compliance, litigation costs, losses which could have been or were not insured and the loss of customers due to diminished trust. Lack of trust can undermine and ultimately destroy the business altogether. Compliance costs are unavoidable in today's business environment, but they are hardly a measure that the deployed security is sufficient to protect the business. Simply put, a company may comply with a regulation, but that doesn't mean that the right security measures are in place.

Incident costs

It is difficult to understand the service creator's security incident costs since the little data that exists forms an incomplete picture. Compared to many other measures of business costs such as bank theft, auto accident losses, losses due to fire and other physical disasters, information on the costs of security incidents is scarce and often not reported. The CSI Computer Crime and Security Annual Survey, one of the surveys that is quoted most frequently in the press, indicates that it is difficult to get information on losses due to security incidents. Few businesses are willing to share this information even if they have it since it could negatively influence customer and partner perception.

In its 2008 Annual Survey, CSI found that the average loss per respondent was $288,618 – down from $345,005 in 2007, which appears to be a positive sign and counter to the argument that the investment in security is yielding poor value.[9] The 2008 Rotman-TELUS Joint Study on Canadian IT Security Practices, a Canadian survey of security losses, found Canadian losses in 2007 at US$423,469 per incident.[10] It is unlikely that the costs reported are the actual costs since the companies surveyed are typically uneasy about discussing the incidents in a public manner.

Costs from the loss of personal data resulting in identity theft provide another measure of the cost of security. The Identity Theft Resource Center of San Diego, California,[11] reported there were 656 reported breaches in 2008 – a 47 percent increase from the 446 incidents reported in 2007. In another study by Ponemon Institute LLC of Elk Rapids, Michigan, the cost of dealing with data breaches was estimated to be $4.8 million per incident. The cost of a breach was derived from an average cost of $182 per lost customer record and an average number of 26,300 lost customer records per breach.

---

[9] www.gocsi.com

[10] www.rotman.utoronto.ca/security/rt2008-fullstudy-final.pdf

[11] www.ponemon.org/press/strongmail-ponemon_survey_press_release_final.pdf

Service outages resulting from denial of service attacks were not reported as a cost in the CSI Survey. However, they need to be considered in the cost impact of security. The increased threat of organized crime using tools such as botnets[12] poses a real concern for Web 2.0 service creators. The cost of botnets is unmistakable but also uncertain.

A security breach can threaten the very existence of a company, particularly one whose entire business model is to deliver online services; such companies cannot afford to be offline for any length of time. A service provider can lose customers permanently after a significant service outage, and can find that regaining customer confidence is next to impossible.

The costs of compliance

In most industries, the cost of regulatory compliance is an unavoidable fact of business life. Estimated spending for Sarbanes-Oxley compliance was approximately $6.0B in 2007, and spending associated with governance, risk management, and compliance (GRC) was estimated to be $29.9B in 2007, up 8.5 percent from 2006.[13] In governments, it is often in the form of compliance audits that result in publicly announced report cards. The Federal Information Systems Management Act (FISMA) serves as the regulation for departments in the U.S. federal government. Sarbanes-Oxley was developed in response to the excesses of the financial reporting scandals such as Enron, Global Crossing and MCI.

Section 302 (Internal Control Certification) and Section 404 (Assessment of Internal Control). Hence Sarbanes-Oxley compliance for US companies has an implied security cost component. Most of the costs are associated with the access, confidentiality, and integrity of sensitive financial information. Many companies have established market

---

[12] Botnet is a jargon term for a collection of software robots, or bots, that run autonomously and automatically. The term is often associated with malicious software but it can also refer to the network of computers using distributed computing software. While the term "botnet" can be used to refer to any group of bots, such as IRC bots, this word is generally used to refer to a collection of compromised computers (called Zombie computers) running software, usually installed via worms, Trojan horses, or backdoors, under a common command-and-control infrastructure.

[13] Kevin Reilly, *AMR Research Finds Spending on Sarbanes-Oxley Compliance Will Remain Steady at $6.0B in 2007.* http://www.amrresearch.com/Content/view.asp?pmillid=20232 (Feb. 22, 2007).

add-on security capabilities in order meet certification requirements. These solutions typically provide for strong authentication of users, the application of Role Based Access Control, digital signatures for integrity and encryption to protect against unauthorized disclosure of data. Without a consistent security framework to work from, it is difficult to understand what security capability is already available in the current IT systems and what additional security capability is needed for compliance.

Companies chafe under the burden of this cost. Many claim that such excessive regulation has led to a delisting of companies in the various U.S.-based exchanges in favour of listing them in less burdensome countries. At the heart of this regulation is the question of integrity and how to ensure the integrity in financial reporting, in the protection of privacy and generally in the data used to report the state of the company, is maintained free of unwarranted manipulation. The table below identifies the regulations enacted to address business functions, and all of them depend on information security to achieve the needed controls.

Laws and Regulations

• Sarbanes - Oxley Act of 2002	• California (SB) 1386
• Basel II Accord	• OFAC–OCC Rules
• Privacy	• USA Patriot Act
– Gramm Leach Bliley Act	• SEC Regulations 10b(5)
– HIPAA	• FTC Do-Not-Call Law
– EU Directive on Data Protection	• Digital Millennium Copyright Act
– State, Country & Municipality privacy laws	• Super-DMCA
• FTC Act	• Foreign Corrupt Practices Act
• Bank Secrecy Act	• FDA CFR 22 Part 11
• General Negligence Law	
• Electronic Communications Privacy Act	
• Bank Secrecy Act	
• Anti-Money Laundering	
• FFIEC Authentication Guidance	

Source: Echelon One, LLC

One consequence of these regulations is that audit companies that maintain armies of young auditors[14] now need small armies of information security practitioners. These regulatory requirements have been driving considerable expenditures in security capability to meet the compliance demands. Increased attention to system certification has been one of the natural consequences – a way to put a seal of approval on the products placed into production. The costs to strengthen the security, to certify and meet compliance requirements are substantial.

The costs of security infrastructure

The costs of security infrastructure at the Point of Purchase - Service Creation are substantial. It is a heavy burden on the cost of running the business and it is difficult to measure the return on investment (ROI). It is not just the investment in network security capabilities that is of concern; all aspects of the business incur infrastructure security costs. It is a 24/7 demand where the race to detect and respond to system threats is a race to save the business and the attacker has virtually all the advantages. If technology vendors don't build security into the components that make up the infrastructure, the race will be lost before it even begins. The cost of building infrastructure grows with the additional burden of trying to protect systems inherently vulnerable if security was not applied at the Point of Creation.

The end result is that detection and response will be too slow to provide the protection required. It is not just the risk in technology systems that organizations need to be concerned with, but also the physical and human risks.

There is the cost of building up a security infrastructure itself with security equipment intended to filter, block, control access, validate usage, provision and de-provision, control configurations and be resilient to minimize the risk of disasters. The options fall into one of two categories: build it up as internal capabilities or outsource the task to a managed security service provider (MSSP). Most companies can't afford to build and maintain this security infrastructure and increasingly find the MSSP option more attractive.

There are also additional costs in conducting risk assessments, where critical assets are identified and then are protected based on the risks identified. An organization needs to take into account its business partners with whom it exchanges information. The challenge

---

[14] MBAs and CPAs

can grow substantially, depending on how the systems used are designed to allow the exchange of information while maintaining the controls its security policies require.

The costs are even higher if business processes and human elements are included. For example, the cost of setting up and maintaining a 24/7 call center can be significant, especially if the business requires multiple languages. Additionally, the cost of conducting and maintaining an inventory of all legal and compliance regulations applicable to the company's global activities can be an expensive overhead yielding little more than to avoid the cost of regulatory penalties. Purchasing and maintaining security insurance is a critical ongoing cost because traditional corporate insurance policies will not cover the losses associated with a network security event. Finally, creating and maintaining an incident response plan is often a forgotten cost.

Security Cost at Point of Service

The third box in the SVL is the Point of Service – the endpoints and users. This is the cost of security for the users and their network devices (includes both individual consumers and enterprises) such as servers, desktop computers, laptops, and smartphones. This is increasingly important, particularly as use of Web 2.0 applications broadens.

There are generally three cases that cover how the user receives services. There are user endpoints under the service creator's control (such as a PDA) where the device and the service are provided, endpoints not under their control (such as laptops) and a hybrid arrangement with a mixed degree of control (such as next generation

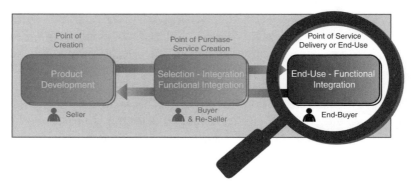

Figure 2.5 Security Value Life Cycle

PDAs) where some of the services are from Web applications delivered by third parties.

Whether the device is controlled by the service creator or not, security costs include the protection of business and personal data, compliance with regulatory requirements, and protecting the infrastructure from hostile parties both inside and outside of their networks. The costs vary depending on how much security is built into devices. Web 2.0 services by their very nature can be accessed in a variety of ways with a variety of devices.

The cost at the Point of Service starts with authenticating and authorizing users. In order to comply with Sarbanes-Oxley and other regulatory requirements, access to applications and services needs to be tightly controlled. Thus there are costs of strong authentication techniques, authorization and perhaps the deployment of a Public Key Infrastructure to apply cryptography to ensure the confidentiality and integrity of user identities and data. These types of security solutions are also applied to ensure that service customers legitimately receive the service value they pay for. If copyrighted content is part of the service offering, then protection of digital rights is part of the security costs at the Point of Service. Security awareness training for employees and business partners is important but is no substitute for providing security in the system design. A good example is a single sign-on solution that eliminates the need for an end-user to remember multiple IDs and passwords.

Protecting a network, preventing data leaks and managing end-user behavior are all part of the mix of costs to the enterprise. Assessing the true nature of these costs becomes increasingly difficult when work and private lives merge. This blended lifestyle is at odds with the assertion that end-devices be strictly used for business. The blurring of business and personal time makes it more challenging for companies to provide the appropriate level of controls.

Impact of Security Costs on Security Decisions and Investments: Network Security Risk Management

Every corporation recognizes the long- and short-term value of technology along with its impact on productivity and business process. However, with great rewards come great risks, and as discussed, there has been no significant understanding or effort within companies to calculate the financial risk for cyber systems until now.

Making sound cyber security investments is difficult when cyber security costs and impacts are not properly understood and so often remain unaddressed. Effective business practices look at different metrics for calculating value, including ROI, which directs investments to increase profits, increase savings and create competitive advantage that is reflected in the bottom line. Businesses cannot elect to simply ignore security in order to invest in revenue-generating opportunities without taking a high degree of unwarranted risk. As presented, the SVL model reveals the costs of cyber security are substantial and they are difficult to assess as these costs exist not just at one point but ripple through the stages in the life cycle. The difficulty does not, however, remove the need to exert the time and effort to establish an estimate of security value, its impact and how much to expend in protecting the cyber presence of the business.

It is well understood that security failures can have costly indirect consequences, including but not limited to civil and criminal lawsuits, lost trade secrets, breach of contract, breach of privacy, reputation damage, business interruption and lost income. Ultimately, it is much more likely that it will be these costs, rather than the direct costs of security, that can harm and potentially even compromise a company's reputation.

This is a sobering concern that every CFO faces. There are financial consequences to cyber security, or more pointedly, of cyber security "events" that can be substantial. The total average cost of a data breach grew to $197 per record compromised in 2007.[15] Since January 2005, the Privacy Rights Clearinghouse has identified more than 230 million records of U.S. residents that have been exposed due to security. The cost increases are measured in terms of lost business, legal defense and public relations. An organization that is unprepared to avert or manage a data breach can suffer significant financial losses and potentially cause irreparable damage to its reputation and customer base. This is no longer just a potential, but a reality, with recent cases making the point in the United Kingdom, United States and Germany where public confidence has been badly shaken by these incidents.

---

[15] Cyber Security Industry Alliance - http://www.csialliance.org/resource/csiadatacompilation.html

As there are real and significant costs to cyber incidents, it is also the case that the organization that has done the prior planning and structuring for such incidents can recover quickly and largely avoid any consequences. As in any moment of crisis, the organization that responds with speed, transparency and skill can even enhance its customer loyalty and improve brand image.

This is an area of discussion critical to understand in the context of how risk plays out at the speed of the cyber event. There is far too little understanding of this phenomenon, with few that have taken on the task of a serious analysis. Rod Beckstrom's recent work on this point was presented earlier, and Ty Sagalow's work presented here is another analysis of importance to this topic. It is, nonetheless, a topic at some offset from the central message and additional materials are provided in the appendixes at the end of this book.

By looking at security costs at the Point of Creation, Point of Purchase - Service Creation and Point of Service, new perspectives can be applied that shed light on how to consider security costs for specific Web 2.0 applications. The model clearly shows that the security costs of the product creator directly affect the security costs of the service creator. If the product creator does not build security in, it is the service creator that bears the additional costs of securing the service by adding expensive security overlays which may or may not be effective.

Security costs at the Point of Service are changing rapidly as ubiquitous access models supplant paradigms of total end-device control for Web 2.0. A common thread in all of the points in the model is the cost of compliance and the necessary certifications that go with them. The Sarbanes-Oxley regulation contains implicit security requirements for technology driving business investment in security capabilities. This trend is spreading internationally, and it is expected to continue.

This impact is taking a heavy toll on the financial bottom line. The message is clear, and it is not to stop investing in the necessary security, but rather to make the investment up front in the life cycle. Deterrence remains the key to alter the decision of criminal syndicates where cost and reward are the calculus. Better metrics are needed to justify security investments. This will help ensure that security investments are in fact producing the right assets and the right results. Ultimately, even metrics such as improved confidence, growth in customers and avoidance of costly incidents such as data breaches, are only indirect measures of security's value to the business. As the world of Web 2.0 poses greater challenges, it is time to start using these metrics.

3

Protecting Web 2.0: What Makes it so Challenging?

"Houston, we have a problem"

Executive Summary

In his futuristic cyber crime novel *The Halting State*,[1] Charles Stross takes his readers on a trip through Second Life in the year 2019 (not coincidentally) and describes an environment where the events in a *grid-crime*[2] can cross over and inspire crimes in the real world that have real consequences and global impact. Although a purely fictional account, Stross' crime novel, nevertheless, provides an inkling of how Web 2.0 might evolve and shape a world in which virtual tools redraw the relationship between humans and machines narrowing distances between the two and heightening the interaction between them across all senses. The novel also gives the reader pause for thought by demonstrating what can happen when reliance on technology that was considered a source of power suddenly turns into a vulnerability in the wake of a system failure. The source of the failure is a compromised encryption key that has been implemented to protect all commercial and government functions. The repercussions are far-reaching and absolute. No border is sacred and no business or government agency is spared. But before we speculate any further on the evolution of Web 2.0 in 2019, and concern ourselves with the potentially apocalyptic

---

[1] Charles Stross, *The Halting State*. (Phillips and Nelson Media, 2004)

[2] Crime that takes place in Second Life. Catherine Holahan, "The Dark Side of Second Life," *Business Week*, November 21, 2006.

consequences that it implies, let's take a step back and take a closer look at just what Web 2.0 is as a way of getting a better understanding of why it should engender such concerns about security?

There are many definitions of Web 2.0, though any differences likely stem from differing perspectives. In the telecommunications community, it can be defined as next-generation networks in high capacity wireline and wireless broadband. By collapsing the separate legacy and proprietary systems into a single technical infrastructure, a system based on packet switching, the Internet Protocol networks deliver the expanded capacity needed for ubiquitous, unconstrained and un-tethered communications. It is also unified communications where e-mail, voice, text messaging, and facsimile can reach a person as a voice message on any device.

Social networking and collaboration applications such as Facebook[3], wikis and blogs are examples of Web 2.0 applications. Companies will expand from their traditional reach in the marketplace; application companies will enter the traditional telecommunications market and telecommunications will deliver Web 2.0 applications. The silos will break down, competition will increase, the traditional information stores from companies in different business verticals will blur with a high potential that privacy controls may be lost in the process.

Like the proverbial blind men describing the elephant, those who attempt to define Web 2.0 are bound to arrive at different conclusions. Web 2.0 is multi-faceted, and it is all of the perspectives of Web 2.0 combined that deliver the next generation of information systems. The promise of the information revolution continues; the first generation was only a taste of things to come.

What makes security so challenging in this new world of Web 2.0 communications and applications? More and more information and applications from both individuals and companies will be delivered in the cloud, not just behind personal or corporate firewalls. If security is partly defined as controlling the system and information assets, in cloud computing, third parties manage the assets. These third parties are expected to deliver services for free (or almost free) in exchange for information that can be used for target marketing. Where are the boundaries of business intelligence derived, and what assurances can these companies make to ensure that their boundaries can't be breached?

There is complexity inherent in making voice, video and data work together over the same infrastructure. The adage that complexity is the breeding place for vulnerabilities applies as much in this case as it ever did before. Add this to the fact that technology companies have historically treated security as a minimal set of design requirements reliant mostly on physical and perimeter isolation. Security in this form is supposed to be provided by a set of aftermarket technologies such as firewalls, detection and prevention systems. With physical isolation in IP networks no longer possible, the conditions are different; highly complex solutions that fail to take security risks into consideration have created an opportunity for those who understand how to exploit this complexity and find vulnerabilities.

---

[3] Facebook is a trademark of Facebook, Inc. All other trademarks used throught out this work are trademarks of their respective owners.

Take a close look inside this technology and the complexity appears in its full clarity – like viewing microbes, invisible to the naked eye, but exposed in detail through a microscope. Aftermarket-based security never did work effectively and it will not serve to protect information systems in the world of Web 2.0, but to change the way the market works will require a sea change. This kind of sea change does not happen by chance or without a significant business driver changing the conditions of how the market behaves.

And, upon closer inspection, there are security challenges posed by the un-tethered communications offered by 3G today and 4G broadband wireless communications soon to come. These next-generation broadband wireless technologies deliver a compelling freedom, yet they harbor a new set of problems for the security community. Wireless broadband delivering services across the full range of voice, video and data has a range of challenges operating together in the shared medium of a radio frequency signal where one bad connection can impact traffic for all the participants on the same Radio Access Network (RAN).

Taken together, these challenges call for a new consideration of how security is applied. The "aftermarket" delivery must change to one in which security is a design consideration at the Point of Creation, and is undertaken at the solution-hardening level and applied consistently. The only parties who can change this relationship are the buyers. The current model is too deeply rooted to be able change of its own accord. The notion of an SVL was introduced earlier to help explain how security works today, and serves to illustrate why this form is so flawed.

Security *designed in* using a standards-based approach is about product and solution makers taking an interest in the security challenges of their customers who face a tremendous set of challenges to secure their respective services, many of them codified in certification and compliance requirements. The SVL introduced in this chapter is a simple concept used to illustrate that systems are tied together like a traditional supply chain. Security must be applied at the beginning or there is no security value to pass downstream to the end customers. The entire process is stuck on the ineffective perimeter security. Technology developers owe it to their customers to get the security right and at the right point. Customers of this technology need to stop buying into this failed form of security, **stop buying complex systems piecemeal and stop acting as the integrators of security**. Push this responsibility back to the developers of this technology and see if the market of product and solution developers won't respond in a positive way.

In Ray Kurzweil's *The Singularity is Near*,[4] humankind reaches the ultimate point at which the gap between technology and biology no longer exists, as technology reaches deep inside the cortex of the human mind. Never mind the man-machine interfaces for the human senses. It makes for interesting science fiction, and it's an idea that some entertain as a possibility in some very distant future. Yet Mr. Kurzweil speaks of it not as science fiction but as the acceleration of science made real through innovation on a trajectory in near reach for the Millennial generation and even for some baby boomers. It is a mind-boggling analysis

---

[4] Ray Kurzweil, *The Singularity is Near: When Humans Transcend Biology* (Viking Adult, September 22, 2005).

not easily discounted given the strength of his construct. As innovation has *intertwined risks with benefits*, what are the consequences from the inevitable clash when the worlds of Second Life and the real world collide?

These are interesting questions for the future, but given that the future is shaped by the present, the questions are of more immediate concern. Is this future state attainable where the risks are understood and the measures put into place are a guide for achieving equilibrium? The present path for securing technology has no metrics and has little in the way even to scope the size of the problem. The CSI annual report states year after year that the information gathered is so insubstantial that it makes it difficult to arrive at conclusions with any degree of confidence. One is left with only the anecdotal evidence.

The challenges of securing the technologies and processes of Web 2.0 are significantly larger than the present challenges of strictly enterprise-based technologies that have defined boundaries. It is not that the means and the methods do not exist for securing the present generation of the Web or the future Web 2.0 generation. It is rather that they are not applied in a consistent (and highly transparent) manner. The current path will continue until such time as technology buyers change the dynamics for how technology is acquired from the vendors of the technology by the use of standard methods for security that create transparency in the process.

In this chapter, the authors examine the world of Web 2.0 and the course of its evolution to Web 3.0 as a way of bringing out the inherent vulnerabilities associated with this new development in Web computing that far exceed the security-based practices built around controlling the assets of a local area network. The present models of perimeter and aftermarket-based security delivery are nowhere near adequate to address the complexities in Web 2.0 computing. These models have no notion of how to secure the content of Company A, stored in the network cloud of a Web 2.0 provider in business to support not just one company but to create efficient data centers hosting the data from hundreds of companies.

How will companies resolve the storage issues created by cloud computing while still meeting the compliance regulations required by various vertical sector markets? Further, how will this impact privacy and accountability embodied in the laws of countries with different regulations? The same question can be asked of millions of consumers, individuals seeking to use these new Web 2.0 services for personal or family use and wanting to feel confident that their privacy is protected.

Identity protection is at once a personal matter and an issue for business and government interacting with customers and citizens. The world is interconnected commercially and financially, a fact learned the hard way in 2008. In similar fashion, but on a deeper level and more tightly, the world is interconnected with the technologies of the Web – a World Wide Web that is growing up, expanding its reach creating new paradigms for everything in its wake.

Chapter 2 proposed a way to start by considering the notion of the SVL. In this chapter the authors make the case that Web 2.0 is a complex set of networks and applications delivered in new ways that cannot be protected by security applied after the fact.

The start of the World Wide Web has key markers in the historical record – a series of events all leading to this most serendipitous integration of technologies: the Internet, the Web browser and the rise of personal computers in the early 1990s. Web 2.0 contrasts as a series of enabling technologies for increased collaboration, more an evolution than a specific moment in time leading to the future concept of a Semantic Web.[5]

---

[5] The Semantic Web is an evolving extension of the World Wide Web in which the semantics of information and services on the web is defined, making it possible for the web to understand and satisfy the requests of people and machines to use the web content. www.wikipedia.com

Not to dampen all that can be said for the wonders of these innovative technologies, the concern in this chapter is with *the intertwined nature of the risks with the benefits*. It is whether these concerns can be understood in a manner sufficient to propose ways that counterbalance the risk. So Web 2.0 may be described as a series of small but momentous leaps forward in the innovations of connecting people and processes, with each leap forward leading to Web 3.0. It is in some respects a *"we will know we are there when we get there"* situation. In this chapter, the authors start with a short analysis to ask and answer the question, what is Web 2.0? It is not just about social networking Web sites.

Defining Web 2.0

When defining Web 2.0, the parable of the *blind men and the elephant* comes to mind – each sector of the technology world defines Web 2.0 in terms that underscore its unique perspectives on the market. Just as the parable concludes that it is only when the blind men combine their perspectives that they are able to truly understand what an elephant looks like, so it is through the combined technologies from the different sectors – the telecom industry, application and content providers – that one can better understand and define Web 2.0.

As an example, a wonderfully clever new PDA application has little value unless the mobility part of the network has sufficient bandwidth capacity to allow the application to run with satisfactory performance. Take notice of the recent gush of new commercials from the various mobility companies delivering the new innovations of Web 2.0 and see the small 3G designation made ever more prominent. The commercials are sending a message, "3G = good interactive performance." None of these "really cool" applications will survive for a moment if the network stalls with poor performance.

It's the network

The definition must begin with convergence – the combination of different media represented in voice, video and data formats delivered by an integrated IP-based infrastructure and combined business models. To the consumer, convergence is the *triple play* or *quadruple play* deliveries of broadcast, Internet access and telephony (fixed and mobile) packaged through a single home network interface device and, increasingly, services are also intermingled – a television set (as in IPTV) that can answer the telephone (Voice over IP) and surf the Net. This is just the start; it continues with video-on-demand and other services bundled by a service provider – one bill from one company for all the communications and entertainment services.

Web 2.0 is also partly defined as a wireless network that achieves true broadband capacity in mobility and is implied in the language of 3G for third generation, LTE for Long Term Evolution or Worldwide Interoperability for Microwave Access (WiMAX). All of these standards are leading to a, as yet to be formalized, 4G standard – the fourth-generation mobility standard in which speeds range from 100 Mbit/s to 1 Gbit/s – the norm for outdoor and indoor wireless networks.

The cloud must also deliver new SaaS applications and deliver them in a manner that reaches the threshold of a satisfactory user experience. One can argue that, without the high broadband wireless networks, there is no Web 2.0 in the car, at remote locations, while in public transit, at small vendor sites, with other embedded devices, for utility metering and so on. A Web 2.0 without the advances in next-generation mobility is so anemic that it can hardly be the heir to the first-generation Web.

And the definition must also include federated identity management to negotiate access control and authentication in the cloud through the exchange of credentials that happen seamlessly and agnostically (without proprietary interfaces) across technology domains (video such as television, voice such as telephony, and data) and geographic boundaries (see figure 3.1).

Once again, if no steps are taken to resolve these challenges, and in light of the fact that there is no global entity in place that can deliver all these solutions from a single source, the interchange and exchange must be part of the "solved" set of challenges, or the Web 2.0 experience will become so frustrating, significantly limiting world-wide adoption.

The network cloud is extended into the customer business premises, to the home and through mobility to the advanced end device able to serve more like the *tricorder* of science fiction movies with a multiplicity of functions where multi-modal is the norm. The network cloud chooses the best available connection automatically and can be presence aware. Access to system resources can be tailored according

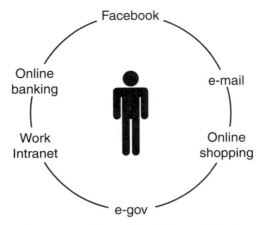

Figure 3.1   The need for federated identity

to the available network connectivity, the context of time of day, location and role.

Applications and content in the cloud

A central tenet of Web 2.0 is that the delivery of new applications issues from the cloud and is provided by service *providers* whose definition is quite broadly defined and can include any company or individual anywhere who has a server that is connected to the Internet who decides to share the fruits of his or her creativity with the rest of the world. Some of the most popular applications for this creativity are Facebook and YouTube, but there is no end to the providers for the creativity coming forth and to the integration of these applications delivered with *mashup* services that combine in derivations impossible to fully predict.

It is just a small step from SaaS (applications in the cloud) to the storage of the information – the content in all forms also kept in the cloud (content in the cloud), stored and accessible as needed. The content can be anything from personal medical records with X-rays and blood laboratory results, to the full range of business applications, databases and documents. For the right service level agreement with the right contract, the imperative of a reduced cost to "lease" technology infrastructure versus acquiring and operating a technology infrastructure becomes compelling for individuals from all walks of life and for businesses of all sizes.

Personalization is another way to define Web 2.0, with companies gathering information that tailors the marketing to the customer with greater and greater precision. The data collected at the supermarket when goods are purchased ties an individual to certain tastes and a certain level of spending for quality. Web sites visited for news, for online purchases, for entertainment, places and people called over the Web phone all yield valuable pieces of information that can be used to build a profile of an individual and accurately gauge behavior. This information has monetary value so it is collected, sold and re-sold multiple times over to any number of businesses, creating a more precise image of the consumer and the business. It is only a small step to the point where this kind of information can shape the type of insurance to price the service on a more precise understanding of the risk. This applies to the automobile that is purchased and even to the health of the individual that is gleaned from the information contained in medical records.

Greater precision of information yields improved customer intimacy, lower friction in the business processes (supply channels) and reduced latency (connected all the time). These are the fruits of adopting Web 2.0 and beyond. The companies most agile with lower points for friction and latency with greater precision in how they deliver goods and services are the companies that will succeed over the competition.

Unified Communications (UC) connects the workforce with a blending of communications and translation between what is currently a juggling act of e-mail, text messages, voice at the desk and on mobile devices, and facsimiles on separate domains. UC provides a way for individuals to seamlessly integrate personal functions with work functions without the need to carry a basket-load of different devices.

The culture for this new world of Web 2.0 is already here and taking full advantage of these freedoms. Facebook, the video content on YouTube and Twitter are, in certain respects, the attributes that define the Millennial generation. It is the citizen, private person and workforce employee all together as one – *alles zusammen* as they say in German.

One area where developing social networking mores have been taken to the extreme is Second Life, an environment where one can assume other identities through avatars – an alter ego, a virtual person (see figure 3.2) that is not connect to one's real world personality – and

Figure 3.2 Avatar

explore social interactions with other avatars in cyberspace. It is also a cyber place, *the grid*, where these virtual interactions take place, and the content of all this creation is controlled with real ownership rights, not unlike physical property. It is virtual, but it is not without real value as the Linden Dollar $L becomes the currency of exchange bought from *brokerages* who charge real money.

So, the working definition of Web 2.0 for this analysis is a series of technologies evolving with time to deliver a ubiquitous (always-on in all locations), un-tethered (mobile and served by both the enterprise LAN and the services Internet cloud) and unconstrained (broadband capacity bandwidth in all situations) experience rich in multi-modal media and where the information can be exchanged and blended as in *mashups* where the participation is interactive.

The analysis of the security challenges of Web 2.0 begins with a short look into *motive, capability (or means) and opportunity*, followed by consideration of the technology: the network (both fixed and wireless), applications and content storage. Throughout this discussion the authors touch on the issues of policy, including management and governance alongside the considerations of the government entrusted with protection of national infrastructures, the enterprise business and the individual consumer.

The Challenges of Web 2.0 Security

In this section, the focus is on the risk side of the risk-and-benefit equation, explaining why the security defenses of LAN-based enterprises are inadequate protection for business functions that exist outside the enterprise perimeter. Present security defenses have been designed to control enterprise assets; in the world of Web 2.0, the issue of control concerns systems and data that reside outside the sphere of enterprise control.

Motive, Capability and Opportunity

Criminologists assert that crime comprises three elements: *motive, capability (or means)* and *opportunity*. This tri-partite framework is equally applicable in cyberspace even as the enterprise of crime syndicates shifts its attention from physical targets to online commerce and e-government functions.

Cyber criminal capabilities are formidable, affordable and yielded with impunity, and protected by distance and international borders. An excellent step for cyber law enforcement came with the development of the Center for Strategic and International Studies Commission for Cyber Security (CCIS). However valuable such an effort is in developing solutions to law enforcement initiatives surrounding cyber security, its reach is only as far as the countries or nation-states that come forward to participate in extradition treaties and the prosecution of such crimes. Few doubt that the capability of the threat against LAN-based systems exceeds the capabilities of defenses to detect and respond in time to stop the impact of an attack. One indicator of the sophistication of the threat (or capability in the crime triad) is how it operates as its own vertical market where services and tools for sale are openly marketed.

On the motive side, the reasons are reaching new plateaus. Where once they were for rather benign interests (fame), these now stretch to a level of importance that are now part of the considerations for national defense strategies as in *information operations.*

Of the three ingredients in the crime triad, "opportunity" is the one that is of greatest relevance to this discussion as it is the only one of the three that is amenable to some form of control by the business interests. By shifting the enterprise processes and data stores to Web 2.0 functions (delivered by service providers with only an SLA to provide assurance of protection) the gap of risk has the potential to turn into a veritable chasm of opportunity for crime of all kinds.

What makes this even more challenging is that whereas telephony and video today still operate within largely separate infrastructures, make use of proprietary protocols and are physically isolated from one another, all these domains are rapidly fusing into one IP protocol stack and often into one mega infrastructure with the advent of Web 2.0. The benefits of Web 2.0 cannot be realized without this convergence, which handles the edge of the network in all its complexity of multi-modal service delivery and the increased capacity in the backbone of the network. It cannot be delivered without the expanded capacity of next-generation broadband wireless to support the multi-modal formats and the hundreds of millions of new handheld devices joining the Internet to make calls, catch the sports game by mobile-TV, or participate in a video conference.

Securing the Web 2.0 Network

The story begins with *the Network*. As previously stated, the network of different media is becoming a single entity. It is IP-based – delivery by packet switching – no longer circuit-based. It is also clear that Web 2.0 does not exist as the heir to the information revolution without an advanced network, one that is far more capable, more nuanced and streamlined for differences between competitive providers.

Where is the complexity in the network, and by extension, where are the vulnerable points that are hidden in the complexity? Consider that there are more than fifty network elements that must interact in the IP Multimedia System (IMS) architecture (see appendix, Ch. 3, Ref. 1). These network elements interact to process the access, session setup and billing for the edge of the network that makes IP telephony, IPTV and the other services that must work together over a common infrastructure.

The architectural complexity of the three separate infrastructures in legacy systems, if added together, is made dramatically simpler with IMS, but as an all-in-one-architecture, IMS is more complex than any of the other three alone. This is not criticism; it is simply a fact and a reflection of the demands to deliver the service where the media formats require differences in handling signaling control, management and quality for different end-users and end-user devices.

The devil is in the details – starting with the protocols

HTTP and the HTML data that it carries are the underlying technologies of the current Web as well as Web 2.0. For criminal elements intent on getting deeper access to the network, increasingly their focus of attention is on the protocol and the content held in the network.

IMS uses the Session Initiation Protocol (SIP) for signaling – a control of communications between end-users and among IMS functional elements, including the application servers. SIP messages are ASCII-based; easy to read, create and modify; and therefore amenable to eavesdropping, interception and forgery. The ease of access to broadband wireless networks (no longer needing to have physical access) means that the inside of the network is more readily accessible for those with the right tools and so the concern is with protecting the protocols (see appendix, Ch. 3, Ref. 2).

Protocols such as Extensible Markup Language (XML) and Simple Object Access Protocol (SOAP) are used extensively in Web-based transactions and are examples of protocols that are currently applied to end-user self management. Self management is a trend that will, by necessity, greatly expand in Web 2.0 networks as a less costly and more efficient means for provisioning of services that can achieve a reduction in the costly expense of establishing customer service centers. As both XML and SOAP are open, text-based protocols, they also are easy to read, create, modify and therefore subject to eavesdropping, forging and interception.

The risk is that without adequate protection, the protocols are open to disclosure of Personal Identifying Information (PII) as well as theft of service. The RADIUS/DIAMETER protocols that perform the authentication exchange between the end-user and the Authentication, Authorization and Accounting (AAA) servers also play an important role in service access and need to be secured or otherwise are also an open invitation to fraud, identify theft and theft of service (see appendix, Ch. 3, Ref. 3).

Security required end to end

IP-based end-point devices connected to a publicly available network are accessible from anywhere around the world. These threats are often beyond the reach of legal protection or recourse; there is no physical isolation of international boundaries on the Internet. As core network devices are merging with edge network devices and applications servers, and these previously isolated network elements are increasingly finding a place in people's homes and customer premises, the need for designed-in security becomes ever more important than before. The more intelligent these end devices become, the higher the level of security that will be required to protect them; these devices and their services need to be managed, a condition that must be accounted for in the overall system design and operational model. The net result of this trend is to move portions of the network cloud into the customer premises (either residential or business)(see appendix, Ch. 3, Ref. 4).

Securing the interfaces and why they need to be secured

Device IP interfaces provide attackers entry into the network and it is typically the first parts of the network attacked. An attack sequence typically consists of the following:

- Network reconnaissance consisting of scanning the network for interfaces with visible IP addresses

- Port scanning consisting of scanning the discovered IP interfaces for active protocols and services

- Software foot-printing to determine what software is running on the device based on responses to running services to probing messages

- Attack known software vulnerabilities in the running software

Interestingly enough, the need to secure the device management interfaces has only recently been recognized. This stems back to the days of out-of-band management using proprietary protocols over a private network. In-band management has brought the need for device management interfaces to the fore. Even local asynchronous management ports are connected to IP networks these days, by means of terminal servers, for example. A reliance on physical security to protect these ports no longer suffices (see appendix, Ch. 3, Ref. 5).

Virtualization is not necessarily a security net gain

The current trend toward virtualization can serve to reduce risk as a strategy for disaster recovery and configuration control. It may, however, increase the complexity surrounding securing devices by increasing the number of layers that need to be secured. Each virtual machine must be secured individually, and it starts with the hypervisor[6] that has supervisory access over every virtual machine. Finally, security of the physical host systems (server) is more important than ever; everything associated with each virtual machine resides on the host system's disk, runs in the host system's memory, and utilizes the host system's processor.

The Wireless Data Challenge

Driven by major advancements in technology and fueled by the insatiable demand of customers to be connected to the World Wide Web 24/7, even when on the move, wireless networks are quickly evolving to be more like IP networks. If global market penetration statistics are any measure, one might argue that wireless networks have already completed their transformation to IP networks, and did so seemingly overnight. In fact, most mobile devices in the market today are not only IP-enabled, but also are used by an increasing number of subscribers to gain access to the Internet and run data-intensive applications while on the move. The global build-out of 3G networks and initial deployment of 4G networks promises to deliver an undisputed "true" wireless broadband experience for subscribers that enables a Web 2.0 experience to be realized seamlessly across all access technologies.

Designing, building and securing an IP network is an art whose significant challenges are well known. The challenges will certainly grow in complexity and magnitude as data applications evolve with the rollout of Web 2.0 services. Accordingly, the construction and operation of the data communications network and access must take that into account. However, often overlooked is the fact that wireless data networks introduce significant *additional* challenges that must be considered to ensure the overall viability of the network.

---

[6] Hypervisors are classified in two types: Type 1 (or native, bare-metal) hypervisors are software systems that run directly on the host's hardware as a hardware control and guest operating system monitor. A guest operating system thus runs on another level above the hypervisor. Type 2 (or hosted) hypervisors are software applications running within a conventional operating system environment. Considering the hypervisor layer being a distinct software layer, guest operating systems thus run at the third level above the hardware.

Ensuring *network availability* is one example of an additional security challenge for broadband wireless (see Figure 3.3 below) with its different forms of traffic. The highly optimized and shared radio frequency means that systems designers must ensure that all users gaining access communicate within strict usage parameters or the shared medium becomes vulnerable to a denial of service disruption. Bandwidth utilization is certainly one of the key considerations. A wireless network is not simply a wired IP network without wires. It behaves very differently from traditional networks with the additional requirement that it interoperate with all of the current and evolving data applications so as to provide subscribers a technology-agnostic and seamless Web 2.0 experience.

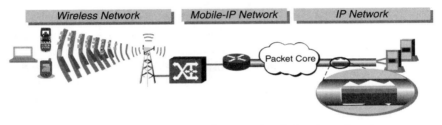

Figure 3.3   Security considerations in wireless broadband

In preparing for the transformation of the wireless network to a wireless *data* network, we can apply lessons learned from the use of earlier wireless network generations that were responsible for transmitting simple traffic (such as voice). These networks were predominantly concerned with regulating "minutes" of usage as capacity of the wireless network is physically constrained by the allocation and use of air spectrum and can only support a finite number of instantaneous phone calls. It is easy to recall any number of times where simple voice call congestion resulted in a dropped or failed connection. These incidents occur regularly in emergency situations, during popular events or even during rush hour at the end of the busy week on Friday afternoon. This is a simple reminder that a wireless network can only support a finite number of users who are instantly using it – and was designed and architected with the understanding that voice subscribers are mostly *not* making phone calls. It is fundamentally a shared infrastructure, where only a fraction of the subscribers are expected to use the network at any instant in time.

Now take that infrastructure and upgrade it to support data delivery and then map the data application bits and bytes to their consumption of wireless resources (such as minutes). In wireless networks it is not enough to understand how *much* data is sent, to whom and from what source, but it is equally important to understand *how* the data is sent. The method by which an application is transmitted – the "how" – has a profound influence on the performance and availability of the wireless network. In the context of Web 2.0 applications transmitting over a wireless infrastructure, there exists a new potential for seemingly simple and low-volume data applications to break the network and cause widespread congestion and DoS conditions.

Stated simply

All bytes are not equal in a wireless data network. In particular, the applications that subscribers use today transmit over the network in ways that result in widely varying Radio Access Network (RAN) usage efficiencies that span at least five orders of magnitude – an uncertainty range that becomes larger as networks become faster. Two identical packets can consume a significantly different amount of capacity in the network simply because of the transmission properties of the session to which they belong. Accordingly, the underlying network infrastructure must account for traffic models that not only vary during the day, but also vary from one day to the next as subscribers introduce new applications that may or may not be wireless-friendly and have highly variable network cost to deliver in a way that is intimately linked to the network design and loading.

The following examples illustrate this in more detail: a subscriber session where a 1 MB file is downloaded consumes *on average* 30 seconds of radio resources (maximum rates would result in shorter resource usage – as low as a few seconds given optimal resource conditions and available wireless data technologies). Compare this with a subscriber session that again downloads 1 MB, this time made up of many small e-mails. This behavior, *on average*, consumes 240-times more airtime and 1500-times more signaling load on the Radio Network Controllers (significantly larger resource consumption is not only possible in theory but also realized in practice). Today's reality, where IP applications can have such pronounced and varied impact on network performance, departs dramatically from the "good old days" of predictable wireless voice applications and this trend will only become more pronounced and significant as the full potential of Web 2.0 is realized. New solutions, designs and application qualification processes are required to comprehensively support efficient, profitable and secure delivery of current and next-generation applications over a wireless IP network.

The good news is that wireless operators can leverage vast industry knowledge and experience about building, operating and optimizing wired IP networks to efficiently build, operate and secure these wireless IP networks. Moreover, many IP network event policy and traffic management tools are readily available and can be used immediately in wireless IP networks.

The bad news is that traditional IP network management technologies are still implemented based on the assumption that the usage of Network Minutes equates to Volume/Bandwidth, an equation that is clearly not applicable in a wireless framework and prone to substantial errors when applied. In a sense, the existing tools have not yet transformed themselves to be sufficiently wireless-aware. As such, wireless networks across the globe are often architected to minimize tonnage and bytes but not to maximize use of radio resources (which include bytes, minutes and signaling resources). Given that much of the cost in building and operating a wireless network is tied to radio resources, in some cases up to 80 percent of the operator's investment, it follows naturally that RAN optimization is not only critical for the delivery of current and evolving applications, but also provides an opportunity to differentiate network performance and the subscriber experience (by alleviating congestion), while maintaining a best-in-class cost structure.

What does this all mean for the end-user? While perhaps an over-simplification, there is no question that users have become conditioned to assuming that the network is always available and unconstrained for the emerging applications they use. This assumption is believed to be true whether a subscriber is using Web 2.0 applications for personal reasons, or a business professional that is increasingly leveraging wireless network resources to break the barriers of a brick-and-mortar office and realize the true benefits of a transparent mobile office. But as discussed above, assumption of an always-on, always available network of infinite capacity is not valid. This is especially the case in the context of emerging wireless networks which are just now beginning to legitimately support a broadband experience, while having to support a highly astute subscriber, and a very rich set of applications that are continuously evolving. With the *mashup* of current and Web 2.0 applications in the network, it is essential to recognize the critical dependencies to ensure that the objective of a successful and ubiquitous rollout of Web 2.0 indeed materializes as being successful and ubiquitous.

Securing the Web 2.0 Applications and Content

Securing the data exchanges - and why they need to be secured

One only needs to look at the current situation with the prolific abundance of malware to understand the need for secure data exchanges. The early viruses attached themselves to files or diskette boot partitions exchanged by individuals. Network worms became the next generation of malware propagating through the network by scanning for vulnerable hosts, creating copies and consuming network bandwidth and device resources until the network collapses. In contrast to the present threats, those were the good old days. The current generation of malware, typified by drive-by infections where an IFRAME in an invisible text area of a Web page (height=0, width=0) transparently downloads malicious code to a user's device, is insidious and more difficult to prevent. Web 2.0 and its ultimate evolution to Web 3.0 continues the prolific free exchange of data represented by peer-to-peer, and targeted advertising, which creates even greater opportunity for malware to propagate in ways entirely invisible to human detection.

For Web 2.0, the business model has been set: revenue is generated from creating intelligent ad-targeting. As content in all forms becomes more commoditized (as in free telephony), advertising becomes the primary source of revenue – with the advertiser paying per the number of clicks on an ad. These *referral* forms of revenue creation are volume-dependent and increasingly dependent upon how relevant the advertising is to the individual. The ability to personalize the advertising is a *killer application* – and is achieved from collecting and analyzing an increasingly large amount of information about the individual. This type of information is in the gray zone between legitimate marketing and a breach of personal privacy. It is information that shines like gold to criminal syndicates able to compromise the existing methods for authentication used in the transactions of everyday life.

The SaaS model generally associated with business software is a low-cost way for businesses to obtain the same benefits from commercially licensed, internally operated software that offers a reduction in cost from the associated complexity and high initial cost of purchase. Application areas such as customer relationship management, video conferencing, human resources, technology service management, accounting, Web analytics, Web content management, and email are some of the initial markets showing success.

> In the SaaS model, the customer relinquishes control over software versions or changing requirements; the cost to use the service becomes a continuous expense, rather than a single expense with its associated infrastructure at time of purchase. The burden of securing application software and the content now shifts to the SaaS service provider. The customer relinquishes control over the software and the protection of the content; a situation where all the eggs really are in one basket and under the control of a SaaS service provider *(see appendix, Ch. 3, Ref. 6).*

IPTV network-based devices such as video servers and video repositories must be protected due to the high value of their content. The digital rights management systems must also be protected or the entire set of controls is compromised. The distributed nature of these services makes security more complicated; there is typically not one video server in an IPTV network, but multiple video servers deployed geographically closer to the customer in a content delivery network. Local video servers may even receive content that is not ready for general release, in anticipation of the expected demand when it is released.

E-mail makes use of best-effort delivery and is highly adaptable to variations in bandwidth and other connection quality capacities with the various links in the delivery route. This is not the case for voice and video where quality-of-service and jitter matters greatly and must be considered. Without a full consideration of the points of vulnerability and a well constructed secure design, the IMS architecture is vulnerable – open to all the well known IP-based attacks: DoS, worm propagations, theft of service and data loss. The list is long. The transmutation of these threats that are well known in the *data* side reaching into what has been relatively (in contrast with data) absent from the other media is happening and can be expected to continue (see appendix, Ch. 3, Ref. 7).

Protecting privacy

The benefits of storing information in the network cloud are clear: information is available any time, anywhere, thus enabling a truly Service Oriented Architecture where the infrastructure is independent of the service (see appendix, Ch. 3, Ref. 8).

> Keeping medical records with a content service provider is a good example of where there are significant benefits and where there are significant security concerns. A person needing medical attention while traveling outside access to their health provider could simply make their records available to the attending practitioner online and potentially avoid a misdiagnosis or costly lab work – the records, including current medications, allergies, etc., would be readily available to them. The health industry can also benefit from improvements in the efficiency of information flow and ultimately improvements in overall health business efficiency. In the wrong hands, the most personal information about an individual can be compromised – the kind of information that can be used to determine insurability or even limitations for jobs. There is probably no more contentious issue than this one; the potential for misuse is almost without limit.

There is no limit to the methods and dangers that can result from storing content in the cloud that can be compromised by accidental or deliberate commingling with other customer's data, the deliberate misuse or release of information, identity theft and even corporate espionage. Encryption alone is no longer sufficient as a barrier and security for the network. Security for content in the cloud must be thoroughly integrated into the information contained in the network at all levels with multiple levels of protection that include integrity checking, more rigorous authentication and disaster recovery techniques.

Any business that is considering using the network cloud to store corporate information, particularly customer data, runs another risk that exceeds simply confronting customers with the loss of highly personal data. Regulations abound with clear penalties for lack of compliance. Described earlier, they include HIPAA, Gramm-Leach-Bliley (GLBA), Sarbanes-Oxley, the Family Educational Rights and Privacy Act (FERPA), Payment Card Industry Data Security Standard (PCI-DSS) and more. Equivalent, and often more stringent legislation exists in many other countries, particularly some of those in Europe where provisions for privacy protection is more stringent than elsewhere.

All of the above argues for institution of a consistent, network-wide, run-time enforcement of information assurance policy by the network cloud operators that is supported by mechanisms that provide data privacy protection and facilitate legal audit. It will always be an environment in which trust is never complete – and there is a need to verify and verify again.

Integrity checking

Maintaining the integrity of systems and information is a key technique to the solutions that resolve the challenges of security in Web 2.0. It has been largely missing from the present toolkits, but is essential to overcoming the risks of botnets and rootkits and other forms of attack that rely on stealth and speed. This is a subject that merits its own lengthy discussion – addressed here to point out simply its absence in many present day systems and in assuring that the digital information resident in the databases is associated with some measure of security.

In present and evolving Web 2.0 systems, there is simply not enough knowledge available that would make it possible to judge integrity of the software, the boot up or of the information kept in the network. This inability to gauge software integrity opens up the opportunity for spoofing and fraud, and the list of methods that have been employed to compromise this lack of integrity is long. Systems slowly degrade, filling and consuming the resources of the computers and the databases until the system fails altogether. Along the forensic path to what happened to cause the crash is a trail of litter – all the points in the path where the integrity was compromised – but without the ability to detect the unauthorized change, it simply goes undetected until the system fails and the business or government function supported by that particular technology also fails.

Of greater concern is the data that is used to make decisions. The system can be restored, but decisions may not be able to be reversed; the consequences of this are limitless. Are the technology companies delivering Web 2.0 designing integrity checking into their systems? It is not that the technology is not available (See appendix Ch 3, Ref 9).

An aspect of maintaining the integrity of information stored in the cloud is related to SaaS. Malware infection of application software violates the integrity of the software; can the SaaS provider distributing to customers assure that the software is free of malware? Also, what about uninterested third parties – parties that are infected by enterprises who were infected by the SaaS application provider? These are issues that need to be worked before SaaS goes mainstream in Web 2.0 *(see appendix, Ch. 3, Ref. 9).*

Other considerations

It should be clear that the topics presented here warrant a great deal more analysis than the short commentary offered here. System performance in reliability and manageability and overall governance are among the other topics that need addressing in the challenges to securing the world of Web 2.0. There are also views to be considered for national infrastructure protection. Virtualization is a topic garnering a great deal of attention for its benefits; only more recently has the discussion also picked up on the risks – particularly those that result from vulnerabilities in the hypervisor. Even though virtualization is in a nascent stage it is already evident that the risks are only starting to be understood and companies should proceed with caution. To close this discussion, consider the viewpoint of the end-user – the different generations of people using or impacted by the world of Web 2.0.

The view from the end-user is one of very little knowledge regarding security issues and at the same time being very susceptible to its risks. Privacy is a prime consideration, but the concerns go deeper and attach to individual economical viability, including the ability to get work and insurance.

It has always been the case that individuals are defined in the abstract – by what is owned, by a reputation and by a certificate. In the digital world, the definition of "I" is more potent and more vulnerable. It's time for individuals to ask and get the right answers for how to gain control of the data that defines them. The repercussions of losing control of this to agents – even well meaning agents – means that one can lose the very set of things that defines the person.

There is a risk to putting all of that personal information willingly, or unwillingly as in targeted marketing, in the network cloud. There will be a price to be paid and what a dear price it will be. Individuals, businesses and governments are equally subjected to the intertwined nature of benefit and accompanying risk.

4

Limitations of the Present Models

The cost of poor security in the United States alone is between $22.2 and $59.5 billion *per year (NIST)[1]*

Executive Summary

Information security surveys are released on a regular cycle revealing what should not be surprising – security breaches increase and there seems to be no end to the rising impact. Could it be that the reason is the way information security and technology organizations approach protecting their information?

As the products that are purchased for technology operations are not consistently measured to any given hardening standard (government certification as the exception), one must consider the current models for hardening as complicit in this problem. One needs to look no further than the "aftermarket" security model for applying security. What does this mean?

Hardening is accomplished at two levels. The first level of hardening is supposed to be accomplished by the manufacturer of the technology product. At this level the product development teams should be driving out of the designs the known vulnerabilities in operating systems that can be exploited by criminals and attackers. This includes buffer overflows and back doors left in by software developers during testing. These vulnerabilities such as back doors create the need for a never-ending routine of security patching applied

---

[1] http://www.nist.gov/public_affairs/releases/n02-10.htm

to operating systems, applications and product software. The second level of hardening involves the information security teams configuring the systems to meet the requirements of the organization.

During product development, the engineers, system designers and architects need to assure their products and solutions with security as a basic property so that critical infrastructure is less susceptible to common attacks. Government agencies have been applying these principles for some time with a degree of success requiring that product vendors harden the equipment and software they sell. There is no such well-followed parallel for systems and software developed for normal business use. Indeed as government agencies also started following the same process of buying technology products as *commercial-off-the-shelf*, there has been little difference in government from business in vulnerability announcements, followed by patching frenzy. For most businesses, it is an ad hoc process, as it is with most governments.

The aftermarket approach to security is the opposite of the hardening described here. As most technology buyers are ill-equipped to redesign the product-solutions they employ to meet their enterprise security requirements, the lack of critical security hardening by product manufacturers and application developers forces information security professionals to react accordingly by applying the approach of protecting their systems at the network perimeter. In this model, the operation utilizes separate specialized components placed at strategic locations in the network such as at the entry-exit points. This self-preservation form of protection involves a growing litany of firewalls, intrusion detection and protection systems (IDS/IPS), separate software protection by employing antivirus detection, content filtering, and so on. But in many cases, the very sophistication incorporated into the security systems used to protect the perimeter and the constantly changing number and types of threats encountered daily make them difficult to configure properly and thus prone to defeat.

In addition to the problem of maintaining perimeter security to protect the enterprise, this model is in direct contrast with the business direction and technology operations movement called deperimeterization.[2] Most organizations have contractors, consultants, and business partners in addition to their own employees who need to access the systems, and they don't all work behind the same perimeter defenses. This undermines what used to be clear borders around computer networks and makes it much more difficult to protect information. The impact can be seen by the losses of critical data not from within the perimeter of the enterprise but from outside the perimeter on laptops, data being transmitted to outside sources or data storage facilities that are outside of the network they can protect.

Not unexpectedly there is a constant tug-of-war between how to adequately protect users' sensitive and confidential information and corporate intellectual property, while still being able to provide a ubiquitous mechanism to transact business. One reaction from these stresses has been for national and state governments to impose security regulations, while other industry bodies have developed industry-based security standards to impose a baseline for security within the various industry verticals. Despite this well intentioned reaction, the problem is that these standards and regulations have provided only high-level

---

[2] Jericho Forum, www.jerichoforum.org

principles greatly lacking in more specific implementation details. As such, they leave much to the interpretation of the implementer. Depending on the experience, knowledge and capabilities of each respective security practitioner and how they help to develop the policies, practices, standards and controls the outcome is sure to vary from instance to instance. System audits have helped, but many audit findings continue year-after-year with little in sustainable security improvements.

As discussed in earlier chapters, the issue boils down to one of risk. In today's business world, technology is intertwined with all business processes and transactions. Thus, most information that needs to be protected will touch some type of technology systems or network component during its inception, use or destruction and as such needs to be protected appropriately. Also stated earlier are how these risks pale in comparison with what is coming with Web 2.0, a world where the challenges of protecting information are significantly larger in scope.

There is a solution and it begins with metrics embodied in standards that reach deeper in guiding not just at the policy and process level, but to how products and solutions are actually designed, engineered and developed. On the practice side of this problem, one clear goal is to make it so that it does not take a specialized security expert to apply basic security principles in product and solution development. The security features and techniques for the most part already exist – what has been missing is the consistent application of the same. Security *designed in*, not passed to the buyer of technology to purchase aftermarket is good business in the long-term. The practice of applying an ad-hoc, minimum set of hardening controls lacks a well constructed business rationalization, so the default of saving the cost has persisted. This lack of business rationalization cuts across every cycle of technology development, such as requirements, specifications, design, acquisition, installation and operation. If security could be measured, a baseline of its current state could be understood while making better judgments for design, purchase and access.

There are answers to this dilemma that deal with measuring security that will be answered later in this book. It will require a change in the models in use today and the development of new ones based on the ability to measure security and apply the correct business rationality on the use of technology.

Aftermarket Security – A Broken Model

The current model used to protect technology systems is a "bolt it on" operation, or, aftermarket model as already described. For whatever reason and by whatever name, everyone expects software bugs and security issues to be found after deployment. The fact is that there are few legitimate reasons, only the absence of disciplined code development and an attitude if one can call it that, of a responsibility passed. As an example, there are software scanners on the market today that will scan application software in development for known security issues. Yet, software for technology equipment continues to be shipped containing buffer overflows and other basic security issues. Why?

What If Civil Engineers Built Bridges Like Developers Write Code?

So how does an organization deal with these vulnerable products? Patch management is the bane of the existence for too many network and information security professionals. The technology buyer cannot remedy vulnerabilities in commercial products, so it creates the conditions for a relationship with the technology developer reliant on their ability and willingness to do the right thing and fix such post-sale vulnerabilities quickly and efficiently. For the most part, this remains out of the buyer's direct control.

With patching the only recourse, sophisticated change-management systems must be implemented to manage all of the patches that need to be applied each month for a typical network or technology infrastructure. There may be scores of patches that need to be applied for a given maintenance window and the occasional crisis patch that puts the ICT department on an overnight drill. The operational costs for the administration and maintenance of the products throughout their life cycles are significant.

On the product development end, the Point of Creation in the SVL, the working perception is that security is an unwarranted cost that reduces the competitiveness of the product. This is the short-term thinking behind the problem with the practice of security. For the buyer, this short-term thinking sets up the patching operation described above.

There is a second level of hardening that takes place where the information security teams configure the products to meet the organization's requirements. A simple example involves fitting the security hardening implementation of various products in the network to the requirements of the company as with password complexity. The degree of hardening in the products and the requirements (potentially driven by governing regulations) are likely not consistent so work-arounds are in order. The technology and information security teams must install and harden a number of different products in order to produce a workable system or service. It is a situation ripe for complexity in which lie other potential vulnerabilities that could be exploited. It is easy to see how this gets complicated rather quickly and it calls out for a standardized security framework that scales from the product to the solution level at the first level of hardening (within the point of product creation) and in the enterprise where the second level of hardening must take place (at the point of technology integration).

By starting with an unhardened product and the inconsistencies that abound at the point of integration it is hardly surprising that enterprises are left with an aftermarket approach to protecting an organization's ICT infrastructure. It all starts with the lack of critical security harden-ing by the product manufacturers and application developers coupled with the fact that technology buyers are ill equipped to redesign additional security into the products they buy.

This is referred to as the perimeter security model. In this model, the ICT operation uses separate security products acting separately or in concert to protect the enterprise, such as utilizing firewalls, intrusion detection and protection systems (IDS/IPS), and separate software protection by employing antivirus software. Often the very sophistication incorporated into the security systems used to protect the perimeters and the constantly changing number and types of threats encountered daily make them difficult to configure properly and open to defeat. As an example, firewall rule maintenance represents one of the most significant problems for an information security operations team. A firewall administrator can spend a large portion of the day in just validating and complying with requests for port openings; an exercise ripe for human error where a port remains open that should be closed setting up the opportunity for a network penetration.

Each perimeter protection device can cost thousands of dollars to purchase and maintain and despite its cost these defenses are insuffi-cient to guard against the highly sophisticated threats that abound. The advantage is with the criminal and attacker – organizations have a target-rich environment of vulnerable points, and can be easily compromised since the data they seek may not even be within the perimeter. It could be on unprotected laptops or when information is transferred to business partners.

Regardless of the complexity of the enterprise's technology infrastructure and whether information resides on the machines of the mobile workforce, vendors, suppliers or customers or the Web 2.0 applications that are being implemented, it is an aftermarket security model pervasive in the ICT industry and by all accounts it is a broken model – one certainly unsuited to the challenges of the expanding use of Web 2.0 computing. By building products that leave security for later, the resulting behavior is in continuing to build and implement perimeter security – a contradiction to how networks really are and need to be.

Standards and Regulations

Aftermarket, bolt-on product-based security and the use of perimeter security continues, and organizations continue to suffer from ever increasing and costly security breaches. Businesses and users know that something needs to be done, but are at a loss how to correct a systemic problem.

Industry and trade groups, as well as national and state governments and their agencies, have developed their own brand of "relief." This relief comes in the form of standards and regulations. Standards are the guidance provided by industry and trade groups to aid organizations in developing policies and practices with which to apply security and to provide a gauge for application completeness. The International Organization for Standardization (ISO), the International Telecommunications Union (ITU), the National Institutes of Standards and Technology (NIST) are a few of these industry, trade and government organizations that have developed and published security standards.

Standards are an established norm or requirement. They are usually a formalized document developed by a team of people that have expertise in a particular discipline. The standard is usually open to public review and comment before it is formalized. The standard, when finalized, usually contains a formal consensus of technical experts. Some standards are voluntary and others are utilized to allow an organization to meet a standard of practice on par with others in the organization's industry. Free market forces mostly govern enforcement of a de facto standard. Other standards are mandatory and are meant to ensure consistent practices that can be defined and measured to ensure the safety and security of a given industry, its customers and stakeholders.

Standards and guidelines vary in specificity and may or may not have defined metrics to determine adherence. They are generally reviewed periodically as the industry changes its processes and technologies to keep the standard up to date. Standards are policed informally either by internal or external auditors and many times are formally assessed by technical experts.

The ISO 27002 "Code of Practice for Information Security Management" standard is utilized by many businesses across many industry verticals (such as finance, utility, petrochemical, telecommunications, insurance and pharmaceutical) to provide the policy framework for establishing security controls within the operation. The Federal Financial Institutions Examination Council (FFIEC) provides guidance to examiners for the Federal Reserve, National Credit Union Administration, Office of Thrift Supervision and the Office of the Comptroller of Currency. These are the regulatory bodies that oversee the majority of financial institutions. The FFIEC creates handbooks, and these handbooks are used by auditors to evaluate the institution's risk management processes, point to specific areas to review, how to measure compliance and a review of oversight obligations. Audit reports are then used to get the institution's compliance with the standards of practice defined in the handbook.

NIST also provides special publications/guides such as the SP800-100 *Information Security Handbook*,[3] the SP800-53 *Recommended Security Controls for Federal Information Systems*[4] and the SP800-82 *Guide to Industrial Control Systems Security*[5] to provide guidance in the development and protection of mostly federal systems. These guides have been used successfully by corporations to develop and maintain comprehensive security management programs.

Organizations that wish to develop security programs and are not under any specific regulations often utilize standards and guides to aid

---

[3] http://csrc.nist.gov/publications/PubsSPs.html

[4] ibid

[5] ibid

them in that effort. Other organizations that are under specific regulations use these standards and guides to provide specific metrics and direction often lacking in governmental regulations.

Lawmakers or attorneys working for a governmental body generally draft regulations. Even though they utilize technical experts that are very knowledgeable in their industry, the regulations usually take on a legal approach instead of a technical one. The purpose of a regulation is to communicate the government or agency's expectations as to a level of conduct and practice.

There are always some negative aspects to not following the regulations, such as monetary fines or cessation of operation for a defined period, which could end up being permanent. The positive aspects for following a regulation are usually twofold: better, safer or perhaps less expensive operational practices for the public, user community or employees and for the company being regulated the ability to continue in the business they are engaged in. Regulations do not always keep pace with fast changing industries such as e-commerce.

Regulations are usually a product of a gross failure of some segment of the industry and are a government's reaction to that failure. There are several well-known regulations that have information or cyber security as their basis for being. The Healthcare Information Portability and Accountability Act (HIPAA) was enacted by Congress in 1996 and is a regulation that governs all healthcare providers, payers, clearing houses and insurance providers who utilize personal healthcare information. It was enacted to provide simplification of healthcare records (to reduce cost) and protection standards for the storage, use and release of personal healthcare information. Sarbanes-Oxley was the legislation and regulation enacted in 2002 in response to the Enron, Global Crossing and MCI financial scandals. It established rules on the creation, modification and destruction of financial reporting information and placed many security restrictions on technology data and practices. On August 8, 2005, the Federal Energy Regulatory Commission passed through Congress the Electricity Modernization Act of 2005,[6] which certified the North American Electric Reliability Corporation (NERC) with establishing reliability and security standards for all of the electric utilities in the United States and Canada. NERC immediately released its cyber security regulations, NERC-CIP

---

[6] http://www.congress.gov/cgi-bin/bdquery/z?d109:SN00010:@@@L&summ2=m&

002-009,[7] which spelled out cyber security compliance requirements, timeframes for compliance and set fines for failures to comply within the specified timeframes.

All of these regulations caused a great deal of concern when enacted. Because they are written to be legal documents, they lack a degree of specificity and are often left vague to allow flexibility in their application. Each has been addressed differently by the regulated organizations they control. With HIPAA, ISO 27001 was used to provide a better and more comprehensive mechanism for compliance. NIST developed SP800-66 *An Introductory Resource Guide for Implementing the HIPAA Security Rule*[8] to aid in compliance. If an organization can show compliance to an internationally recognized standard or guide, the organization can usually meet its regulatory requirements. However, compliance with a regulation or standard does not guarantee that an organization is secure. For example, a major supermarket chain that had recently undergone and passed a rigorous Credit Card Industry Standard of Practice was breached at a cost of millions of dollars to the company.

Regulate Yourself into Good Security?

Compliance regulations, certifications and standards exist to guide and drive a consistent behavior. Without a means to determine effectiveness, they may turn out to do more harm than good. So it is a fair question to ask, with respect to security: Is it "process to the rescue" or is it "process overload"? For the moment, one can make the case that it is process overload with little hope that these regulations will diminish and they may, in fact, get even more stringent. Regulations are needed, but the regulatory maze that exists is creating an undue burden to business. A more efficient and comprehensive regulatory framework from a consortium of governments working together would be helpful. Solutions to this problem may also come from pushing the burden to the developers and providers of technology where the differences of compliance between countries can be satisfied in the algorithms of software code.

---

[7] http://en.bcmpedia.org/wiki/NERC_CIP_002-009

[8] http://csrc.nist.gov/publications/PubsSPs.html

Regulations have sprung up in all vertical markets. The nature of global commerce and the intertwined nature of businesses relating to other businesses make for a dizzying complexity of international regulations. A business person working in Switzerland, traveling to Germany and to the United States must abide by different privacy regulations – the same person working for the same company in one country can access certain information, while in another country it is different. Some countries allow encryption of data using a particular key length and others do not – and the penalties for violation can be quite severe. If one were to encrypt data in China, the Chinese government must be provided with the ability to access the keys. In the UK the Eighth Data Protection Principle of Data Protection Act states: "Personal data shall not be transferred to a country or territory outside of the European Economic Area unless that country or territory ensures an adequate level of protection for the rights and freedoms of data subjects in relation to the processing of personal data."[9] So, moving data, encrypted or not, from one country to another is also a challenge.

Below are some of the Privacy and Data Security regulations in effect for several countries. The legislation describes *what* is to be protected, but the *how* is left to the security professionals to determine and then establish within their respective organizations.

Table 4.1 Privacy and Data Security Legislation

Country	Privacy Legislation
Australia	Privacy Amendment Act of 2000
Canada	Personal Information Protection and Electronic Documents Act
European	Union Personal Data Protection Directive of 1998
New Zealand	Privacy Act of 1993
Hong Kong	Hong Kong Personal Data (Privacy) Ordinance of 1995
United Kingdom	Data Protection Act of 1998
United States	Gramm-Leach-Bliley Act of 1999
	Health Insurance Portability and Accountability Act of 1996

---

[9] http://www.e-lindsey.gov.uk/council/dp-and-foi/dp-principles.cfm

Silos of Risk

Another reason that regulations do not always provide the level of security that was intended can be traced back to silos of risk. In this case, a regulation focuses on a specific area and ignores potentially surrounding or interdependent areas.

One example that comes to mind is the HIPAA regulation. It is focused specifically on personally identifiable patient information. When security and compliance personnel set forth to comply with the HIPAA regulation, they inventoried all systems where Protected Health Information (PHI) was stored or at least in all of the known areas. Because of the silo, only systems managed by the technology department were inventoried. However, buried in the bowels of a particular hospital was a cardiac imaging unit that was run by a group of doctors who used a PC to hold all of the catheterization images and associated PHI. Even though the hospital achieved HIPAA compliance (as attested to by the hospital's compliance director) the PHI was breached a few months after compliance when a hacker performed a war dialing exercise on the hospital and found a lone PC and modem. The hacker downloaded the PHI and sold it to a mailing list company. Clearly the hospital was performing only enough security work to meet the regulatory standards and was not "securing the operation."

Many times, regulations are applicable to a specific organization, entity or operation like a bank, insurance or utility company. As was the case with the hospital described above, these entities never considered the impact of overall security risks and often overlooked third party suppliers and partners. The regulations often do not always spell out external entities. The real issue is that for security to be inclusive and comprehensive it must look at all possible risks and then apply control to mitigate risks as appropriate. Data at rest and in motion and the technology systems that provide those services must be protected and included within the umbrella of the security architecture.

Another area where silos of risk can impact an organization is outsourcing. A business decision to outsource operations may not take into account the full risk considerations – how to limit the risk of business partners, for example, and still retain control, particularly if the partner is operating under a different set of laws and regulations. Outsourcing to another country can create additional risks, and the loss of data is like ringing a bell. Once it has been rung and data has been lost or compromised, the bell cannot be un-rung and information cannot be recovered. The physical and network infrastructure in other countries may not be as secure as in the country of origin.

There are many examples of data used by the outsourcing partner being misused, sold or not properly protected. In one example, a company retained an outsourcing application software developer to develop a proprietary program. The offshore developer utilized "live test data" (real data from a different company) that was also a client of the outsourcing company to test the program. When the software was delivered to the first client, unintentionally the test data of the second client was also provided – the second client's data had been compromised.

While companies can outsource a function, the risk and responsibility cannot be outsourced. In fact, as a general rule, Partner A in an outsourcing agreement inherits the additional risk of Partner B if not otherwise limited and controlled.

Absence of Metrics to Define Trust

One can argue that the present-day practice of security is more of an art than a science. Security practitioners must deal with such nebulous and un-measurable metrics as "secure" and "insecure" that are based on possibility and probability rather than in-depth analysis. In the meantime, security professionals need to operate within an organization and produce acceptable results, which cannot be quantified other than, to wait and see if a breach occurs and then to see how bad it was.

The absence of metrics to define levels of security and trust has repercussions throughout the technology life cycle. The repercussions are unnecessary costs, operational inefficiencies and a lack of transparency as they all perpetuate the current problems with the aftermarket security model. In order to avoid this dilemma, security needs to be integrated into the business process and, in this case, the product development and manufacturing life cycle. Examples include:

Design

Security designed to a particular level based on a risk model. It considers all the elements of security, applies enough security – not more than needed – and can assign a score. These things are not part of the development methodology in most current product designs but they should be.

Acquisition

The buyer-seller relationship is currently a process without structure and gets re-invented each time. There is no standard basis by which to evaluate the security between competing vendors. Security standards need to be integrated into the acquisition life cycle.

Integration

The burden of security integration is with the buyer of the technologies, but begins with the technology developer who is in the best position to integrate their technology with the other products that make up the overall solution. The integration activities include:

- Integration between the Prevent-Detect-Respond components of security

- Integration with the certification and compliance elements

- Integration with the technology management frameworks such as ITIL

- Integration with enterprise risk management

This burden is laid at the feet of the enterprise and is typically the responsibility of the CIO or CISO. This is quite a burden, particularly, as has been repeatedly established; when the providers of the different parts of the technology apply an inconsistent and ad hoc approach to security design considerations. Vendors, the creators of technology, would do well to design their products and solutions using a known, understood and industry accepted set of quantifiable standards. With these standards in mind, the buyer can better evaluate to what degree the partner is secure and whether their technology equipment and services meet the standards with sufficient rigor. This topic will be discussed in the ensuing chapter.

Operation and maintenance

Being able to measure the integrity of the system code and configurations to establish the principles of provenance – the validation that the code in operation is from a legitimate source is what provenance is about. Is it valid code, or is it a fraud from a gray channel or man-in-the-middle form of attack? The state of integrity health at boot up and in operation to thwart rootkits, botnets and other stealthy code needs to be measured. From this information one can make determinations about what level of access is permitted. Not trying to detect the malware via signatures, but rather the presence of change to operational code or configurations that have not been authorized that could be malware or more likely a mis-configuration. Both are detrimental to the health of the computing environment – the integrity of potentially critical data – and the major cause of outages.

The Current Model is Broken – Now What?

The ever-increasing frequency and cost of security breaches is the symptom of this deeply rooted problem and the problem is unresolved in large measure by the absence of a new workable model to the reality of how security should be applied. A recent ASIS[10] survey indicates financial losses from proprietary information and intellectual property theft or loss in the area of $50 billion per year worldwide,[11] and losses seem to involve critical or private information that was supposed to be protected by the corporation or government entity that held it.

Only through the use of metrics applied in a consistent manner can an organization understand the adequacy of their security controls, policies and procedures. Metrics provide the ability to aid management's decision of where to invest in additional security protection resources or to identify and evaluate non-productive controls.

Metrics in the development and implementation process can also be used to justify security investments. The results of an effective security program, which uses metrics, can provide useful data for directing the allocation of information security resources and simplify the preparation of performance-related reports, which ensure the proper selection of mitigation strategies and controls.

Given the information presented thus far in this chapter, the current model does not work in relatively simple computing environments.

---

[10] http://www.asisonline.org/

[11] www.asisonline.org/education/securitybooksasis.pdf

This means that the chance that this model will work in the more complex, more communicative world of Web 2.0 applications is even lower. Security professionals know the problem well enough. It cannot be solved by everyone "doing their own thing." Standards that aid in the implementation of controls that are fit-for-purpose, measurable and sustainable is the right direction, the right course of action. This is the only way that Web 2.0 can be as secure as it needs to be.

5
Defining the Solution – ITU-T X.805 Standard Explained

> "The nice thing about standards is that there are so many of them to choose from."
>
> —Andrew S. Tanenbaum

Executive Summary

There are no shortcuts. As explained in Chapter 4, aftermarket security means the end- user is resigned to perimeter-based security, dependent upon detection capabilities that cannot overcome the zero-day threat. The only remedy is a seemingly endless patching process. This model simply doesn't protect e-commerce environments of the present nor of future Web 2.0 in which data control is further diffused.

Applying security appropriately starts when the product is designed and engineered. This is the foundation for secure technology solutions and services and continues through the Security Value Life Cycle as defined earlier. The need for security metrics is paramount, and it is time to engage in the *how* part of this discussion.

Security design starts by applying the eight security dimensions of the ITU-T X.805 ("X.805") standard model and building products as component parts in an overall network solution with a direct relationship to the process and policy of certifications and compliance. Chapter 5 starts with a brief examination of the landscape of standards, certifications and regulatory compliance frameworks, postulating that the combination of X.805 and the ISO/IEC 27000 series standards is the right approach.

The X.805 standard starts to answer one of the primary concerns: a framework to guide beyond the policy and process level to how the security gets applied in practice. The right level of access control, authentication, non-repudiation, communications security, system and data integrity, data confidentiality, system availability and privacy are critical and all of the security dimensions have a key role. As a framework for designing security during product development, it is the missing link between secure product design, secure applications for the end-user, and the standards, certifications and compliance rules.

From theory to practice, it starts with determining the assets that form the product components, the risk profile that allows the engineer to establish the risk zones, and lastly, determining the vulnerabilities and completing the necessary hardening to achieve *sufficient* security. Sufficient is the operative word, as it is well recognized that the right level of security is always relative to the risks that will be present in the environment.

The X.805 standard framework is foundational as it is prescribed at the start of the development life cycle – when and where the products get developed, integrating them in combination with other products constructing systems and functional services. In this process, one can actually start answering and being responsive to the demands of all the security and compliance requirements by embedding security as an integral part of overall technology and business management.

This often-used quote from the executive summary about "so many standards to choose from" gets to the heart of the problem with standards, certifications and compliance regulations that form the myriad "choices" and spawn the unintended consequences of overwhelming process bureaucracy. Figure 5.1 conveys this picture. With a wide range of standards, certifications and regulations, there are questions about which regulations apply and how they integrate with standards and certifications.

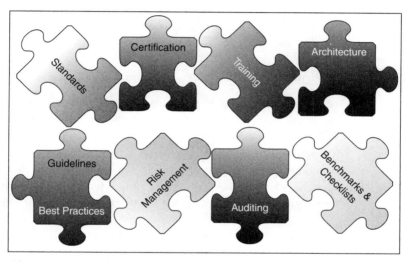

Figure 5.1   A wide range of risk management demands on the enterprise

The answer is not more standards, but rather to select one for product development and assessment. Starting with product development, the X.805 standard is *extensible* as illustrated with the arrow in Figure 5.2: projecting to the right, encompassing the ISO/IEC 27000 series standard certification occurring within an enterprise implementation, and further to the right at the point where compliance is mandated – the service delivery endpoint. It is *extensible* and also *demanding* in the sense that it asks the product engineer to consider the full range of security dimensions and activities performed – a standard that serves through the full SVL.

Consider the SVL in Figure 5.3 to explain the link from making products secure during product development through the selection process. The key to success is technical integration at the first point of purchase through functional integration when the product is placed into production.

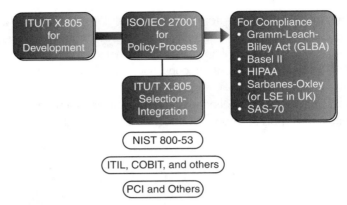

Figure 5.2 Standards, certification and compliance

From the left, the X.805 standard is the prescription for product developers designing security into the product as one part of an overall network solution.

By using the X.805 standard framework, the *product developer* has a structured and complete list of the security considerations. Part of the product development life cycle is deciding which security features to implement across the security value life cycle. Mindful of the certification and compliance requirements across the value life cycle, the product developer not only needs to design the right measure of security, but should also represent precisely how the set of choices made at the design-development step satisfy the ISO/IEC 27000 series standard requirements and the various compliance requirements needed downstream. Transparency and interoperability are the positive results, and with transparency comes accountability for the decisions that determine the security features included in the product or solution.

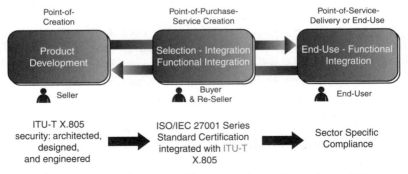

Figure 5.3 Hardening, certification and compliance in the SVL

At the point of *selection, security and functional integration,* in the center of the SVL, is the buyer and potential product-solution re-seller. The X.805 standard becomes the basis for evaluation and selection. The buyer now has a means by which to evaluate competing vendors and how the respective sellers consider and apply security to manage the risks in a production environment. The vendor (seller) who provides the specifics of the security *designed in* to the framework, and the certification and compliance requirements and framework for traceable change control, is the vendor to select. Security factors are obviously not the sole basis for the final selection decision, but security can be a key driver in the selection process.

For the first time, there is now a reference-able expectation for both buyers and sellers. Network security design becomes a structured process and not just a set of ad hoc choices. Technical and functional integration is enabled by the choices a product developer makes, knowing that the product will be part of an overall system serving a customer's needs (see figure 5.4).

On the right side of the SVL, the end-user is defined. This can be a consumer, an enterprise employee connected to a local or wide area network, or it can be a set of services accessible directly from the application end-points on the Internet. The SaaS and cloud computing models discussed are part of the Web 2.0 + world. Responsibility and accountability for security does not diminish but rather accumulates, as now there may be millions of real end-users or customers using a service.

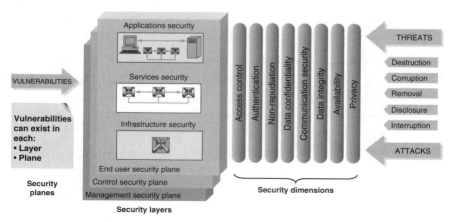

Figure 5.4   The ITU-T Recommendation X.805

The ITU-T X.805 Standard Explained: Building a foundation for the Security Value Life Cycle

In physical science the first essential step in the direction of learning any subject is to find principles of numerical reckoning and practicable methods for measuring some quality connected with it. I often say that when you can measure what you are speaking about, and express it in numbers, you know something about it; but when you cannot measure it, when you cannot express it in numbers, your knowledge is of a meagre and unsatisfactory kind; it may be the beginning of knowledge, but you have scarcely, in your thoughts, advanced to the state of Science, whatever the matter may be.[1]

A bit of the history

It was a question for which there did not seem to be a ready answer. The year was 2002 and the question was simple enough: "What standard should the Bell Labs scientists and engineers use for securing the next-generation networks?" A second question quickly followed: "How much security is enough and how does one measure security?" After conducting a search and finding no published standard to answer these questions in sufficient detail, a small group of Bell Labs scientists embarked on a task that eventually led to the creation of the Bell Labs Security Framework[2] that further made a recommendation to the International Telecommunication Union committee. The Bell Labs Security Framework became the ITU-T Recommendation X.805[3] standard defined as "Security architecture for systems providing end-to-end communications" in October 2003.

The introduction provides a clear problem statement:

"The telecommunications and information technology industries are seeking cost-effective comprehensive security solutions. A secure network should be protected against malicious and inadvertent attacks and should have high availability, appropriate response time, reliability,

---

[1] *http://www.todayinsci.com/K/Kelvin_Lord/KelvinLord-Quotations.htm*

[2] International Telecommunications Union, Telecommunications Standardization Sector, "Security Architecture for Systems Providing End-to-End Communications," Rec. BELL LABS SECURITY FRAMEWORK, 2003, http://www.itu.int

[3] http://www.itu.int/rec/T-REC-X.805-200310-I/en

integrity, scalability, and provide accurate billing information. Security capabilities in products are crucial to the overall network security (including applications and services). However, as more products are combined to provide total solutions, the interoperability, or lack thereof, will define the success of the solution. Security must not only be a thread of concern for each product or service, but must be developed in a manner that promotes the interweaving of security capabilities in the overall end-to-end solution. To achieve such a solution in a multi-vendor environment, network security should be designed around a standard security architecture."

Notice that nowhere does the introduction speak of protecting the network with an externally developed security system. Rather, the focus is on network security design. That simple declaration is what is different about how the industry secures networks at the present time and how they need to secure networks in the future. Further, the standard is clear from the start that individual products themselves do not provide technology services; products are part of the system (or solution) that provides the service and it is the system that should be designed securely from end to end.

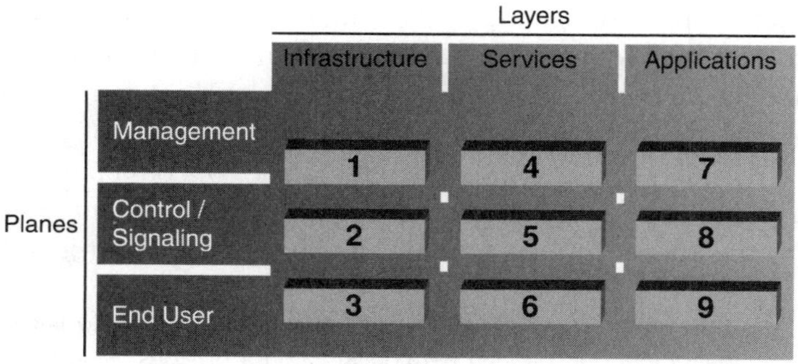

Figure 5.5 Decomposing the security framework (Part 1 of 2)

The standard defines a network model consisting of three layers (infrastructure, services and application) and three planes of communication (management, control/signaling and end-user) as illustrated in Figure 5.5.

– The **Infrastructure Security Layer** contains the fundamental building blocks of networks such as routers, switches, servers and the communications links that tie them together.

- The **Services Security Layer** consists of services that the network provides to end-users. These services range from basic connectivity such as Frame Relay, ATM and IP to advanced, value-added services such as VoIP and VPN.

- Finally, the **Applications Security Layer** consists of network-based applications accessed by end-users such as Web access, voice mail, e-mail and e-commerce.

Starting with the security layers, the model treats them separately to recognize differences in the vulnerability points – the different threats, methods of attack and ultimately the need to integrate the appropriate security controls.

As an example, a DoS attack launched at the infrastructure layer can flood a particular network port with malformed packets. A different form of DoS attack can be performed at the services layer by gaining access to the authentication server and deleting the files containing user IDs and passwords. One can readily see that the controls needed to be deployed to prevent these DoS attacks would be disparate for each different layer.

A network element serves a role in one or more of the layers exchanging information on one or more planes of communication. In combination with other products, all the products (assets) are identified and the security is designed for the system level solution. The security architecture and the appropriate design protect an end-to-end service.

The model clearly shows that the planes of communication have different objectives and consequently comprise different sets of security measures that must be isolated either physically or logically.

As an example, a typical end- user should not be able to access the management console of a network switch for obvious reasons. Legacy public switched telephone systems have physical isolation for the planes of communication. A technician has to gain physical access to the tightly controlled facilities of the phone company to see or gain access to the management console.

In IP-based networks with addressable network elements, the physical barrier doesn't always exist. Isolation must be achieved logically to ensure that an end-user has no ability to even see the network switching, much less gain access to them. One can readily see the heightened need to ensure a hardened design for isolation and the need for stringent authentication controls since physical isolation is not always possible.

- The Management Security Plane is concerned with the provisioning and management of network elements and services. It may be implemented in-band or out-of-band with respect to general network traffic.

- The Control/Signaling Security Plane typically consists of machine-to-machine communications, such as routing updates that enable a network to function efficiently. The control/signaling plane may be implemented in-band with end-user traffic such as IP, or out-of-band with respect to end-user traffic such as secure sockets layer.

- The End-User Security Plane represents how end-users access and use the network, which could be for basic connectivity/ transport, value-added services such as VPN, VoIP and so forth, or access to network-based applications, such as e-mail.

The basic architecturemodel is set. The individual products (collectively called assets) serve specific roles exercised in the network solution leading to a network service. To determine the appropriate level of security, the model defines five threat parameters, which are described in detail in ITU-T Recommendation X.805 standard.

- Destruction of information and/or other resources

- Corruption or modification of information

- Theft, removal or loss of information and/or other resources

- Disclosure of information

- Interruption of services

In combination these threat parameters form the risk model for the product to be designed or assessed. After understanding the risk profile, the next step is to determine which of the eight security dimensions applies at the product level and at the interface between products that interconnect in a network (for example, a Web service call to the application layer coded in a database server). The eight security dimensions listed earlier

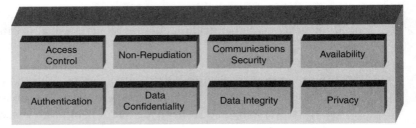

Figure 5.6   Decomposing the security framework (Part 2 of 2)

envelop the full range of security considerations – good for the security of present day and future solutions. By stating that the definitions "envelop the full range of security considerations" the intent is not to mean that this is some finite security features list. The definitions are broadly stated, creating a high degree of flexibility in determining the appropriate security features to be implemented in the system design.

In the example of the network switch serving a role in the infra-structure layer, the product engineer must consider the eight security dimensions for the three planes – a total of twenty-four possible points of consideration to be made. This notional switch stores no personally identifiable information, so privacy is not a prime consideration for any of the three planes. The twenty-four possible is reduced by three, leaving a total of twenty-one areas for consideration. These considerations include how stringently to apply *authentication* controls, whether or not to encrypt the data exchange channels (*communications security*), what security technology to apply and so forth. This is a detailed approach to security performed as a series of design considerations at the product and solution architecture levels. Made with the understanding of the use case, the design team brings forward a product to market as part of an overall solution that is secure by design.

The eight security dimensions are defined to be expansive, broadly worded definitions, creating a comprehensive framework of considerations to be made by the product developer that covers all aspects of security for technology systems. The definitions were derived from an analysis of pre-existing standards,[4] which were viewed as best practices. The appropriate use of security tools, techniques and processes supports the best practices to mitigate vulnerabilities that may exist in a particular use environment. The security dimensions are concepts already well

---

[4] ISO 7498-2, ITU-T M3106, IEEE 802.10a, ITU-T X.800

known, though in the X.805 standard they are formed within an overall network model. A short definition of the security dimensions follows:[5]

Table 5.1 X.805 Security dimensions

Security Dimensions	Short Description
Access Control	Protects against unauthorized use of network resources by individuals, devices or system calls.
Authentication	Confirms the identities of communicating entities, ensuring the validity of the claimed identities such as a person, device, service or application.
Non-Repudiation	Provides means for preventing an individual or entity from denying having performed a particular action related to data by making available proof of various network related actions.
Data Confidentiality	Protects data from unauthorized disclosure and covers the information that can be gained just by observing network usage. For example, a large number of calls between two parties may imply a prelude to a significant event.
Communication Security	Is concerned with ensuring that information flows from source to destination without opportunity for diversion or interception. Unauthorized wiretapping is an example of the type of threat this security dimension is intended to address.
Data Integrity	Ensures the correctness or accuracy of data, protecting against unauthorized modifications, deletion, creation or replication.
Availability	Ensures that there is no denial of authorized access to network elements, stored information, information flows, service and applications due to events impacting the network. This dimension is directly related to network reliability, which, by itself, is its own discipline.
Privacy	Provides security for the protection of personal and network information that might be stored in databases or derived from the observation of network activities such as Web sites visited or geographical location. This dimension is different from data confidentiality as its privacy pertains to specific personal information while confidentiality pertains to more general network traffic.

---

[5] http://en.wikipedia.org/wiki/ITU-T

In practice, there are clear efficiencies that can be achieved in a product house to streamline the selection and implementation of security decisions. In not making these decisions and not applying the right measure of security hardening at the point of product development the vulnerabilities remain in the products and solutions.

The notion was postulated earlier that one can measure the degree of security relative to a risk profile. This is achieved in eight vectors formed by the eight security dimensions. By taking the basic construct of the X.805 standard model, the team at Bell Labs developed a tool (patent pending) that allows a product developer to model the risk into three zones.

Figure 5.7 is a representation of the output report that can be used by a product development house both in the design stage for new products and as an assessment tool (patent pending) for existing products. The graphic is a representation designed to help communicate the relative states of security implementation. Arrayed against a Kiviat chart (see figure 5.8) on a zero-to-one point scale, the chart depicts three bands of security hardening and the actual product assessment overlay. The outermost band (from gradient level 0.9 to 1.0) represents an "ideal" implementation of security, where the security hardening is made specific to an individual customer's needs that go beyond the norm of hardening. A product developer would not be expected to design their product to this zone level except in individual and specific needs. The middle zone (from the edge of the inner zone to 0.89) is defined by the boundary between the

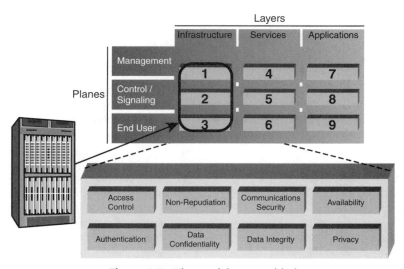

Figure 5.7 The model reassembled

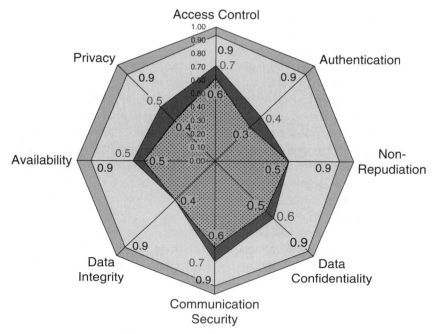

Figure 5.8   The Kiviat chart report

outermost zone and the inner-most zone, also called the "red zone." The product developer would harden products in this zone reaching a higher standard (as in a stronger encryption algorithm) driven by either competitive market demands or once again by specific individual requirements.

The innermost band, known as the red-zone (from gradient level 0.0 to a boundary determined by determining the product role), represents the minimum standard of hardening and is bound by the parameters of the role for that product. A technology product that stores personal account information would be expected to have an extended red-zone boundary (closer to 1.0) than one that does not contain any of this type information.

The actual product assessment overlay represents the degree of actual hardening or in the design stage can represent the actual hardening designs. Using the example of a notional product, the results of the X.805 standard assessment are shown overlaid on top of the bands. Without much explanation one can see the security gaps in meeting the "sufficient" or "minimal" threshold (the edge of the red zone) in six of the eight security dimensions. Only data integrity and non-repudiation mitigations meet the requirement to have no red-zone gaps.

This shows a product engineer and other stakeholders where the gaps exist, and, depending upon the detailed data behind the report, provides the basis for making business-rational decisions about which gaps to close first, which ones need to be addressed urgently and those that can be resolved in a future product release.

In practice, this is a methodical process of taking a full consideration of the security dimensions against the backdrop of a product's role in the network. By applying these design steps as gates in the product development life cycle, one can be assured that the product has met the minimal standards for release. Taking the example of a customer call center server with a high degree of risk for the role that it plays (designed to contain thousands of personal data information), by applying this methodology, one can determine that in fact the encryption algorithm was of a strength sufficient to protect the personal data storage, that the authentication and access control was designed sufficient to the risk that one system administrator could not, on their own, compromise the system. And through the other six security dimensions, one can see the results in a clear transparent way. The engineers behind the product are clearly identified with how they hardened the product or failed to harden their product to the sufficient level set as the benchmark for product release.

It eliminates the guesswork of determining which security features to apply, it communicates by means of the Kiviat chart in figure 5.8 whether the right level of "sufficient" security is being met and it is "executive" friendly as a means to represent when that benchmark has not been met.

The importance of having a relative way to measure security hardening in a product cannot be overstated. It is also important that it be based on an openly available standard one that measures the state of security in a product as part of the overall solution.

As in the physical science that Lord Kelvin spoke of, the " *first essential step in the direction of learning any subject is to find principles of numerical reckoning and practicable methods for measuring some quality connected with it.*" The Kiviat chart is merely a representation with specific details behind it to support the findings. The network model forces consideration of the overall solution to a risk profile established on the basis of various factors. Further, it is a framework that allows for transparency as it provides a common view that all participants in the SVL can use to question and review. It is a *numerical reckoning* applied to security that can serve in a number of ways; the most apparent is the ability to baseline the products' security using a numerical score. By using this graduated scale, the product engineer can see a clear way to where and to what degree remediation needs to be made. The business manager can perform a cost-benefit analysis and gauge a business-rational decision. Business development personnel have the means to communicate to the customer how and to what degree security was considered and applied.

It is not a cookie cutter approach, since the remediation needed in the security implementation steps is specific to a risk profile. The score is relative to the associated risk for each security dimension in the model. For authentication, there is a 0.1 gap. The gap is an indicator of the authentication dimension insufficiently applied. The reason may be insufficient password strength or a password file that is not encrypted. It could be a number of things but the details are merely represented in the gap. The remediation in this example is straightforward: allow only selection of passwords that are sufficiently strong and encrypt the password file.

Coupling to the ISO/IEC 27000 Series Standard: Complementary Standards that Enable the Process and Policy Leading to Compliance

The primary documents in the ISO/IEC 27000 series standard focus on information security and on *process* and *organization*. These apply primarily to the middle and end-points in the SVL depicted earlier in Figure 5.3.

The ISO/IEC 27000 series standard has a number of documents focusing on various aspects of information security techniques and Information Security Management Systems (ISMS). This discussion proposes that the X.805 standard is a framework that is complementary to the ISO/IEC 27000 series standard *designing in* the security during product development.

Figure 5.9 shows the focus of the ISO/IEC 27000 series standard, breaking it down from overview at the top layer through the general requirements and into sector specific requirements. The graphic also helps define the existing components and those still under development.

At present, four of the standards in the ISO/IEC 27000 series are publicly available – ISO/EIC 27001, 27002, 27005, 27006 – while several more are

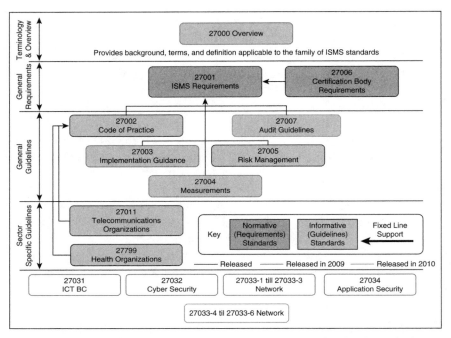

Figure 5.9 Information security management system family of standards

under development. This family of standards is intended to address all aspects of information security from the organization to implementation of ISMS. The intent of the standard is that security integration can be achieved by implementing a set of suitable controls, including policies, standards (practices), procedures, organization structures and software functions. Two of the well-known standards in this area are:

> ISO/IEC 27001 series standard is an international certification standard which contains controls and recommendations by which an organization can certify their Information Security Management Systems (ISMS). ISO/IEC 27002 series standard is a code of practice containing controls and recommendations for the ISMS.

A number of companies are taking the important step of establishing ISO/IEC 27001 series standard certification as a minimal requirement to do business. Many have also implemented the ISO/IEC 27001 series standard certification internally. This is a critically important step, a trend that will continue and grow as more companies see the importance and benefits of certification.

The process of certification is a series of steps that includes risk assessments and leads to deciding the set of security controls to be applied to meet corporate compliance requirements specific to the market sector and the associated regulatory requirements reference: http://www.27000.org/ismsprocess.htm.

Of particular interest, and importance to the success of the ISO/IEC 27001 series standard certification, is the definition of policies, scope and limits of the information security management framework. A security policy states management's commitment to information security to meet the business objectives and regulatory requirements. The top-level security policy is supported by subordinate policies. These subordinate policies are typically developed based on the expertise from the organization. However, ISO/IEC 27001 series standard does not provide guidelines on how to meet these objectives and/or what the security objectives should be.

This is how the X.805 standard is complementary – by providing the specific requirements needed for what the security objectives should be and how they can be achieved. For example, Figure 5.10 shows some key questions that would be asked if using the X.805 standard to define the boundaries of the ISO/IEC 27001 series

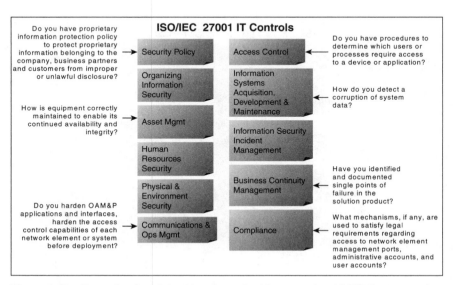

Figure 5.10   Example of applying X.805 standard framework to ISO/IEC 27001 series standard controls

standard controls in order to make this more prescriptive. Note in Figure 5.10 the example questions that one can ask (using the security dimensions of X.805) that drive ways to protect key user, operational and maintenance activities.

By asking these key questions, the implementation of controls needed to address these ISO/IEC 27001 series control objectives are realized. Controls are implemented based on the eight security dimensions as applicable to satisfy the needed security implementation. The ISO/IEC 27001 Access Control is met not just by implementations of role-based access control, but also by addressing the authentication and non-repudiation security dimensions.

The general objective is to extend the information security management guidelines provided in ISO/IEC 27000 series standard with the details provided in implementation of the X.805 security framework that implement network security safeguards across a wide range of network environments. In some sense, it provides a bridge between general information security management issues and network security technical implementations. In fact, X.805 can be used to conduct a detailed network security analysis to meet the ISO/IEC 27001:2005 communications networks control requirements.

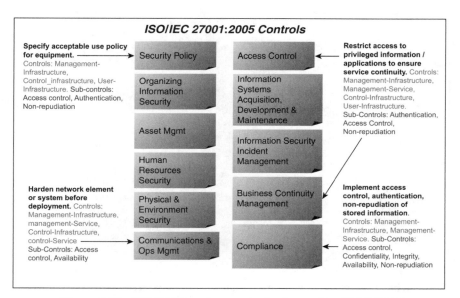

Figure 5.11   ISO/27001 series standard enhanced by ITU-T X.805

ISO/IEC 27001 establishes the organizational, policy, process and general technical scope. The X.805 security framework helps determine the critical assets and relevant technology as well as determine the risks and appropriate compensating controls.

This is done by answering the following questions:

1. What kind of protection is needed and against what threats?

2. What are the distinct types of network equipment and facility groupings that need to be protected?

3. What are the distinct types of network activities that need to be protected?

The answers to these questions produce a list of critical assets, key threats and mitigations from a user, operational and maintenance perspective.

The risk assessment determines the organization's risk exposure, its risk profile and subsequently is used to establish the management controls. The controls themselves can then be implemented as appropriate leading to certification by an accredited third party.

With respect to encryption, the ISO/IEC 27001 series standard A.10.3.2 Encryption says: "*Encryption shall be applied to protect the confidentiality of sensitive or critical information.*" The ISO/IEC 27001 series standard control is not specific where and how to apply encryption solutions. The X.805 analysis takes this process to the needed level of granularity by examining if the measures are adequate to minimize the impact of threats in the different security dimensions for the layers and planes of the model. X.805 complements the ISO/IEC 27001 Encryption Control, by helping the product engineer determine how encryption is applied, in what measure and at what places in the different network layers and planes.

Password management is another example of system control. In this example, ISO/IEC 27001 series standard specifies a password management system and X.805 authentication specifies the authentication capabilities needed. For example, there should be authentication in: (1) mechanisms for hardening administrator and end-user passwords, (2) the application at various layers of centralized vs. distributed per layer, change frequency and audit frequency. ISO/IEC 27001 series standard requires a password management system and X.805 assures the appropriate coverage.

The two standards work hand in hand to provide the detailed and comprehensive security coverage that is needed by both buyers and sellers of technology solutions. This must start during product development with the buyer making it clear that an X.805 prescriptive design for security is a requirement for all product purchases. Without this clear statement, the buyer in this relationship is left with making choices among the various sellers with no rule of measure for evaluation.

The positive action in the security value chain carries forward from product development (the seller) to the security technical integration (the buyer or re-seller) that is expected to certify the systems using the ISO/IEC 27000 series standard.

Security is an integral part of network design, whether it is adding new services, expanding network services or making technology changes, it all needs to be addressed based on customers' needs. Network changes affect security and security can impact performance, reliability and operations. By understanding these impact priorities, security can be balanced with other considerations such as business operations, customer trust and business continuity. From certification to compliance, the groundwork is in-place.

At the end of this value chain is a business operating in a market sector with its various regulatory compliance requirements. There is no getting away from this – regulations are part of the business environment; those entities who certify and require its business partners to be certified as a pre-condition of their partnership will in the process be taking care of the major share of compliance requirements.

This is as far as one can take this point in the discussion without going into a level of detail better left for another book. On close examination of the many compliance requirements, the premise of each of them is that both businesses and governments are accountable at the highest levels to ensure that information is safeguarded, that the right security controls are in place and that transparency is achieved. Transparency cannot be achieved without the needed specificity at a level of granularity that the X.805 standard implemented with the ISO/IEC 27000 series standard can provide.

Enterprise Risk and IT Management Frameworks

In the broader scheme of business operations, information security is an integral part of two related disciplines: enterprise risk management and technology management. While there may be a separate information security organization with independent reporting, the governance functions are so closely inter-related to enterprise risk and technology management that one cannot think of security functions as entirely separate. Rather, they are best considered as interdependent processes. In this case, the authors provide only a brief discussion mostly to state the obvious relationship and the need for integration at the process level at a minimum.

> Starting with enterprise risk management, the very definition is about considering risk holistically. For an organization to understand the risks it faces, it must take into account economic risk, legal risk, compliance risk, credit risk, geopolitical risk, operational risk and technology risk. Without a comprehensive understanding of these risks, an organization may face unanticipated events that can negatively impact its financial health.

> Approaches such as the Factor Analysis of Information Risk (FAIR) allows an organization to objectively comprehend the risks it faces, what the financial implications of risk might be if the proper controls aren't in place and have a consistent approach to understanding an organization's risk across the enterprise.

One can see the common approach to the discussion presented so far with the X.805 standard framework for viewing inherent vulnerabilities that are identifiable and correctable up front. By doing so, security vulnerabilities can be corrected before going downstream to the buyers and technology implementers.

There is also common ground with the technology management frameworks of which there are many: IT Infrastructure Library (ITIL®) and the Control Objectives for Information and related Technology (CoBIT®) are two of the most broadly adopted in organizations globally. The correlation is to the ITIL Information Security Management component where the functions of policy, governance and vulnerability assessment are defined. For CoBIT, the correlation is with the CoBIT Security Baseline.

Both of these technology management frameworks provide an overall approach to policies, process and governance supported by best practices. They are not meant to provide the level of details needed for security implementation at the level provided by the X.805 standard, but clearly serve to provide an overarching and complementary management structure in which security is one aspect of controlling risk consistently.

Security is not a separate process but an intricate part of a larger management context. Whatever the choice, ITIL, COBIT or others, the task is to find and conduct the integration that supports the policies and processes with the details of implementation to ensure a consistent and rigorous application of security. The X.805 standard is a good fit for this purpose.

6

Building the Security Foundation Using the ITU-T X.805 Standard: The ITU-T X.805 Standard Made Operational

---

"By any chance, do you know if this particular solution has been assessed for security using the standard?"

Executive Summary

The transformation of applying security in a product company is no easy task. There are up-front costs in capital, design and engineering effort, and in the long term, the company needs to have the determination to get on and stay the path. Yet this investment has a real benefit that pays for the cost of product differentiation and the ability to compete better and in other intangible ways. For now, consider some of the practical issues with taking the X.805 standard from good theory to real practice.

The experience to date with applying the X.805 standard is still in a formative stage within Alcatel-Lucent. While there is still limited experience (and much to learn as the program matures), the results are already clear enough to draw some early conclusions. This approach is transformative and can identify vulnerabilities consistently. Thus far, they have ranged from those that would have minor impacts if exploited, to security issues that could have significant impacts on an organization. Some of these vulnerabilities should never have been there in the first place. The process to catch these and correct them was missing.

One lesson learned is something already known but not well applied with the global nature of product development: A product development house must adhere to strict quality metrics. The metrics of security apply not just to individual product hardening but to all the components that are part of the overall solution. To have the appropriate level of security, security needs to be part of the fundamental specifications and requirements – right up front in the development cycle. Product hardening can be measured using the X.805 framework and will yield a product that has a higher level of integrity and fewer security issues. As the X.805 framework is used in the long term and more broadly adopted by organizations, the lessons will be better understood and assimilated.

For now, consider this short but helpful story to illustrate the power of this transformation.

In discussion with a business development team about the process and the early results from assessing products with the ITU-T X.805 standard, the question was asked, "By any chance, had there been an assessment of a particular solution?" The answer was "Yes, as it so happens, that assessment was recently completed and the solution yielded excellent results." The product engineers had done their homework and had been diligent about applying security. What had been up to that point courteous but only mildly interested business development people in the conference room all of a sudden came alive and the questions came fast and with great interest. It turned out that a large and important request for proposal was in the last days of the bid development process and the customer had asked specifically for proof of the security design. The benefits are clear, crystal clear.

Now imagine if the answer had been the opposite: "No, not yet," or "Yes, the assessment was conducted but the results were not good." The detriment to the company in this scenario is also clear: opportunity lost.

In another example, a product assessment using the ITU-T X.805 standard revealed a problem that would have been embarrassing had the problem not been discovered and corrected while still in the development stage. Both of these stories are focused on the assessment phase. How much more powerful are the examples with the ITU-T X.805 standard applied not as assessments with the product near completion, but in the design stage? What are the costs that could have been avoided if security had been integrated into the design stage?

At the solution level, the process of system design is expanded, yet remains essentially the same. The engineering team conducts an overall threat analysis, which forms the basis for understanding the vulnerabilities. It continues by taking steps to decompose the solution into the detailed system assets, with each of the assets investigated with respect to the security dimensions for vulnerabilities. Both inherent weaknesses that can be exploited (such as a maintenance interface unprotected from tampering in an end-user device) and well established attacks such as cross-site scripting or buffer overflows.

The identification of assets is followed by a set of decisions to mitigate the vulnerabilities based on criticality and market demands. For each of the system assets and the interactivity between them, a three-step process – *investigation, assessment, appropriate remediation* – delivers a solution hardened to reflect the environment in which it will be implemented. There is no shortcut, but there are clearly efficiencies to be gained by the repetition of a consistent process. There are really not many unique security situations – just different degrees of applying the security dimensions and factors, such as cost and time, to deliver a solution for mitigating risk.

In the long term, preventing vulnerabilities from being implemented in a customer environment will provide not only a better product, but it will also reduce long-term costs for both the product company and the consumer. Some of the costs that can be avoided include retrofitting security, distributing software patches and legal liability. This will create a competitive advantage for those enlightened companies that truly embrace a fundamental change in mind-set.

The standard made operational

Once a repeatable, consistent security engineering approach is deployed across a company immediate benefits occur. This has been the clear experience and a key lesson. Common vulnerabilities are identified, lending themselves to remediation that only needs to be developed once per vulnerability and applied across the different products and solutions. This results in increased efficiency and reduced cost for the corporation.

Key lesson: Complexity breeds insecurity

The axiom that a chain is only as strong as its weakest link is particularly true in complex systems. As discussed in Chapter 2, there is a great deal of complexity in the technology of convergence carrying the traffic for voice, data, and video – so it is particularly important to establish and maintain trust relationships (encrypted channels, exchange of certificates) between networks and end-user devices, signalling and transport elements and service and user profiles.

It is interesting to note that the X.805 standard has already been described in some circles as overly complicated. This point is usually made as a prelude to promote the idea that security can only be designed when one buys the network from one company – never mind that the world of networks and information systems is a hybrid of many different technologies from different companies. X.805 is complex in the practice for the simple reason that the network is complex as are the services that the network delivers. The tools used to design and examine security for complex systems must be sophisticated enough to deal with this complexity. This is where the X.805 standard is so effective. For network security to be effective, it is measurable trustworthiness that is the goal; trustworthiness achieved through hardening and transparency in the processes.

Consider the IP Multimedia Subsystem (IMS) as the perfect example for the implementation of convergence. In the initial versions of IMS it contained approximately fifty functional elements, dozens of interfaces and protocols, and it was only concerned with the call control and billing functions. The X.805 standard security framework helps by decomposing the IMS solution into its security layers and planes, and evaluating what security measures need to be applied at each layer and plane.

Taking the examination of complexity even deeper, the technology trend is moving toward architectures where a single device functions as an entire network collapsed into a small box. The trend toward integrating multiple functions into one appliance has simplified network architectures but has also increased the complexity of individual devices. Previously, a security engineer was only concerned with securing the protocols and data associated with one function; one must now secure multiple sets of protocols and data in order to secure a device. An IPTV set-top box is a great example. In addition to providing a network interface for the delivery of television programming to the consumer, a typical set-top box also contains digital video recording capability and digital rights management. Both of these represent high value assets in themselves and are now embedded into a consumer appliance. Again, the X.805 standard with its layers and planes quickly drives a security analyst or product engineer to identify these assets and realize the need to protect them. Whether it is next-generation broadband wireless networks, VoIP or Web 2.0 applications, the complexity is unavoidable and the vulnerabilities must be discovered and addressed.

Key lesson: The cloud has entered the building

Significant portions of the network are moving closer to subscriber endpoints within the subscriber residences and business offices. The Femto Base Station Routers (BSRs), as an example, will place an entire telecommunication access network inside a consumer's home, supporting a variety of expanded functions for wireless broadband communications. A virtual home office is a trend that continues to grow in popularity. Up to this point, this functionality has been within the physical premises of carrier networks. It now enters the customer environment that introduces potential security vulnerabilities (such as tampering) that were not in older networks where the engineer could count on the physical separation of the network cloud. With the device now fully accessible, a variety of threats must now be considered such as occurs with Wi-Fi devices where neighbours can gain access to the network or even to the owner's personal computers. In this scenario, it is not hard to imagine a wireless access point sharing the home's high-speed Internet connection (cable or DSL) with the Femto BSR. The security concerns for this environment are considerable, particularly as experience teaches that consumers are often unable or unwilling to secure their computers and networks.

With direct physical access to these devices, the threat of tampering is a consideration. This is a well known problem in the cable industry, where kits are available over the Internet that allow one to access enhanced services free of charge.

> For example, it was discovered that a certain cable modem make and model had electronic leads on its circuit board that provided a local management interface for the cable modem. This management interface allowed for the cable modem's quality of service policing to be changed and therefore have much more bandwidth than the Multiple System Operator intended. Note that these were internal electronic leads, not an internal or external connector. This is an eye-opening example of the types of things that can happen when enough people are given enough time to exploit vulnerabilities.

The business implications of these types of threats require a new approach. In one scenario, tampering disables the set-top box, but it may mean that people would just return it to the merchant as a defective device and place additional costs on the business unit. The task is to make it secure from both physical and logical tampering. These capabilities must be *designed in* to the device. The alternative is that the network cloud would otherwise be accessible by millions of end-users. The ITU-T X.805 standard plays a critical role in going through a systematic and rigorous process of identifying and remediating all the vulnerable points. Access to the network cloud was an unthinkable situation in the past but not any longer.

Key lesson: Address common vulnerabilities

The existence of vulnerabilities commonly found across different parts of the network and within different network elements only reinforce the need for a consistent, repeatable security engineering approach. In large corporations that develop technology products, there is typically no consistent way of identifying and mitigating vulnerabilities or sharing this information across multiple business divisions. By using the X.805 standard in a consistent manner such as cataloguing vulnerabilities, a common set of security capabilities can be deployed across an entire product line. Positive business impacts include improved efficiency and lower costs. The more an organization uses this approach, the less time will be spent by each business unit to identify and implement security capabilities for their products. The time to market is also improved with the added benefit of an improved customer relationship as the security developed in the product has favourable results with the technology buyers.

Key lesson: Not all vulnerabilities are created equal

By looking at the vulnerabilities through the prism of the X.805 security dimensions, one can determine which ones are of greater priority for resolution. To a large extent, the priority of vulnerabilities in a particular product release is determined by the associated risk. Risk is a function of two intersecting vectors: probability of occurrence and impact. By applying a curve fitting process, one can calculate a numeric value for risk, and the vulnerabilities can be mitigated by security capabilities that reside in one or more security dimensions.

> For example, administrator passwords reside in the Authentication Security Dimension and Non-Repudiation Security Dimension. Tying these relationships together allows one to graphically represent the product or solution risk along each of the eight security dimensions; the larger the risk area shown, the higher the risk for the product or solution.

Deciding which security gap to remediate first and in what order to follow the other risk gaps then becomes a business decision. It becomes obvious that the absence of antivirus software represents more risk on an application server containing customer credit card numbers than it does on a core IP router that doesn't store this information. The risk equation would formally bear that out as well by assigning the appropriate values to the attractiveness of target – the ease of attack and impact. Applying this process of risk and vulnerabilities provides a consistent set of metrics that can then be represented on a graph, and business-rational decisions can be made for the priority of remediation.

Key lesson: What is reportable and when is it reportable?

The discovery of vulnerabilities poses a new wrinkle about what, when and how to report. There are technical and legal issues that confront all technology companies and software companies in particular. New processes and even entirely new services have entered the marketplace for alerting and disseminating security patches.

The unspoken assumption is that the technology vendors had no prior knowledge of the vulnerabilities in their products. The current aftermarket process allows an inconsistent assignment of responsibility. A practice of applying security engineering and design during product development places primary responsibility for security with the product developer.

There are no easy answers to these issues; if the vulnerability is reported, how many customers will be affected? Is there a countermeasure that will mitigate the vulnerability? What is the cost of deploying a compensating control?

One thing to keep in mind is that security by obscurity no longer applies in a converged network that is based on open protocols and where there is no physical isolation. There are a great number of "third" parties working to find and exploit these vulnerabilities, many of them financially motivated and possibly associated with organized crime. The odds that these actors uncover *unknown* vulnerabilities continue to increase. Once they have uncovered something, it is simple to perpetuate a crime. The "head in the sand" approach is a game no company can afford to play. The expectation is that the product company is designing with security in mind and actively tests its products and solutions to find, correct and develop a disciplined process to remediate vulnerable points for new releases and deployed systems.

This requires a lengthy engagement with the company's incident response team to expand the process with emphasis to resolve when and how to communicate the discovery of vulnerabilities in a consistent and transparent manner. The X.805 standards-based assessment serves to find vulnerable points where they can be corrected without having to send out patching alerts. The buyer-seller relationship is enhanced by this demonstrated commitment to making security engineering and design part of the product creation and development process.

Key lesson: Security mitigation is also a business risk management decision

By addressing the problem of security as a set of choices to be made, the security questions become business decisions around risk management. This goes back to the repeatability of security assessments used to determine the degree to which security is implemented in a product or solution based on quantitative risk. Using a tool-assisted (patent pending) approach (developed by Alcatel-Lucent) based on the X.805 standard security framework helps eliminate the subjectivity and unevenness currently associated with security assessments, and it can identify the risk associated with unimplemented security requirements.

Experience shows that the use of a tool eliminates the dependency on the security engineer to a large degree. No tool completely eliminates the need for security experts when performing a security assessment or for security design, but the role shifts from that of primary person to one of consultant. The framework makes it possible for the product engineer to take the first step in the security design and security assessment.

Key lesson: Performing the assessment with confidence in the results

A questionnaire-based security assessment is only the first of many steps needed to determine the security posture of a product or solution. From this foundation, the baseline security in a given product or solution is improved with additional testing measures. These additional measures improve confidence that the assessment accurately reflects the security baseline. They include commercially available security auditing tools that check for instances of code that is susceptible to buffer overflow attacks and other vulnerabilities. The product development team with support of a security expert can accomplish this additional testing.

At the solution level, when the products are combined to create a solution or service, the assessment needs to go into the test labs with the aid of security experts. This is the level of assessment that starts to give the first indication of the state-of-security hardening in field operation – the critical implementation at customer locations. The application of additional methods of assessing the security of a product and at the solution level increases the product engineer's overall confidence level. Organizations that have mature security programs consistently follow these best practices:

- Governance

- Policies and Standards

- Security Awareness Training

- Security Architecture Review

- Secure Coding Practices

- Integration of Security into Code Review Process

- Code Analysis Tools that Include Security Analysis Capabilities

- Vulnerability Test Tools

- Incident Response Procedures

- Patch Distribution Procedures

These activities provide a feedback loop from product concept to maintenance and serve to increase the confidence in the security of a product as it proceeds through its life cycle.

Key lesson: Convince the product unit

It is no easy task to convince a product unit that is always under the stress of delivery schedules with tightly controlled resources to apply time and resources for security design and hardening. The convincing works best when the process is made as simple as possible. Automation helps drive down the level of effort and improves overall acceptance that security can be applied without overly committing tight resources.

The obligation of security practitioners is to aid the product units by making the process as painless as possible. This eases the acceptance, adoption and automation, and common security capabilities can play a large role in adoption. A library of security capabilities can provide off-the-shelf compensating controls that can be used by the product units to close their security gaps and this is a critical breakthrough. Using an automated tool to identify missing security capabilities has been a key to this success. Leveraging the results from this tool, the process now allows a company to identify common security capabilities that can be included in a library accessible to all product units with the appropriate remediation. Once organizations see the positive results, the use of automated tools starts to snowball. STEPS is an acronym for Security Tool (patent pending) for Evaluating Product Security.

Taking it in STEPS is the motto, recognizing that security must be first addressed in a disciplined and consistent approach by technology vendors. Conducted one step at a time, the tool can help transform a

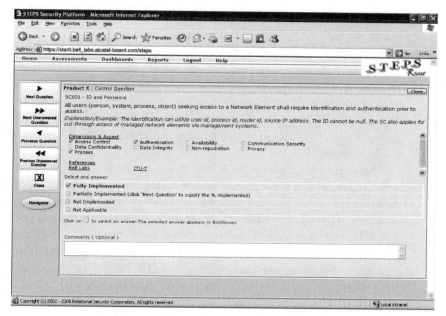

Figure 6.1   STEPS screen snapshot

company and maybe, when others participate, can help to transform an industry still dependent on the aftermarket security model.

Closing thoughts on the key lessons

Technology companies sell into different vertical markets, each with its own regulatory requirements. Despite the best intentions of organizations and standards committees, inaction and unclear direction eventually lead to security breaches; some that make it into the press and most that don't.

A product supports a function as part of an overall solution – such as a Web server or an application server. Where security isn't integrated into the product it creates vulnerabilities resident in the solution that is placed into production. Ideally, a product engineer should be able to trace a control element back to a compliance requirement and clearly understand what feature has been applied to satisfy that requirement. The X.805 framework allows an organization to consistently address these security or compliance requirements and communicate this to its stakeholders. If this framework is used, an organization has end-to-end traceability to validate that they have met regulatory requirements consistently.

Taken to its logical conclusion, all parts of a network, including those that contain the corporate data outside the firewall perimeter, should be accounted for and all compliance elements met. There should be accountability of all assets – the physical ones and the logical ones that include the data. It must apply for SaaS and for cloud computing, which includes applications and storage that are part of the Web 2.0+world.

The implementation of the X.805 standard at Alcatel-Lucent continues to provide a great many lessons on how to take a concept and make it a reality with the benefits addressed here. The key lesson remains in the future, where this process results in the growing trust earned by the transparency of the processes and the details of implementation. Nothing else will do to ensure that our present and future information systems are trustworthy. Without the ability to measure the security using a consistent process, the situation is as Lord Kelvin described it, "*when you cannot measure it, when you cannot express it in numbers, your knowledge is of a meager and unsatisfactory kind.*"

7
The Benefits of a Security Framework Approach

Executive Summary

Transparency at the Point of Creation permits transparency at the point of product evaluation and product selection, and it permits transparency at the point of delivery – when the product is inserted as part of a system delivering service in the network. Without transparency at the source of this life cycle, ambiguity and obscurity persist throughout and it creates the problems discussed in previous chapters.

In this chapter the benefits that can be derived from applying the rigor of a good security framework will be addressed. It is primarily to argue that the notion that security is too hard is no longer defensible. Investing in hardening the products at the start does not need to be a business disabler; it is quite the opposite. Security can help businesses and organizations promote quality, lower operating costs, compete better and engender trust. Who is against good quality, lower operating costs, competing better and being considered trustworthy?

The X.805 standard is such a framework – a framework that allows the product and solution developers to establish what kind of security should be applied by first determining the role to be played. For instance, a computer server is generally assigned a role and the security should be appropriate for that role. A network switch is the same. These roles begin to define the needed security measures, as do other factors. The developers must take into account all eight of the dimensions in the X.805 standard, such as privacy, authentication and integrity checking. These

113

judgments include business decisions as to what environment the developer will market and sell the product in, expecting for instance that for government clients the requirements for security may be more stringent than for a medium size enterprise.

Because these judgments were made within a security framework, the eventual buyer of the technology gets transparency to make better choices and to differentiate not only the functional value, but also the security value of the product. This can now be done without having to recreate a long, specific list of needs; the list is already clear within the framework of the security standard.

It changes the entire dynamic of the seller-buyer relationship by removing the mystery and dealing with the facts, and ultimately making the best choices among the options offered by different vendors. In many respects, as conjured in the image of Figure 7.1, applying the security framework is about recognizing that it takes a closer-in inspection to find and remediate what are inherent vulnerabilities in complex systems. This is transparency at work.

Figure 7.1   Looking through a microscope

Make no mistake about what this means to the product or solution developer; it will take a great deal of effort to adopt the X.805 standard. Yet, it is effort that pays for itself when the product competes and wins in the marketplace – a marketplace that uses the same security framework to remove the mystery of security and is able to apply a better decision in the technology selection process.

The buyer of the technology also benefits from the transparency by being able to insert the technology into a business solution with the knowledge of how the security design satisfies certification and compliance requirements. One can see all the cost savings without much explanation. The added benefits transfer further to the buyer of technology, (Point Two in the SVL) who is further responsible for providing secure systems and services with accountability in customer relationships. Compliance is made simpler by this transparency, where overall quality is improved and the customer relationship is reinforced.

Those who consider only the up front development cost of the effort to *design in* the security are making a fundamental and strategic mistake; the true cost is the combined cost of product recalls, liabilities, loss of sales – lost opportunities. Imagine going in to pitch a particular product to a customer and facing the question:

"Please tell me how your product was designed for security using the ITU-T X.805 standard security framework," and your response is, "Ah, can you spell out the name of that security framework one more time?"

That is the end of the sales call and the end of the relationship. Imagine now the opposite situation, your response being:

"Yes! I am pleased to do that. Our engineers considered with great precision the risk parameters in your operational environment for this product using the ITU-T X.805 standard model; they have a complete listing of how all eight security dimensions in the standard were considered within your use environment and can, with that same precision, demonstrate how, as an example, access control, authentication, privacy and system integrity are applied commensurate to the risk model. We can also demonstrate that the security designed-in to our product allows you to meet and maintain your ISO/IEC 27000 series standards certifications and also support your Sarbanes-Oxley Act compliance requirements."

This is a relationship that the buyer will value – no mystery, no obfuscation, no tap dancing – the sale is made, the relationship strengthened, a happy salesperson, a happy CEO and CFO and a more prosperous company. This is opportunity gained, not lost and the cost of the security design recouped many times over with strong profit margins.

Wherever one may be in this life cycle, having transparency in the security design just makes good sense, but it starts at the Point of Creation. In the world of globalization, outsourcing and products made in multiple places, without the use of the security framework there is no way that a product can end up designed secure to its use. Security does not happen by chance – it must be *designed in,* and the downstream elements in the life cycle are the points of enforcement and carry-through.

That is what this chapter is all about – not the problems but the many ways that following the security framework has real benefits, those that look good on your top line as well as the bottom line in the company's balance sheet. For the government agency it removes layers of bureaucracy to deliver more cost-effective and secure services – the things that engender confidence.

In this chapter, the many benefits of using the X.805 standard security framework to deliver a more secure Web 2.0 will be discussed. Web 2.0 is repeatedly referenced for the reason stated earlier: Web 2.0 is transformational and it is happening right now. It implies a new technical infrastructure – convergence – and new services; Facebook is a good example.

Web 2.0 applications and services create the great potential for businesses to evolve, bringing a virtual connectivity to customers and business partners – the disintermediation or elimination of the so-called middleman between product-services creator and the end customer. The reduction in latency and cost, and the improved operational efficiencies are the benefits and the differentiation for companies. The concept of making explicit the specific security challenges in data storage in the network cloud, as one example, with a third-party company that might have significantly different business agendas and stresses than your business, brings the discussion full circle. It is about transparency.

How does one secure the data in the network cloud when the interests of the client company may vary significantly from those of the provider of these data storage services? It should be clear, the interests are different, but they are not necessarily incompatible. Different is OK; incompatible is not OK and can create great risks.

The specific security solutions for the most part already exist to create the compatible interests within an acceptable level of risk. Other security technologies may be needed – an opportunity for enterprising security companies. The X.805 standard security framework does not prescribe what the solution is in this specific case in the same way that it does not prescribe any of the security solutions. It does, however, name the requirements; it causes developers, sellers, buyers and service providers to acknowledge its presence and creates transparency in how it is answered – or not answered. The choices are now whether the provider of these services is providing methods of security that despite different business models can still be compatible. The power of transparency is clear and it needs to be used to solve the challenges of present-day and Web 2.0 security.

The previous chapters developed the reasoning – a path from problem to solution. There is no such thing as a technical silver bullet that can solve the world's cyber security problems. No, this problem is less an issue of technology and more a question of how to approach the problem. The present methods leave the vulnerabilities in the system complexity to be protected by a perimeter security unequal to the task and an aftermarket security approach for the buyers and implementers of the technology – the point in the life cycle least able to solve the problem.

Chapters 5 and 6 proposed the idea that the security resolution for complexity requires attention and remediation at the point of product solution creation. It is about getting back to basics – security *designed in* to the product and in consideration of its role within the overall solution or service. The X.805 standard is a simple model to understand but places the hard work of applying security where it belongs. It positions an irrefutable claim that security in complex systems must come from within; no suit of cyber-armor can protect against the sophistication of current threats. It proposes transparency and nothing more. The actual security implementation remains a set of choices made by the system developer and driven by role. It should be driven by how the technology will be used and by business-driven considerations.

What is needed is enough security – enough to counterbalance the risk and not more. Aircraft are not sold to airlines with the expectation that the security to ensure the proper functioning of the aircraft gets added after the sale, at an additional price with its integration the responsibility of the airline company. Airbags in the automobile industry are another example. Our own biology, with all its complexity, has an embedded immune system – an intrinsic function of sustaining life.

These are strong reasons, but they are not enough. Businesses do not survive by security alone; they survive and thrive when they succeed in the competitive marketplace. Can one make an argument for security as a business enabler, one that generates increased revenues, improves the reputation, and strengthens customer relationships? Absolutely. These things matter in the long haul if businesses are intent on being around during good and tough times. Government offices are no exception, not for reasons of revenue creation, but for something yet more valuable – to protect the public and to keep its trust.

There is another reason and it has been discussed throughout this book – the world of Web 2.0 +. In just a few short years, Web 2.0 will transform every paradigm of life known today more completely than its

Figure 7.2   Benefits of the Security Value Life Cyle

predecessor generation. What if the ICT industry fails to design and integrate security inside the more complex world of Web 2.0? The idea that all things that depend on communications for the basics of life are wholly dependent on a complex web of technologies riddled with vulnerabilities is alarming.

There are multiple benefits in business value for taking an X.805 standard approach to cyber security. Call it *"Convincing the CFO."* To aid the discussion, consider once again the chart above, first used in Chapter 2, illustrating a view of the SVL. Chapter 2 discussed cost and impact at each of these three points and the interfaces in between. Chapter 7 considers the benefits that the ICT industry and businesses can derive from a proposition that starts with security *designed in* using the security framework at the Point of Creation and carrying it through to the Point of Service Delivery.

From the Point of Creation through the Point of Purchase - Service Creation to the Point of Service Delivery or End-Use, the top (right pointing) arrow represents the many benefits that transmute forward. As discussed in Chapter 2, the implications are clear – the more often this discipline of security *designed in* through the X.805 standard security framework is applied, the less likely that the business will see the return (left pointing) arrow, which represents all the activities that eat away at corporate profits, such as product returns, patching, brand but also cost avoidance – a language that any CFO understands and appreciates.

Convincing the CFO

Point of creation

As noted, the Point of Creation represents the place where innovation first takes place within a company, developing products that make up the elements in complex networks that, in combination, deliver a new

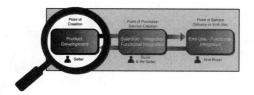

Figure 7.3 Point of Creation

service or automate a process. It is the point of provenance – the root of the life cycle – where it is so critical that security be applied.

Get it right here and the benefits can carry through to the endpoints. The transmutation principle applies both ways: vulnerabilities hidden are not somehow cleared up downstream; they carry forward, and the potential impact multiplies as they become embedded in operational systems. Fail to apply it, or get it wrong and the remedies-fixes are no more than bandages, never fully meeting the risks and costing more in the long run. Consider the many ways in which applying the X.805 standard security framework at the start benefits the company:

Threats are defined up front: Extends the definition of the use-case to include the corresponding threat environment. From this starting point, the engineers can develop the appropriate security controls and features as a roadmap for implementation driven by the production schedule. The benefits are primarily to drive a process so that security can be considered in the right measure to the risk and as part of the product development life cycle. It forces the engineers to establish up front not only the role, but also the market and its associated certifications and regulatory compliance requirements.

Faster to certification: Security certifications will expand with more businesses establishing proof of secure practices as conditions for partnership. Following a security standards-based approach within the product and solution development process can drive the needed efficiencies that secure-by-design can achieve at a lower cost and at the speed the business demands. The current process defined in activities such as Common Criteria suffer from cost and speed problems that, for whatever the reasons, are not meeting the needs.

Better testing results: Standardizing the process to *design in* the security has the benefit of standardizing the test methodology and eliminating the guesswork. Test laboratories can directly measure the degree of compliance to the corporate targets – even to the customer expectations. For any product development house, the test laboratory is the final point in the development life cycle, the place where efficiency counts in meeting delivery schedules. A standard process, following a published industry standard for security, will have the added benefit of improving the test results and reducing the time to bring the product to market.

Removing guesswork: There is an obvious benefit to reducing the guesswork when it comes to security design. When all security dimensions are considered, implementing the appropriate ones and in the right measure becomes clearer, and products can be designed to better serve the solutions. The use of an international standard brings the process of what is in the standard to an open forum for review and improvement. The corollary benefit is in the transparency – the standard is not owned by any company – yet companies can still compete on the basis of implementation.

A common language between the component developers, the product and solution developers: By using a stepwise methodology to identify the assets in the product (components), and at the solution level, the overall security requirements are developed internal to the product and between the products that make up the solution. The product owner is able to specify to its component providers the security asset to be covered and the level to be applied: software testing for security vulnerabilities established up front, encryption levels, methods of key exchange and even code-checking specified up front. The security standard provides a common framework for defining the parameters, the security features and protective measures. Extending this concept to the relationship between developers and buyers of the technology, having a common language embodied in a standard for what and how the security was *designed in*, has significant benefits again in removing the ambiguity – transparency is enabled and a clearer set of expectations is communicated between the two parties.

Prioritization: Not all security dimensions in the standard apply in equal importance for all products and in all situations – a variety of factors play into the considerations. For existing products assessed against the security standard, the assessment report may expose a number of gaps in meeting the targeted levels of protection, but it is not always possible to apply a remedy to all of the gaps at the same time. As an example, the X.805 standard *privacy dimension* for a Web server that contains personal account information is likely to be of greatest importance among the eight security dimensions in the standard. Choosing where the security dimensions should be applied from the perspective of the overall solution, one can prioritize which security features to apply and in what order, and the product development team can rationalize its decisions against production schedules. The benefits are in making better and more consistent choices as to what security is enough, when it should be introduced in the product development life cycle, determining overall cost and product pricing.

Re-use of security features: Security hardening procedures, features and techniques can be shared and re-used without reinventing the wheel. It is not as if these security technologies don't already exist. From encryption for data at rest and in transit, to integrity-checking techniques there is a wide range of tools and technologies that can be applied by product and solution developers. As the security process embedded in the framework becomes increasingly familiar, the developers can achieve a greater comfort level. The security framework represented in the standard provides an anchor point where the appropriate security technology can be applied and thereby reduces the uncertainty. Once again, the improved efficiency lowers time-to-market, reduces re-work and most importantly, security features once developed can be applied many times over.

Improving the teaching of security: An understanding of the science of protecting complex IT systems is needed as much in the general computer science and systems engineering curricula as it is in the security-specific disciplines. The X.805 standard puts security into the context of the overall system, the specific techniques for the mitigation of risk applied in a consistent manner that builds from the highly detailed to the system and business function level. The benefits to the overall IT industry is a community of computer science and systems engineers more likely to understand how to apply and consider security in their designs, removing the notion that system security can only be designed by security engineers at some point after the product is developed. There is also a learning curve to understanding security, one that can be significantly flattened by simply following a standard approach, the curve to learn and apply is shortened thereby leading to lower cost in development.

Educating the business development and sales professional: Few things strike more anxiety into the technology business development and sales professional as being faced with IT security questions from a potential buyer. This anxiety stems from a lack of understanding – what is needed to meet customer requirements, what degree of hardening has been applied and what are the specific security attributes. A product or solution designed with these considerations up front can remove the uncertainty and make clear the risk model that was applied, the inherent vulnerabilities and mitigations *designed in* to the product, and how the product interfaces into the overall solution from a security perspective. Improving the understanding means that the business development and sales professional can approach the sales meeting with a high degree of confidence. The security standard is, by definition, consistent, so it can be taught at a level for the sales pitch; the choices made to harden the product into an overall solution makes it clear that the company selling the technology is mindful of the security needs and has demonstrated competence in meeting those needs.

Reducing patching: It really is quite amazing to consider the question of whether a particular patch sent out worldwide to fix a vulnerability could have been completely avoided – the problem caught and fixed at system design. The cost to the company developing and sending out patches is significant (the lower left pointing arrow in the SVL), but it is dwarfed by the cost of IT specialists around the world and individual consumers going through the exercise of patching systems. The number of vulnerabilities continues to increase on an annual basis. For example, the Identity Theft Resource Center states that the number of security breaches has increased to 656 in 2008 versus 446 in 2007.[1] This is a 47 percent increase on an annual basis. Vulnerabilities can be discovered at design and all the cost and loss could be avoided altogether. The benefit is as simple as the reduction in the cost and damage caused by the lack of attention and investment at the point of design.

Improvements in cross-selling: Despite conventional thinking, there really are few unique needs in security across the different markets. Government needs are increasingly the same as those required for businesses that have millions of customers and, in the aggregate, make infrastructures of national and even international importance. Privacy needs to be protected in business transactions as much as in government ones. Designing for security for one market means that the very same approaches, the same security features, can be re-marketed for other markets; changes made in the presentation may be all that is needed. For the company considering the value proposition for investment in security hardening of the technologies they sell into one market, this is an important recognition – the market may be bigger.

Improved channel sales relationships: Channel sales are an important element in the commerce of technologies where local companies make local relationships to deliver technologies from global companies. The benefits of following a standard for security apply to both the product-solution developer and the channel sales company. It can dramatically improve this most important relationship, again reducing the friction to get the product into the marketplace as quickly as possible and delivered with a competent channel sales provider knowledgeable in answering the questions of security hardening.

Transparency in Web 2.0 models: This point has been made repeatedly throughout this book – that Web 2.0 makes ever-more challenging the task of controlling the critical information assets of a company or an individual. Without this control, there is no security, and without the security the foundations of trust and confidence sit on uncertain ground. Transparency is

---

[1] 2008 Identity Theft Resource Center Breach Report, www.idtheftcenter.org

the primary benefit of applying a standards-based approach – transparency that is demanded in all relationships between consumers and businesses. These relationships need to be based on a clear and unambiguous demonstration that Web 2.0 does protect the information assets in ways that can be understood, measured, audited and assured. The benefits of transparency are unfortunately typically understood only after the cancer of hidden processes and hidden agendas reaches a crisis; the evolving financial crisis taking place on a global scale is only the latest example.

Answering the regulator: It is no mystery that the buyers of technology (Points 2 and 3 in the SVL) face their own security demands from their customers. Increasingly, these demands are codified in certifications or regulations. These certifications and regulations ask a series of questions to probe and determine the degree that systems and information assets are assured. Again, no mystery what is in these certification and regulation requirements, and they are, without exception, standard security considerations of role-based access control, assurance of integrity and so forth – nothing particularly unique except the degree to which systems have to be hardened. It stands to reason that the company developing the technology to sell into these markets most attentive to the certification and regulatory environments of their customers can *design in* the appropriate security that makes it clear and easy to answer the auditors. Businesses can prove to their customers that their products satisfy the requirements of regulators and even the government concerned with the protection of national infrastructures.

Improving the brand, improve the business: It was stated up front, security is of no purpose for its own sake; it has to serve a business purpose. The CFO has to look across the conference room to the CEO and make the appropriate nod. Security can be more than a hit on the balance sheet; it can improve the top line as the company's reputation is enhanced, the security concern of the company for its customers is recognized and the brand has a new shine. The avoidance of incidents is part of the dynamic for why security investments are made, but it can also be used to differentiate the company from the competition. Security professionals and business developers need greater collaboration on the latter of these two points. To the maker of technologies, a security standard following a standardized method of applying the security is the benefit of an investment made with full benefit at minimum cost as every degree of efficiency is applied within the corporate product development processes.

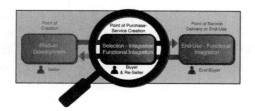

Figure 7.4 Point of Service Creation

Point of purchase and service creation

The Point of Purchase and Service Creation is the place where the technology enables the business to focus on delivery to the market, to lower its cost and compete better. In the context of this analysis, competing better is in two forms: lowering the friction of bringing services and products to market faster (lowering latency) and by delivering technology that also answers security concerns. Both of these goals are satisfied when the product developer, the Point of Creation in the SVL, has taken these factors into consideration up front to answer the questions of how the security was *designed in*. Without these upfront considerations, the result is friction in the processes at the Point of Purchase and it adds latency to the company that the purchaser of the technology can ill afford. Simplifying the acquisition process, the technology integration and the functional integration where the technology and the business function are optimized helps reduce this friction and eliminate unnecessary latency in bringing the products or services to market.

By starting with the simple statement, "Tell me how your technology applies the X.805 standard," the product purchaser pushes that entire burden back to the product and system developer – where it belonged in the first place. Selection then becomes a decision based upon transparency and execution – the salesperson who can demonstrate that they own up to this responsibility, that they have done their homework and are not afraid to be accountable and are confident in their product engineers, becomes a long-term and strategic business partner. Following the standard security framework is advantageous to both parties; listed below are the benefits to the companies where the technology gets purchased, integrated and a service created:

Simplifies the acquisition: Point 2 in the SVL, the technology purchaser, can focus the efforts on a solid definition of the use case with a requirement that potential bidders represent the security *designed in* to the product-solution to the X.805 standard. This creates a straightforward way for the product-solution creator to understand the process for evaluation and for the technology purchaser to evaluate between competing bids. The technology purchaser can validate that the bidders have used a reasonable representation of the threat model for the use case, that the inherent vulnerabilities were adequately identified and the appropriate hardening countermeasures taken. This is transparency at work – a simplified process that lowers the time to express the requirements, understand the bids and make a more informed decision.

Simplifies security integration: The X.805 standard begins with a network model where security is *designed in* as a part of an overall technology solution. Security integration conducted at the Point of Creation becomes part of the implemented solution in the technology purchaser's operational environment with minimal adjustments. The current method places this burden with the technology purchaser or with a systems integrator. Neither of these two parties can successfully resolve the inherent vulnerabilities in the solution if the security was not applied at the Point of Creation. The benefits are clearly to simplify the security integration by making it part of the responsibilities at the technology Point of Creation.

Speeds certification and compliance: A variety of different certification and compliance requirements serve in the different commercial and government markets. Many of these were discussed earlier, including the financial, retail and health markets. On closer examination, there is greater commonality between the security requirements of these different sectors than there are differences. Where there are differences, these tend to the degree, or rigor of, hardening or the extent of validation needed to yield a certification. The X.805 standard provides the framework; the market requirements dictate the degree of, or rigor of, hardening. By identifying these at the Point of Product-Solution Creation, the process of certification and compliance is made simpler, resulting in a faster process to satisfy these certifications – compliance audits at the Point of Purchase and Service Creation. This can apply for ISO/IEC 27000 series certification, for the Payment Card Industry – whatever the certification and compliance demands of the different market sectors. The coupling starts with identification of the target market, followed by determining the market certification-compliance requirements and then mapping these to hardening steps taken at the Point of Product-Solution Creation using the X.805 standard. It takes place where it can best be resolved, the Point of Creation, and the benefits flow downstream in the SVL to the Point of Purchase and Service Creation. Also, by building it from the ground up, there is a much greater likelihood that the certification and compliance audit is represented not just in the paper report but also within the information systems and processes.

A common language: As in Point 1 in the SVL, having a common standard for the implementation of security in systems also serves to establish a common basis of communication. The first of these was discussed above in simplifying and speeding the process of technology acquisitions. The second is between Points 2 and 3 – the relationship between the initial purchase of technology and the subsequent endpoints of purchase where the technology is applied to a consumer, business or government function. The security standard provides the common framework for defining how the security was integrated first at the product-solution level and also as part of the overall service delivery in Web services, as one example. There are significant benefits again in removing the ambiguity – transparency is enabled and a clearer set of expectations is communicated between the three parties in the SVL.

Transparency in Web 2.0 models: Point 2 in the SVL is the Point of Purchase and Service Creation of Web 2.0 services. The X.805 standard applied at Point 2 can serve to deliver the needed transparency so that customers of the service, Point 3 in the SVL, can have a standardized basis to determine the degree of protection considered and applied by the service provider. Between business partners, this allows the two partners a standardized basis for considering the state of security in the planning to exchange information. Partners A and B can determine the degree of automation to exchange information while still maintaining their respective corporate certification and compliance requirements. Once again, transparency is the primary benefit of applying a standards-based approach – transparency that is demanded in all relationships between businesses, between consumers and the businesses. These relationships need to be based on a clear and unambiguous demonstration that Web 2.0 does protect the information assets in ways that can be understood, measured, audited and assured.

Improved coupling to IT management frameworks: The major beneficiaries of the standardized implementation of ITU-T X.805 are the companies associated with Point 2 in the SVL, as it is these companies delivering IT services that are most likely to be following an IT management methodology (examples, ITIL and CobIT) for overall IT management. The benefit is first with tighter coupling between the detailed security hardening practices (following the X.805 standard) and the IT management framework that allows the IT manager to have a single management system for organization.

Measure performance from a standard configuration: IT Security begins with establishing and maintaining control and it typically starts with standardizing the information system configurations. In the same manner, the standardization of security hardening is the first consideration. Without a standard configuration there is no point of reference to use as the known good state that can be compared to changes – and detecting unauthorized changes is central to knowing when systems are being compromised. These are the basics: the benefit of applying a standardized process based on an international standard is the legitimacy and consistency needed between the creators, purchasers and implementers of technology represented in the three-point SVL.

Additional indirect benefits: A number of indirect benefits can be attributed to the standardized practice of security hardening using the X.805 standard. These may include reductions in insurance costs associated with managed risks, less need to depend on expensive IT security consultants to serve as intermediaries to assess and determine the appropriate security posture – the so-called disintermediation benefits – and ultimately to use the improved state of security as a way to differentiate the value of the service between competitors.

Figure 7.5   Point of Service Delivery or End-User

Point of service delivery or end use

The Point of Service Delivery or End-Use is the last stop in this three-stage description of how the benefits accrue and transmute from the point of origin, where the product is designed secure, to a solution that is architected using the X.805 standard security framework. The chain of trust is now complete; where the service delivered to an end customer can be made with the confidence that comes from transparency delivered by the clear demonstration of security applied to a standard that reveals the extent of the protections or the absence of protection.

From Point 1 through Point 2 in the SVL, the end customer represented in Point 3 must be part of the security design, particularly where the end-user activity depends on an IT transaction with a Web 2.0 service provider and where the security of the end-user device is part of the equation. Online purchasing, online banking, and even service registration and creation are among the kinds of end-user activities that must be protected. By using validation techniques prescribed in the security framework, such as system and data integrity-checking and network access control as part of the access dimension in the security framework, the Point of Purchase - Service Creation can protect its interest and that of its customers, assuring that the benefits that come from security *designed in* at the Point of Creation carry forward to the endpoint of IT service delivery.

Ultimately, the security value chain must transmute from Points 1 and 2 to include what has heretofore been an end-user left to be their own security engineer. Using the eight security dimensions in the

X.805 standard to discuss the benefits of the SVL applied from the starting point, the benefits become clear:

- **Authentication:** Spoofing is an evolving art of crime becoming increasingly sophisticated as cyber criminals find easily exploited vulnerabilities in the system designs of individual service providers and of the Internet in general.

  A Web 2.0 service provider offering online banking may implement strong authentication requirements in a simple many-to-one relationship (many customers to one service provider). But this is not the real world. It is obviously a many-to-many relationship (many customers to many service providers) and so the strongly implemented authentication applied many times over gets unraveled – the general population is unable to remember beyond a few passwords but may be interacting with hundreds of Web sites asking for login authentication. As a result, people keep written copies of the authentication passwords and re-use the same password across multiple login accounts. The same password used for the Web site with poor implementation of password protection is likely the same one used to access the strongly protected login of the bank account. With this same password, the cyber criminal can gain access to the bank account, and the personal details of the compromised person opens up in its entirety.

  By considering how end-users interact with the Internet, designing for the real world of Internet use (a many-to-many, not a many-to-one relationship), the system designers can mitigate the inherent vulnerability in the limitations of people. There are now new identity management services available to solve this very problem, a problem that has been there from the beginning of the Internet, to share information and for e-commerce transactions. The security design that considers the real world of the end-user as part of the solution is the one that accounts for the limitations of people, removes this vulnerability and makes it easier for end-users to use IT systems in a more secure fashion.

- **Access control that is context sensitive:** Once again, consider the end-user interacting in the real world of online activity. System developers have historically designed for the many-to-one type of relationship between end- users and network or application access as if it is one openly accessible network and as if each application is the only one in the network The real world is greatly more complex; each end-user having multiple roles, and interacting with multiple systems and applications, inside the LAN and with the Web, often at the same time. Role-based access to the network needs to maintain consistency to the identity for every transaction in the network and with the multiple applications to provide the right context control – the person exercising roles in the context of time of day, location, as employee, member of a team and as a private individual. The benefits of systems designed with this understanding of the complexity of end-users in the overall solution is the system better suited to providing needed security for the real world of individuals exercising roles as employee connecting from re-mote locations, at home and in different countries with different controlling regulations.

- **Assuring integrity:** Integrity assurance is meant in the context of the system and for the data stored in these systems – aspects of system design that have been largely absent.

  The benefits of integrity-checking controls for the end-user are a long list of corrections needed for, once again, how IT systems are used in the real world. The enterprise workstation or home computer, PDA, television or any endpoint device acting to exchange data, voice or video in any combination assumes some degree of integrity. It is a false assumption; current systems have no sense of the state of the integrity when there is no point of reference for the good state of integrity to measure against. By applying integrity-checking techniques in the security design (now coming into use), one can determine, as an example, when some highly stealthy keylogger spyware has compromised the system to steal account information or an embedded rootkit has compromised the operating system to make some external and unauthorized system call. At the data level, having integrity-checking capabilities in the file systems or within applications can provide the information needed to determine the degree of trust, whether the important corporate spreadsheet used for a variety of critical decisions is the right spreadsheet unchanged or whether it has been compromised by an unauthorized agent intent on gaining some unauthorized advantage. The examples of this go from the silly and insignificant, when the "enterprising" student gained access to the spreadsheet of school grades to improve the semester report card, to the far more serious example – parameters in some database used to control utilities affecting thousands of customers.

Designing for integrity-checking of the system elements and of the data stored on those systems used to make all forms of decisions such as billing or in utility control provides one all important benefit: a basis for adjudicating the degree of trust, which in turn is used to determine the degree to which access is granted and transactions get completed.

- **Non-repudiation consistently applied:** Non-repudiation in the security design is frequently absent and yet it is ever-more important in Web 2.0-based transactions where the parties are separate entities: the end-user and the application service provider in the network cloud. To achieve the benefits of transparency, and to build trust between the transaction points, it matters that the information about the exchange (at all layers in the system stack) within the various information and systems logs is captured, passed between the parties and is used as a means to adjudicate access – even to detect anomalies that are the indicators of some form of system breach (such as data theft and system probes). A standards-based ITU-T X.805 approach that takes the end use into consideration can make it that non-repudiation is *designed in* and used for enhancing the trust between the parties in Web-based applications.

- **Communications security:** Once again, the world of Web 2.0 makes it critical for the communications path starting at the endpoints and the information stream whether it is data, voice or video to stay protected from eavesdropping or other forms of interception and misuse. By designing for communications security starting with the endpoint device, the advanced capabilities to blend all the modes of communications can stay protected from threats sure to arise, as it becomes clear what is taking place on these networks and in these endpoint devices. Online banking, micro-payments, billed Web purchases with account information, GPS positioning, sensitive phone calls and even sensitive video conferencing interactions are all parts of the wide range of new capabilities for delivery in next-generation networks – Web 2.0. Design the security for the endpoints as part of the overall systems with a standards-based ITU-T X.805 approach and there is a greater likelihood that these new capabilities can enter into widespread use trustworthy to the high rate of use and the important role these services will provide to consumers, businesses and government agencies.

- **Privacy controls:** Privacy begins at the endpoint with the end-user's personal information input into databases, both in corporate networks and with Web applications. It is also in the network as information flows between the endpoint and its destination. Most importantly, privacy controls are needed in the data center with applications, databases and mass storage systems. The benefit of applying a standards-based approach to the system design is simply that security of all the personal information gets considered in advance where a deliberate and rigorous effort to identify the information, minimize its use, apply encryption where needed and establish how it is used in the context of the differing context settings for access controls as discussed earlier. Trying to correct for privacy controls after the fact is a most inefficient approach that really never resolves the vulnerability.

- **Confidentiality in the transactions:** It is no secret that Web 2.0 traffic derives a tremendous amount of personal information. End-users expect that this information is maintained in confidence. The benefit of a standards-based ITU-T X.805 approach to security design is simply that the end-user's stake in the confidentiality of this information is considered up front by the system designers and by the service providers delivering the Web applications in a Web 2.0 environment. This kind of up-front design thinking pays off not only with meeting end-user expectations but also in meeting the certification and regulatory compliance requirements. Every time an incident occurs where privacy-related and confidential information held by "trusted" companies is lost, mishandled or even sold, the pressure will grow that legislators provide legal protections. The regulatory burden will grow even as the complexity of how to protect against these incidents gets more challenging. The benefit is that with the right design, the confidential information can be used within acceptable boundaries and still remain protected from unauthorized disclosure.

- **Availability of services:** Previous chapters addressed at length the growing importance of broadband wireless communications as all IT users continue the trend to un-tether from the physical constraints of wired systems. The growing demand in network traffic will stress the wireless and wired networks, some argue, beyond the capacity to meet the demand. Add in the potential that these highly capacity-optimized systems can be subject to DoS attacks, and entire business segments highly leveraged on Internet access may fail. As these systems underpin national security, the bar of importance and criticality is raised higher. A standards-based approach with a realistic understanding of the threat can drive the system designers to plan for availability beyond the nominal to extreme conditions of an active hostile attack. It must consider the end-user both in a positive and hostile role – the botnet-generated distributed DoS attacks serve as a good example. Intentional or not, the system must protect itself to assure that it remains available to all and can be exercised in a precedence-structured method, the needs of government in times of crisis carrying out critical services assigned higher orders of precedence.

Together, these eight security dimensions in the X.805 standard security framework provide the necessary rigor to operate and deliver the services that ensure confidence and provide a measurable basis for trust in computing transactions. Following the security framework is advantageous to all parties, but it begins with ensuring that the security is *designed in* at the beginning of the product development and carried forward with Points 2 and 3 in the SVL. In general, the benefits are:

- Improved trust in online services – that converts faith-based reputation to metrics-based reputation, whether that metric is five stars, or some other model, to establish a ladder of trust.

- Accountability becomes better understood. If it's the method of how IT products and services are measured, it improves the confidence that the rating scheme is valid and thereby trustworthy.

- Reduced need to buy security as an aftermarket purchase and installation. This is a benefit in cost – the cost of the added software or services now being sold and in the time that has to be spent downloading the security wares.

- Reduction in the exposure of people to the social engineering schemes that target the unaware – the people least able to detect and resolve these types of schemes.

- End-users can have a higher sense of confidence in interacting with Web sites and can make better, more appropriate judgments of risk.

- When security hardening is embedded in the products and in the service delivery, it reduces the demand to try and make security engineers of end- users.

- The complexity in systems is too great for simplistic perimeter-based defenses and the methods of attack too sophisticated for human (unaided) capabilities. The security *designed in* is the method of tuning the security integration at the speed of electrons and high-speed networks.

- Increased trust in e-commerce and in e-government services all moving to a Web basis of service delivery.

John Maynard Keynes said, "It is better to be roughly right than precisely wrong." When it comes to how security is applied in complex IT systems, the verdict is clear enough: it is a "precisely wrong" situation. Protecting a perimeter defined within a LAN has not worked for a long time now, and with Web 2.0, it doesn't even make sense. Doing more of the same "wrong" changes nothing – the hole just keeps getting deeper. Another adage applies in this case: the first rule of getting out of the hole is to stop digging. In this chapter, one considers that there are more than just consequences, there are actual tangible benefits – the kind of benefits that can convince the CFO in every one of the instances in our three-point SVL: the Point of Creation, Point of Purchase-Service Delivery and at the endpoint.

The benefits are real and they can be achieved across the SVL from product and services creation to the delivery-operational state and end-user experience of sound security. With this framework there is now a basis to measure security, baseline it and make better judgments as to what level of risk to assign. These benefits create other direct benefits to the growth of e-commerce and e-government.

Web 2.0 poses particular and more difficult challenges to security. These can be met with all its derivative benefits with security practiced using a common standard accessible to all industries. The X.805 standard framework is a point of beginning. Without it we should not venture forward further into Web 2.0.

8
Correcting Our Path – What Will it Take?

"To prime the pump it will take organizations coming together"

Executive Summary

The word that best captures the message of this chapter is inertia – the rut in the path so familiar and so ingrained with reinforcing processes that are so difficult to overcome. At the start of this book the story of the frog in the cauldron where the temperature rises slowly to boiling point was another way to make this same point. This path has a name: an aftermarket approach to security placing the security burden where it can least be resolved, with the end-user community, the buyers and users of the technology. This rut in the path is a persistent practice despite a body of people and knowledge well aware that it is an inadequate method; doing something the same way faster with more money will not create a new and better result. It will simply make an inadequate process faster and more expensive.

Inertia must be understood for how it keeps the status quo. But to actually get out of this rut, change the patterns, the habit of familiarity and the market forces with self-interest to keep it the same, it will take more than good reasoning and sound logic or even the loss of billions of dollars annually. To un-tether from the suction and drag of inertia will take a surge of new energy from different groups pulling together. It will take a clear commitment to a new path of transparency in security, one that starts at the beginning in product development where it always belonged. That is the focus of this chapter, correcting our path – what it will take to get out of the rut of the current path and onto a road to practice a new model where security is *designed in* and it is consistent in each stage of its SVL.

137

Who are these forces for change? In a broader sense, there are three: business, academia (including research), and government. Specifically, it is leaders in these areas willing to make the investment and step away from the rut of inertia. Closer to ground, it is key organizations willing to lead within these groups, of which there are many. The change must come from all of them, though not necessarily starting together at the same time. The supply side of the security market (security technology companies) has important contributions that provide the key technologies used to mitigate the vulnerabilities, but the impetus to change from aftermarket to *designed in* will not come from the security industry itself; it is too self-invested in the current model. Not that the security industry fails to recognize the need for change, but the inertia feeds this industry, and the security industry will ultimately respond to the demands of customers. The key is with the buyers of the information technology solutions insisting that security be *designed in* with transparency in the form of the security framework described in these previous chapters.

Government must be one of the primary catalysts, as one can argue that it has the most to lose, with the concern over national infrastructure dependent upon communications systems. There are already signs that government gets it; of note is the attention being paid to hardening critical infrastructures from cyber attacks. Consider the Federal Desktop Core Configuration (FDCC) mandate in the U.S. federal government's Office of Management and Budget. By any other name this is about a large customer acting as one buying body demanding that vendors deliver computers in a configuration where the operating system and applications are shipped patched to current levels and stripped of unnecessary features that may create security issues. It is important to note that endpoint computers alone do not make a large complex network, therefore by no means is desktop computer hardening sufficient. It is more than the endpoints, one that includes the network elements, the overall information service delivered with technologies end to end. But this example is a beginning, and it is consistent with the concept. This is a good and hopeful sign.

Businesses must also be primary catalysts and initiators of change. In some vertical markets, such as the world of investment banks, the technology organizations take the practice of security *designed in* as an absolute configuration control applied in every element of the process, not willing to trust anyone but their own well-developed procedures. They take neither endpoint computers, nor any element of networks off the shelf and install it as is. More of this thinking is needed across businesses, though clearly the technical sophistication found in investment banks is a rarity. Businesses in general will need to apply a model of security where it is *designed in* and delivered securely by the product developers – the vendors of technology.

Academia and research laboratories are the final piece that comprises the change agents – the place where engineers and scientists learn their craft, the art and science of innovation and creation. These are the places where security needs to be part of the curriculum, not as a separate function for security engineers. It is an integrated function of sound engineering principles that all engineers learn, and it is in these institutions where it can grow and mature with greater sophistication as a set of principles that come as a body of knowledge with the students who graduate and enter the workforce in product development companies.

It is the entire technology industry that needs to transform, contribute, learn, adapt and integrate security as part of the basic business process. It must follow a standard that is open to contribution and follow an open-source model not held back by a process that is laggard to the pace of business change and to the politics of standards committees. These are not antithetical points; it can be a standard and it can be open to contribution – really open, not just open to companies vying for advantage. It must be open source so all can participate, using the tools already in use, such as blogs and wikis – a standard that matures in small increments, but faster with greater value as it becomes more precise and with greater specification in the various use cases that derive from business in motion.

It must align with the ISO/IEC 27000 series standard as this is the path to certification and compliance, and with certification the needed transparency is developed so that business and governments have a foundation upon which to apply trust. Technology needs to become more trustworthy to its lofty place in our lives – a dependency to every facet of modern society. That can only come from transparency.

How does this pump get primed and get started with sufficient mass that it reaches the critical point, the tipping point, fueled by its own momentum? This question is frequently discussed as the *digital Pearl Harbor*[1] event, a crisis of such magnitude directly attributable to a culprit that can be named and blamed. To be sure, the potential exists for this very scenario. Cyber events are happening today, and they will continue to grow more lucrative due to a variety of motives along with the opportunity presented by vulnerable systems. Be assured that the problem of how to secure complex computer systems will only grow, and its consequence will be more loss in confidence, trust, money and higher costs in trying to correct an uncorrectable situation; one that was designed to fail, or was not designed for survival in a hostile technology environment.

To prime the pump it will take organizations coming together, saying enough is enough. It will take a community of interest for purchasing might and for communicating to its vendor communities that systems will only be acquired that can demonstrate their transparency in accordance with a standard framework. The X.805 standard framework can serve this purpose and get the industry started in correcting its path – a new road moving away from the rut of the path it follows today.

---

[1] Winn Schwartau, *pearl harbor dot com*, (Interpact Press, 2002)

The transformation of the security practice from a reactive approach to one that applies controls at the point of product development at a consistent level will not happen by chance. This form of industry transformation will only happen by design and positive action in the three domains of business, government, and academia and research laboratories. The role for business is to make security design a set of principles applied as part of the normal course of product development. The government's role is to establish policies supporting a security-framework-based transparency in technology purchasing decisions. The role for academia and research laboratories is to enhance the science of applying security metrics and techniques. Transformative change needs to occur in these domains and develop to a point of maturity to maintain parity with the sophistication and complexity of Web 2.0.

Pertinent to this discussion is the topic of a digital Pearl Harbor. The image is one of a stealthy, but seismic, cyber attack of catastrophic proportions – December 1941 repeating itself, but in the world of cyberspace. This event will finally convince governments to take action. The Internet has ground to a halt, commerce has stopped and economies have started to shut down. The scenario has many variations, but generally plays out as the world wakes up to discover that governments and businesses have been scrambling overnight, unable to stop the cascading devolution of infrastructures that have all become dependent upon vulnerable computer systems. This scenario is the notion of Hollywood Armageddon-type movies playing before a pliable public willing to be entertained with the outrageous. Is it so outrageous?

Convergence and Web 2.0 are happening now, and if industry, government and academia do not set a new course to transform the way technologies and services are secured, it is with near certainty that society will face the scenario painted in the introduction to this book: the slow and steady degradation of confidence and trust engendered over long periods of time that gets compromised in seconds with realized losses. A core set of consistent security values must reach critical mass between the product developer, the seller and the buyer in order to avoid a digital Pearl Harbor from becoming the catalyst for change.

This action can be the combination of two very human predilections – fear and profit making. Fear alone will not compel business to take action. One might argue that this strategy has engendered cynicism, causing decision makers to become almost immune to the cries of fear mongering. Now, argue a case to make security worth the cost of investment – a scenario that even a CFO can love. This model for security will differentiate the company from the competition on the basis of creating brand recognition around quality, reliability and security. The CFO of a business highly organized around its technology would be very interested in the statement that the security organization can improve the overall state of security while not increasing the operational budget.

In order for security to have a lasting impact, it needs to be a priority as much for the development team as it is for the executive team. Organizations need to change their fundamental behavior about how systems are purchased, where the security designed-in is demanded by the makers of the technology – follow the OMB example.

Business process is frequently the action that breaks the bonds of inertia, and it can come from anywhere in the world of business. But in order for it to be successful, it has to come en masse – in the buying power of large numbers. The security industry will listen, and will respond. However, the real target of this message is less security companies and more simply companies that make products for the technology industry. These products include routers, switches, gateways, servers, operating systems, applications, databases, storage and those that deliver technology services in the Web 2.0 world.

Government also needs to be involved. The organizations within the government have the most to lose, as these functions play a very important role in maintaining the ability of modern societies to proceed in an orderly manner. At the time of this writing, this point is being made in very personal ways, as it becomes clear how deeply and widely the thread of finance runs through the economies of nations. The concept is the same with computer systems; the thread of technology runs deeply through everything in the economies of nations. The lesson of the financial crisis is there for us to learn and apply – a future global crisis can be averted.

Governments should be concerned, if they are not already, about the state of security in the national infrastructure, as the functionality is deeply dependent upon commercial computer systems that get bought, installed and placed in production. This product implementation is done without knowing if the products or components purchased were actually sourced from the company that wears the brand label or from a clone manufacturer with no reputation to uphold.

Academia and research laboratories comprise another critical group that needs to be engaged. These institutions are the source of tremendous innovation, and these are the places where engineers learn that engineering is a science for investigating and finding new technological possibilities. These engineers, the ones preparing to become product developers, must learn and apply the principle that security is part of the system design to be applied in a consistent manner. The primary role for academia and research laboratories is to educate the next generation of developers and scientists, to develop better methods, better approaches for how to integrate security into complex network solutions.

Innovation accelerates, as Mr. Kurzweil explains. It will take product engineers to be "mindful of the risks along with the benefits" so that these concerns can be addressed as a set of good practices. The great schools of innovation are the third prime to the pump – teaching the security framework as part of Engineering 101 – getting back to the basics.

The Power of the Customer to Transform an Industry

In 2002, John Gilligan, then an Air Force CIO, decided that enough was enough. Gilligan put a stop to future Air Force purchases of Microsoft software licenses running on Air Force computers until Microsoft provided a secure configuration out of the box.[2] After a period of shock and awe that a customer would actually seek to dictate to Microsoft how it would deliver software configurations in workstations, Microsoft responded in a positive way. They worked with Gilligan's office to come up with a plan that they executed consistently with the very principle that security considerations should be a prerequisite of the product developer, before the sale, not pushed onto the buyer (in this case, the Air Force) to figure out. This example set a very powerful precedent.

"Your most unhappy customers are your greatest source of learning."
Bill Gates

---

[2] "Air Force seeks better security from Microsoft," Byron Acohido, USA Today, March 10, 2002

The Air Force, using its influence as a major customer, was able to create a practice that in 2007 became the FDCC mandate across the U.S. federal government. This mandate must happen across a wider range, not just in hardening the operating system, but also across the networks that deliver the systems and the technology services that enable the businesses. In the discussions that follow, consider the three domains introduced earlier to prime the pump: government, business and academia.

Government

The idea of a prescriptive product hardening leading to certification is hardly new to governments. The Evaluation Assurance Level (EAL), more commonly known as *common criteria*, has been in practice for a number of years. In the U.S. defense department, there are a number of branch unique certification requirements with corresponding policies and with their own test laboratories. In combination, they have unwittingly made it more difficult for the product developers; the parochial approach – each branch of service having its own view – means that there is more overhead. This approach is not mindful of the costs and stresses that it places on the businesses making decisions about how many separate certifications to go through or whether to EAL certify. The consequences are predictable in queuing delays for certification schedules, and uncertain revenue returns have resulted in companies choosing to not go through the government certification process or certified product versions that are out of date. Further, the certifications, as they are not always designed to take a full network model into account, means that the security hardening may not even improve the overall security posture once it is installed.

In contrast, the X.805 standard is, first and foremost, a network security model that gets applied at the component and product level and in consideration of the role to be exercised within the overall network solution. The box is hardened to the solution even when the solution is a hybrid of different manufacturers. The standard does not differentiate between levels of network classifications with strict boundaries but rather, leaves it open to the judgment that comes from determining the ultimate role and environment of use. Further, it is designed to meet the certification and compliance requirements of different vertical markets. Can it serve as a model for government as well as for business? A standard that can be used for both business and government requirements with lower implementation costs and structured as a network model is an idea worth considering.

How can government use its buying power to transform the technology industry from an aftermarket security approach to one where security is designed-in and carried forward through the SVL? The answer is first, by acting as a single body, where appropriate, in the acquisition process and second, by following the Air Force example and requiring that security be part of the standard configuration. Businesses will be more apt to invest in security features when the overall process is simplified and streamlined.

Where it applies to protecting the critical infrastructure, government can also set the bar of security performance. The critical infrastructure not only affects the systems of government, but also the systems that provide vital communications and other services to the population at large. By this definition, government must get involved and become the overseer.

The culture of following hardening practices is already in place within government in the form of common criteria and, as noted earlier, with the FDCC. In practice, however, there is need of extensive reform with common criteria to improve the execution to be more in line with business interests. This, in turn, will improve the speed to market and reduce the cost of meeting the certification. The X.805 standard can serve as a model for these much needed adjustments in the security certification process.

The Federal Information Systems Management Act (FISMA) is roughly the equivalent of the Gramm-Leach-Bliley Act in the financial services sector, and they suffer the same problem – the absence of a corresponding hardening and certification standard that actually works the way that product developers make decisions. Until this situation is remedied, a FISMA accreditation will not mean that systems are secure. This makes the cost and burden of these compliance regulations of uncertain value in actually reducing risk. The following are key steps that need to be followed to ensure security is part of the entire business process:

- Transparency in the requests for proposals

- Influencing the purchase of systems so that they are secure before they are placed into production

- Using the security framework as prescriptive to the solution levels, not as afterthoughts

- Making e-government secure and trustworthy by coupling the X.805 standard to FISMA can provide a basis of measurement for how well the security is applied.

Business

It's a simple question of how the product was designed with security as a primary consideration following a framework that makes it easier to understand the design choices. In the end, it is a set of choices about optimizing a set of factors, one of them being the use environment that helps to define the risk. The other is how the eight dimensions of security in the X.805 standard security framework were considered and applied not only at the product level, but also at the solution level. The choices must make sense together and be in balance with the risk. Business needs to start defining requirements and making purchases not at the product level, but at the system and solution levels with security a prime consideration in the selection process.

Companies that optimize these choices can expect to win more deals and increase profits. Guide the CFO to the understanding that security can actually make money for the company, and the CFO will listen with greater attention. Get enough companies thinking and acting together in this chain of logic, and it will be more than the business CFOs and CEOs paying attention. The entire technology manufacturing industry, whose CEOs became household names, will start paying attention to security as a consideration in their products and will start developing solution-level offers. Security can become a differentiator in selling products, but the demand must come from the buying side of the equation en masse, not incrementally.

Clearly, business is not found just at the point of product development. Business transcends the full range of the SVL. Collaboration between the business that buys technology and the business that makes technology creates transparency in the transaction. The actual decisions of what security features to apply, and what hardening techniques to apply in operations, will be driven by the factors of use and roles.

Collaboration is needed, but the start of the discussion begins with the buyer of the technology. Whether it's finance, healthcare, transportation or even entertainment, all business sectors must make it clear that the buying decision will not be based on just functional features and performance. A full analysis of how security is a part of the solution mind-set as prescribed in the X.805 standard security framework will be a critical factor in the selection process. This is the incentive needed for the makers and developers of the technology to learn the methods of this X.805 standard approach and apply them in their product lines. This is the inducement for transforming the product development end of the life cycle that fear or compliance auditors alone do not attain.

Real measures of trust can be applied throughout the SVL. Security can serve as a basis for a revenue generating service with end customers. Security does not have to be just cost; a well-designed service with measurable value for the end customer is something that can actually return the cost of investment in security and more. This same integrity-checking technology can be applied for machine-to-machine validation to establish the basis of trust between network nodes.

The evidence that security can be a revenue making service is found in the managed security service line of business; an area of growth estimated at $1.3 billion in 2007, an increase of 19.6 percent over 2006.[3] It is clear that there is a monetized value of security to customers who are increasingly cognizant of the threats and the need to protect their systems. This is security value transmuted across the life cycle and builds a value chain based on transparency at product design and through the selection, integration and end-use points.

Businesses will respond where there are opportunities, but, once again, the spark to light this fire begins with customers that ask and demand. It is a spark that can come from a variety of business sectors, specific companies using mass buying powers to transform the way that security is applied.

From this beginning, the benefits find many derivative points of value:

- Risk that can be quantified means that business can make better judgments.

- Insurance premiums are lower as security can be measured and risk controlled.

---

[3] U.S. Managed Security Services Market To Grow By Billions, *securitysolutions.com*, September 30, 2008.

• Security is integrated in and coupled to the detect-respond parts of the security triad so that a system can actually report its state of health – meaning that the detection part can take appropriate response when that state is reporting out-of-band for a healthy configuration.

Academia

Cyber security is, first and foremost, part of an overall risk structure; second, part of an overall network solution that is increasingly defined by a Web 2.0 model of operation; and third, a detailed level of hardening down to the code and component level. Too much of the focus of security has been on creating and teaching security detection as the primary means of protecting the network. To transform how the technology industry applies these lessons in practice will take not just business and government participation, but the talents of educators and researchers developing the skills and capabilities of engineers in the information sciences.

This message is speaking not to the security labs in academia, but rather to the computer and information science departments. Security cannot be the domain of the security specialists when the problem must first be addressed through the implementation of secure design in software code and in the network solutions that create network services. It also speaks to the world of entrepreneurs creating the new applications that drive additional revenue for customers.

The innovations that can grow the concepts and constructs defined in the X.805 standard need to come from within the walls of academia and laboratories worldwide. This standard must become a mature practice of measuring security at the Point of Creation development, in the selection and integration, and at the Point of Service Delivery. The technology industry can start to reduce the number of vulnerabilities in its products by applying security in the product development phase and throughout the SVL. Academia and research need to start with this as the main lesson. It is far too easy today for the hackers and criminals to take advantage of system vulnerabilities.

The sophistication of the threats currently exceeds the ability to protect today's networks. The reasons are clear and have been discussed at length. Academia, with the research labs, have much to contribute to reverse this condition by creating ways to measure security and creating engineers skilled in the hardening of information technology solutions.

Where is the innovation needed? Creating technologies that solve the challenges of maintaining data controls in a data sharing environment is key to securing information in the Web 2.0 model. Another area of needed innovation is in security design at the solution level in a hybrid, multi-vendor environment to minimize the security integration at the end-user point. Maintaining end-user control of personal information stored at different points of service is yet another needed innovation to create conditions of measured trust. Additionally, security for storage in the cloud and SaaS that is based on measurable security must not be neglected. The list is long, but it must first begin with recognizing that quality designs begin with creating transparency by using the security framework.

Summary and Conclusions

When it comes to accepting the principle of transforming the implementation of security, neither logic nor fear are sufficient motivators. Inertia is the other enemy to overcome, and, given the size of the task, it will take a great deal of energy and leadership from a variety of domains to break free and take a new course.

The domains were named and the tasks delineated to make it clear what needs to be done. The implementation of security standards is what remains. This process is not going to come from the security industry, as the problem does not start there. The problem starts with the technology industry at large, because this industry has behaved as if the end-user is responsible for securing the systems they have purchased. Let's be clear: We are the technology industry. With convergence, it is all IT, voice, video and data. The security discipline needs to transform, and the change must come from the buying side of the buyer-seller relationship. Until customers demand a standardized approach using a security framework, the technology industry is expected to continue pushing security as an endpoint responsibility that can only be done with perimeter security, detection technologies and non-ending patching. That is no way to run a business or government.

The proposition is to transform using a little known, but very useful, tool called the ITU-T X.805 standard. It belongs to everyone, as it is an internationally published standard available to all product developers at large as well as the buyers of the technology. This simple fact can initiate the basis for transformation, but it will take a spark to light this fire.

Who will start this fire and begin the needed transformation to put the security responsibility back where it belonged in the first place? If there is ever a reason for why this must happen, look no further than the promise of Web 2.0, a promise that cannot achieve its full potential if trust and confidence are not engendered from the point of reference of a measurable foundation.

As important as achieving this promise is, providing a solution to the very real risk of vulnerabilities harbored in the technologies that operate in all areas of the national infrastructure is another important consideration. The financial crisis that started in 2007 and spread across the global economies teaches us the dangers of highly leveraged conditions. In this case of the financial markets, it was credit run amok diffused across global financial services companies and banks without the benefit of transparency in the transactions. Sound familiar? Now is the time to take corrective action in the technology industry!

Appendix A
Building Secure Products and Solutions

Ashok K. Gupta, Uma Chandrashekhar, Suhasini V. Sabnis, and Frank A. Bastry

Many security vulnerabilities in current information technology (IT) solutions and products are the result of a piecemeal "strap-on" security approach. The inclusion of many security add-ons, such as firewalls, antivirus software, intrusion detection systems (IDSs), and intrusion prevention systems (IPSs), may imply that the security objectives were an afterthought, not adequately defined initially, or that the required security objectives were never met by the individual system components. In fact, a "grounds-up" approach to security, where each component is individually secure, in a defined network deployment scenario helps meet the need of minimal risk exposure. Security should not be bolted on; rather, it should be the prime consideration from the beginning and throughout the entire lifecycle – from concept to deployment and ongoing operation for each product in the solution. Given the ever-increasing sophistication of attacks, developing and monitoring secure products have become increasingly difficult.

Bell Labs Technical Journal 12(3), 21–38 (2007) © 2007 Alcatel-Lucent. Published by Wiley Periodicals, Inc. Published online in Wiley InterScience (www.interscience.wiley.com). • DOI: 10.1002/bltj.20247

Despite the wide-scale awareness of common security flaws in soft-ware products, e.g., buffer overflows, resource exhaustion, and struc-tured query language (SQL) injection, the same flaws continue to exist in some of the current products. The objective of this paper is to introduce a technology-agnostic approach to integrating security into the product development lifecycle. The approach leverages the Bell Labs Security Framework, the foundation of the International Tele-communication Union, Telecommunication Standardization Sector (ITU-T) X.805 global standard. Building this framework into the product lifecycle supports the goal of realizing secure products. The security framework can be applied to any product domain to facilitate security requirements analysis and the development of usable tools such as checklists, guidelines, and security policies. The application of Bell Labs Security Framework concepts and its use in the development of secure products are illustrated using the example of a centrally managed firewall product. © 2007 Alcatel-Lucent.

Introduction

According to a recent report issued by IBM's Internet Security Systems (ISS) X-Force research and development team [14], the number of newly discovered vulnerabilities jumped 40 percent in 2006 com-pared to 2005, making 2006 a record year for security vulnerabilities, with an average of 20 new exploitable flaws discovered every day. The exponential rise of security threats has demonstrated that the "strap-on," after-the-fact security paradigm is an ineffective and costly way of addressing security. Modern complex networks and services require that security be considered and embedded in every component of the solution. Still, assuring the security of each network element indepen-dently does not necessarily create a secure network. Each product needs to be inherently secure to realize a secure solution.

Many products do not build security requirements into their plan-ning and design cycle. Security is often addressed as an afterthought, generally in reaction to publicized security incidents or newly identi-fied threats. This results in a piecemeal security approach dependent on a seemingly endless barrage of expensive to deploy security patches. A software bug discovered after product deployment can costs millions of dollars to fix, over and above direct incident-related losses.

Security as an afterthought does not provide a complete and cost-effective long-term security solution. A "grounds-up" approach to security is needed in which security is a prime consideration for the entire lifecycle – from concept to deployment and ongoing operation for each of the components used in the solution as well as in the end-to-end solution itself. Each component needs to be individually secure.

This paper presents a technology-agnostic approach to integrating security into the product development lifecycle. The approach leverages the Bell Labs Security Framework [7] that was adopted by the International Telecommunications Union (ITU) as the framework for the ITU Telecommunication Standardization Sector (ITU-T) Recommendation X.805 standard in October 2003 [5], and also accepted by the International Organization for Standardization (ISO) and the International Electrotechnical Commission (IEC) as the basis of their joint enterprise standard, ISO/IEC 18028-2 [3]. This framework should be used in conjunction with other standards and industry best practices [1, 6, 8, 10, 12, 13] for integrating security in every phase of the product development lifecycle. The Bell Labs Security Framework concepts are presented in this paper and illustrated using the example of a centrally managed firewall product.

Panel 1. Abbreviations, Acronyms, and Terms

3GPP – 3rd Generation Partnership Project
3GPP2 – 3rd Generation Partnership Project 2
BCDR – Business continuity and disaster recovery
DA – Discontinued availability
EOL – End-of-life
IDS – Intrusion detection systems
IEC – International Electrotechnical Commission
IEEE – Institute of Electrical and Electronics Engineers
IETF – Internet Engineering Task Force
IPS – Intrusion prevention systems
ISO – International Standards Organization
IT – Information technology
ITU – International Telecommunication Union
ITU-T – ITU-Telecommunication Standardization Sector
SQL – Structured query language

Product Lifecycle Overview

Every organization has its own customized version of the product development lifecycle. This section establishes one such view (and the associated terminology) for the purpose of discussion in this paper.

A typical product lifecycle consists of five major phases: (1) concept, (2) explore, (3) execute, (4) volume deploy, and (5) end-of-life (EOL), as illustrated in Figure A.1. The phases are the basic building blocks and are not always executed sequentially but allow for overlapping and concurrency. For purposes of discussion, a sequential execution is assumed.

The concept phase establishes the business need for the product and a strategy for the road map. It defines the business case for proceeding to the next stage of the lifecycle. In the concept phase, initial risk assessment and cost-benefit analysis are performed on the basis of a preliminary list of customer requirements.

The explore phase produces a detailed market, customer, and financial assessment enabling a business decision to be made, including commitment of resources.

The execute phase is the actual development phase of the product so that the volume deployment phase can begin at its conclusion. The execute phase is also referred to as the *development phase.* In this phase most of the security is created in the product; it is also when most of the vulnerabilities are created. Thus, the execute phase, which has its own lifecycle consisting of requirements, design, implementation, and test phases, is the primary focus of this paper.

The volume deploy phase is the payoff phase of the process, when the quick ramp-up to significant volume occurs. The end-of-life phase is the commencement of volume ramp-down, discontinued availability (DA), and continued support services for installed base products after DA.

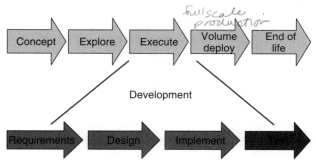

Figure A.1 Typical product lifecycle.

Integrating Security Into the Product Lifecycle

Security is a continuous, living process for ensuring that people, networks, and information have the necessary protection required by businesses for secure, reliable day-to-day operations. Security must be systematically addressed and should be integrated throughout the development lifecycle.

The product lifecycle for the execute phase covers the requirements phase, design phase, implementation phase, and test phase. Detailed requirements are established for the product to meet the demand of all stakeholders (e.g., the customer and business), as well as to meet regulatory/standards compliance and industry certifications. In the design phase, the necessary architecture is developed and the detailed design work is carried out to satisfy the established requirements. Depending on the nature of the product, the implementation phase may include a combination of fabrication, assembling, coding, and integration. In the final phase of development, testing is done to verify the compliance of the product specifications and performance with the established requirements. Developing secure products is a complex and challenging task. However, by integrating security from the start of the development lifecycle, along with the customer requirements, the challenges are better understood and more manageable in the long run. Key considerations in the various stages of the execute phase are listed in Table A.I.

Building in Security

Though there is a growing awareness of common security issues, an organization continues to face several challenges:

- Security may not be a priority in the customer purchase decision.

- The organization may lack a formal security policy and specific security requirements.

- The product development team may lack security awareness and knowledge.

- The organization may lack uniform or widely applicable security considerations, practices, tools, and techniques for the development of secure products.

Table A.1   Security Considerations and Example Checklists in Execute Phase of Product Lifecycle

Phase	Key security Considerations	Example Checklists
Requirements	• Determination of security assumptions, including product deployment scenarios. • Identification of critical assets to be protected and secured. • Identification of security requirements and interface specifications for third-party product incorporated in the design and securely interoperating with the rest of the network. • Identification of requirements for securing the communication, data storage, and configuration for the product. • Performing high-level threat analysis. • Determination of the product hardening techniques to be applied.	• Regulatory list for industry. • List of relevant best practices to be incorporated. • List of standards for compliance. • List of high-level threats.
Design	• Define and design security architectures where product will reside. • Perform detailed threat and potential vulnerability analysis for critical assets. • Principles of defense in depth; least privilege and partitioning should be followed. • Both static and dynamic analysis tools should be used.	• Status per 8 security dimensions (e.g., access control, authentication, confidentiality). • List of advanced secure protocol standards. • Completion of applicable architecture views for management, signaling, and user.
Implementation	• Ensuring a secure development environment. • Adhering to security standards and best practices for protocol implementation, hardening, and coding practices. • Use of secure tools, e.g., compilers, implementation reviews. Code reviews are the	• Configurations guidelines. • List of unused ports to be protected. • List of rules for product hardening to guide implementation choices.

	primary mechanisms for ensuring the security in the implementation phase.	
Testing	• Determine whether security mechanisms are working as designed and whether anything is missing. • Determine whether software implementation has introduced new vulnerabilities that can be exploited. • Defect review analysis is helpful in preventing further security defects in the development cycle. • Apply stress testing for vulnerabilities and penetration.	• List of adversarial test cases to be executed. • List of known vulnerabilities in subcomponents and in the product that have been tested. • Use of secure static and dynamic tools, e.g., compilers, standards compliance, implementation reviews. • Check for open ports.

- The development team may place primary focus on functionality, and security becomes secondary and often an afterthought.

- Security activities in the schedule/project plan may encounter resource constraints.

- Perceived cost and ongoing maintenance of security may not be viewed as affordable.

Risks that are not identified early in the requirements analysis phases lead to a host of vulnerabilities that are only exposed later during the operational life of the product. A systematic approach, as enabled by the Bell Labs Security Framework, is effective in integrating security through all phases of a product lifecycle.

The Bell Labs Security Framework focuses on three essential questions:

- What kind of protection is needed against what threats and vulnerabilities?

- What are the distinct types of network equipment and facility groupings that need to be protected?

- What are the distinct types of network activities that need to be protected?

The answers to these questions will help with analyzing and validating security needs in a consistent, complete, and systematic manner and facilitate the adoption of common security practices, tools (e.g., checklists), and techniques for secure product development.

Bell Labs Security Framework Overview

Bell Labs' Network Security Framework was originally developed to help network operators understand what is needed to design, implement, and maintain a secure network. This framework is now the foundation of the international network security standards known as ISO/IEC 18028-2:2005 [3] and ITU-T X.805 [5].

The framework is flexible so that it can be adapted to the ever-changing world of cyber security and regulations. Network equipment manufacturers, corporate information technology (IT) departments, telecommunications service providers, and business users can benefit from its use.

The framework, depicted in Figure A.2, can be used to divide complex end-to-end network security logically into manageable architectural components. This separation allows for a systematic

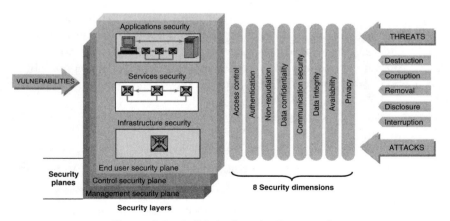

Figure A.2 Bell Labs Security Framework.

approach to end-to-end security analysis to plan new security solutions as well as assess the security of the existing networks.

The framework utilizes the ITU-T X.800 series threat definitions [4], specifically

- Destruction of information and/or other resources

- Modification or corruption of information

- Removal, theft, or loss of information and/or other resources

- Disclosure of information

- Interruption of services

Security layers

The framework defines three security layers, which describe a hierarchy of network equipment and facility groupings. These can be viewed as physical and logical components and separated into (1) the infrastructure security layer, (2) the services security layer, and (3) the applications security layer.

- *The infrastructure layer* includes the basic building blocks used to create the network, services, and applications.

- *The services layer* focuses on services that end users receive from networks.

- *The applications layer* consists of network-based applications accessed by end users.

Security planes

The three security planes defined by the Framework correspond to the types of activities performed over the network – management, control, and end-user activity.

Security dimensions

The eight security dimensions or mechanisms are a set of security measures to assist in countering attacks at each layer and plane:

- *Access control* protects against unauthorized use of resources.
- *Authentication* confirms the identities of each entity using the resource.
- *Non-repudiation* proves the origin of the data or identifies the cause of an event or action.
- *Data confidentiality or data security* ensures that data are not disclosed to unauthorized entities.
- *Communication security* allows information to flow only between authorized end points.
- *Data integrity* ensures the accuracy of data so they cannot be modified, deleted, created, or replicated without authorization and provides an indication of unauthorized attempts to change data.
- *Availability* ensures that there is no denial of authorized access to network elements, stored information, information flows, services, and applications.
- *Privacy* provides for the protection of information that could be derived from the observation of network activities. (Note that privacy can be viewed as a goal realized by combining other security dimensions rather than a separate dimension. However, the model is flexible in that users can choose which dimensions will meet their security needs and use them as appropriate.)

Modular methodology

Figure A.3 depicts a combination of layer/plane perspectives. This provides a rigorous consideration of different sets of security measures.

The Proposed Approach

Recently, a number of security best practices that primarily focus on secure coding principles for products have emerged [1, 6, 8, 9, 12, 13]. The Bell Labs Security Framework can be applied to ensure that the critical assets, potential threats, and vulnerabilities in the product are identified and addressed in a cost-effective and prioritized manner.

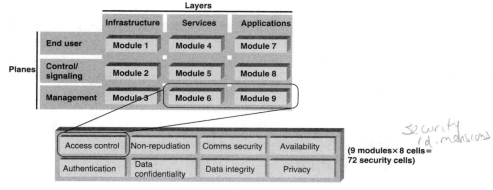

Figure A.3 Modular form of the Bell Labs Security Framework.

Figure A.4 illustrates the improvement to secure product development process. Ensuring that security objectives and commitments are integrated into product realization processes is a key factor in integrating security in the overall development lifecycle.

It is essential that the product be deployed in a secure manner; otherwise many of the security controls integrated in the product may be easily circumvented. Critical attributes required for the secure deployment of the product such as training, documentation,

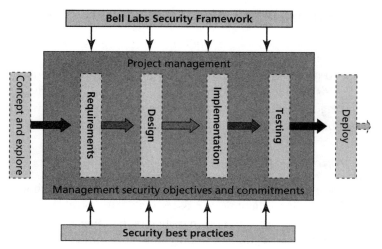

Figure A.4 Approach to develop secure products.

operating environment, and usage consideration should be included in the development process. The Bell Labs Security Framework can be extended to help provide a security checklist for integrating the product in a multivendor environment, especially for the concept and deploy phases. This paper focuses only on the execute phase.

Integrating Security in Requirements and Design Phase

The requirements phase should define the security needs of the developed product. Many products fail to meet the required security expectations simply because adequate security requirements are not defined early on. In this phase, the security requirements are defined to meet the organization's business security objectives and the customer needs. Detailed security considerations for general features as well as security feature requirements are the main outputs of the requirements phase.

The recommended process for definition, design, architecture, and security requirements is depicted in Figure A.5. The diagram shows how the critical input needed for the requirements and design phases can be obtained using the Bell Labs Security Framework.

Security specifications

One of the common oversights in defining security specifications is to consider only the user of the product when in fact activities related to end user, management, and control are equally important.

As an illustration, the security specifications derived using the suggested process for a typical centrally managed firewall product is tabulated in Table A.2.

Asset identification

The next step in developing detailed security requirements for the product is to identity key assets within the product from a security perspective. These assets may include hardware, software, interfaces (internal and external), information stored/processed, and protocols used. Not accounting for an asset at an stage may severely impact the

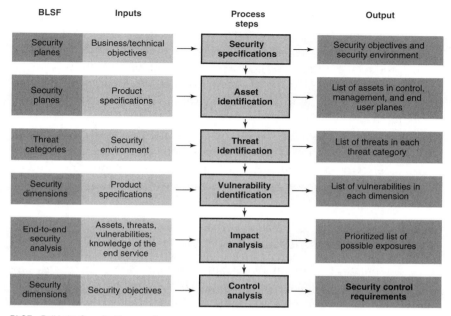

BLSF	Inputs	Process steps	Output
Security planes	Business/technical objectives	Security specifications	Security objectives and security environment
Security planes	Product specifications	Asset identification	List of assets in control, management, and end user planes
Threat categories	Security environment	Threat identification	List of threats in each threat category
Security dimensions	Product specifications	Vulnerability identification	List of vulnerabilities in each dimension
End-to-end security analysis	Assets, threats, vulnerabilities; knowledge of the end service	Impact analysis	Prioritized list of possible exposures
Security dimensions	Security objectives	Control analysis	**Security control requirements**

BLSF—Bell Labs Security Framework

Figure A.5 Security definition, requirements, design, and architecture analysis overview.

Table A.2 Security Specifications for a Firewall Product Using Bell Labs Security Framework

	End User Plane	Control Plane	Management Plane
Security objectives	Protect the resources behind firewall from all known and possible unknown attacks.	Dynamically update the rules and close sessions on the basis of externally detected security events.	The management interface and the traffic should be protected including its isolation from the end users.
Security environment	Direct facing to Internet with no external protection.	Dynamic rule update information is exchanged with the security manager over Internet.	In-band centralized management over Internet.

security of the final product because vulnerability in the overlooked asset might later be exploited by an attacker.

For example, a simple reset switch on the front panel of a firewall product is a critical asset from a security standpoint. On the basis of the environment specifications, it may be necessary to provide adequate (physical) controls to protect it from various deliberate and accidental threats.

Table A.3 lists some illustrative infrastructure assets for a typical firewall in each of the three planes. Service and application layer assets would be similarly identified in each plane. The firewall example focuses on the infrastructure view for discussion purposes in the paper.

Threats identification

"A threat is the potential for a particular threat-source to successfully exercise a particular vulnerability" [7]. Depending on the environment, there could be a large number of threats, and in the absence of a thorough threat model, it could be difficult to account for all relevant threats. Various models based on the source, intent, or type of threats have emerged. The Bell Labs Security Framework uses the ITU-T X.800 threat model, which is based on destruction, corruption, removal, disclosure, and interruption.

The next step is to prepare a list of threats for each of the identified assets on the basis of the five threat categories. A few illustrative threats for assets identified in the firewall examples are shown in Table A.4.

Table A.3 Sample Identified Assets in a Typical Firewall

	End User Plane	**Control Plane**	**Management Plane**
Identified assets	• Network interfaces	• Reset switch	• Management GUI
	• User authentication	• Session table	• Policies
	• Deep screened protocols	• VLANs	• Logs
		• Routing protocol	• Alarms
	• User authentication	• Rules update traffic	• Configuration
	• Traffic passing through it	• State information	• Administrative accounts

GUI – Graphical user interface
VLAN – Virtual local area network

Table A.4 Sample Threats to Few Example Assets

Threat Category/ Asset →	Ethernet Interfaces (end user)	Session Table (Control)	Logs (Management)
Destruction	Cable removal, electrical surge, hardware failure.	Buffer overrun or software bugs can overwrite the table.	Unauthorized deletion of log files, improper log rotation.
Corruption	ARP poisoning.	Ill-formatted IP address or headers can corrupt the table.	Man-in-middle attack.
Removal	MAC address spoofing.	Not applicable.	DOS attack on log server.
Disclosure	Sniffing, rogue access point.	The session table can be dumped using the debugging mode.	Use of syslog, public read access for log files, log unprotected server.
Interruption	Faulty cable, traffic injection, disabling the interface.	SYN flood attack may exhaust the table.	Disk full, network failure, log file access issues.

ARP – Address Resolution Protocol
DOS – Denial of service
IP – Internet Protocol
MAC – Medium access control

Vulnerabilities identification

A vulnerability is a weakness that can be exploited by a threat. Vulnerabilities are intrinsic to any product or solution. If the vulnerability does not exist, then the threat cannot have any negative impact on the asset. Therefore, it is critical to identify vulnerabilities for each of the assets to design a secure product. Now, the obvious question is, How can one ensure that all vulnerabilities have been identified? Though security dimensions as specified in the Bell Labs Security Framework are mechanisms used to protect assets, they can effectively aid in the vulnerability identification process at any given phase of the lifecycle.

As an illustration, Table A.5 summarizes a few identified vulnerabilities for the "sessions table" maintained in the firewall using this mechanism. The sessions table is an internal data structure in the firewall software that stores information about all active sessions (flows) including the action to be taken. Receipt of a packet triggers a scan of the sessions table to determine whether it belongs to one of the active

Table A.5 Identified Vulnerabilities for the Sessions Table

Dimension	Vulnerabilities
Access control	Unau2007thorized modifications to the "sessions table" can be made if a process or person gains access to the firewall's address space where the session table is stored.
Authentication	"Any" process can modify the session table without any authentication.
Non-repudiation	There is no definite record/proof of who made the changes to the sessions table.
Data confidentiality	The contents of the session table can be seen by an unauthorized entity.
Communication security	None, as the sessions table is local to the firewall.
Data integrity	Modification to sessions table, which is difficult to detect.
Availability	Attacks like SYN flooding can quickly fill the sessions table, leaving no space for new sessions.
Privacy	Critical information about the sessions tables can be deduced by examining the sessions log.

sessions. If it belongs, then the corresponding action is taken without referring to the rule set (policy); otherwise, a new session is created.

Impact analysis

The next step is to determine possible exposures (i.e., a threat able to exploit the vulnerability) and their impact with respect to the security objectives. Another important consideration is the likelihood of exposure. The impact is assessed relative to an organization's tolerance for risk. Conventional risk analysis techniques [11] can be used to calculate net impact.

An impact analysis process needs to consider the security environment in which the product is expected to operate. An exposure may not be critical to the standalone product, but after integration into a service, it may have serious implications for service delivery.

Continuing with the example of the sessions table from the previous sections, a prioritized list of exposures is presented in Table A.6. It is clearly evident (high impact, high probability) that protecting the sessions table from a SYN flood attack [2] is the highest priority exposure that needs to be addressed.

Table A.6 Illustrative Impact Analysis for the Sessions Table

Dimension	Vulnerabilities	Impact	Probability
Access control	Unauthorized modifications to the sessions table can be made if a process or person gains access to the firewall's address space where the session table is stored.	High	Low – if there is no mechanism to modify the table from the management user interface. The session table's address space is protected by the kernel's memory protection techniques.
Authentication	"Any" process can modify the session table without any authentication.	High	Low – as above
Non-repudiation	There is no definite record/proof of who made the changes to the sessions table.	Medium – knowing who did it does not help much.	Low
Data confidentiality	The contents of the session table can be seen by an unauthorized entity.	Medium	Low
Communication security	None, as the sessions table is local to the firewall.	Low	Low
Data integrity	Modifications to sessions table are difficult to detect.	High	Low
Availability	Attacks like SYN flooding can quickly fill the sessions table, leaving no space for new sessions.	High	High – considering so many hackers out there.
Privacy	Critical information about the sessions tables can be deduced by examining the sessions log.	Low	Medium – normally logs are accessible outside the firewall.

Control analysis

After identifying and prioritizing the threats, it is necessary to select appropriate security controls for mitigation. The eight security dimensions represent classes of actions that can be taken, or technologies that can be deployed to counter the threats and potential attacks present at each security layer and plane.

In the sessions table example, the recommended controls for various exposures are listed in Table A.7.

Table A.7 Illustrative Security Controls for Various Exposures of the Sessions Table

Dimension	Vulnerabilities	Recommended controls
Access control	Unauthorized modifications to the sessions table can be made if a process or person gains access to the firewall's address space where the session table is stored.	• Do not provide the option to access/modify the session table from the management interface. • Take care of buffer overruns as they might provide access to the sessions table. • Use a secure/hardened operating system.
Authentication	"Any" process can modify the session table without any authentication.	• Implement all modifications to the sessions table using a function call and restrict the access to this function to only select processes.
Non-repudiation	There is no definite record/proof of who made the changes to the sessions table.	• Make a provision of logging all changes to the sessions table.
Data confidentiality	The contents of the sessions table can be seen by an unauthorized entity.	• Not practical to encrypt the table. Rely on access control.
Communication security	None, as the sessions table is local to the firewall.	• None required.
Data integrity	Modifications to sessions table are difficult to detect.	• Compute and verify the hash/checksum every time table is modified – not practical and not required.

| Availability | Attacks like SYN flooding can quickly fill the sessions table, leaving no space for new sessions. | • Remove incomplete sessions on the basis of timeout.
• Use some kind of intelligent purge mechanism triggered by the usage threshold. |
| Privacy | Critical information about the sessions table can be deduced by examining the sessions log. | • Protect sessions logs. |

Integrating Security in the Implementation Phase

The architecture and design phase provides the foundation for the security considerations in the implementation phase. Controls introduced during the design phase are significantly cheaper to implement and maintain than those included during implementation. Security in the implementation phase is merely an instantiation of the recommendations proposed in the design and architecture phase. One of the key areas in the implementation phase is engineering the software such that security is built in.

The value of Bell Labs Security Framework is to provide a systematic approach to ensuring that all security mechanisms are addressed and evaluated in a given lifecycle phase. The eight security dimensions provide a good starting point for enumerating security mechanisms that must be built in. Even though earlier phases of the product lifecycle address security at the architecture and feature levels, the implementation phase requires knowledge of the security goals for the product and an application of the security framework at the detailed implementation level. Some examples of consideration in the software design and implementation phase are listed in the following:

- Use of standard protocols and components for authentication.

- Authorization based on privilege management and compartmentalization.

- Access control by ensuring there are no back doors into the software, having a secure default configuration, and validating user input. Keeping secrets in implementation is extremely difficult and poses a security risk. So security by obscurity should be prevented in the design and implementation phases.

- Communications security considerations such as end-to-end session encryption and secure session management.

- Data confidentiality using encryption and segmentation; ensuring that the operating system utilizes files systems with access controls.

- Non-repudiation or accountability can be implemented to some extent by code signing and code authorization. Logging should be part of the software design for accountability in the runtime environment (and could also be a legal requirement).

- Data integrity for stored software and data should be implemented using encryption algorithms and message integrity code mechanisms. Software design consideration should allow for the integrity of log files to be checked.

- Availability using static code analysis tools for standards compliance and mitigating against common vulnerabilities like buffer overflows. Also, in code design, one must ensure that the code fails securely. In other words, if the system fails in any way, the security of the system should be maintained.

- Privacy by ensuring that control/signaling message headers are encrypted end to end such that the network activity cannot be observed for extracting information about the origin/destination of the transmission.

The implementation phase also requires that the development environment support secure software creation. Table A.8 illustrates an example approach for using the Bell Labs Security Framework for evaluating security controls for three secure development environment processes – change control, software installation/upgrade, and the end-of-life process. The emphasis here is to have a systematic approach to identify all relevant aspects, and the Bell Labs Security Framework supports such a checklist paradigm.

The quality and professionalism in the software development process have huge implications for the security of products/systems that are released and implemented. Security requirements should be assessed systematically for creating a robust security development environment.

Table A.8 Evaluating Security Controls for Three Secure Development Environment Processes

	Activities		
	Change Control	**Software Installation/ Upgrade**	**End-of-Life Consideration**
Access control	Developer access to software is strictly controlled – with special consideration for vendor/contractor access – using uniquely identifiable user IDs.	Access and authorization privileges for software upgrades.	
Authentication	Use of strong authentication for sensitive software access.	Mechanism for software authenticity.	
Non-repudiation	Software access must be logged and traceability of change must be maintained.	Ensuring that actions of administrators installing the software are logged.	
Data confidentiality	Dedicated or isolated computing environments for sensitive and critical projects.	Use of encryption for storage and transfer.	Retention requirements and media sanitization.
Communications security		Secure software distribution, e.g., web download or CDs.	
Data integrity		Integrity of software and patches.	
Availability		Software backup storage and rollbacks.	Migration plans and impact to other systems.
Data privacy		Ensure software is not installed in debug mode.	Provisions for legal requirements.

CD – Compact disk
ID – Identifiers

Integrating Security in Testing Phase

Security testing should be an integral part of any product and service security strategy. It must be incorporated in processes afforded proper planning and support to ensure customers receive the quality that is expected. Testing of any features or capabilities must focus on the proper assets and avenues of attacks.

Typically, functional testing involves verification of the documented implementation requirements. However, for security it is important to include strategic testing specific to configuration/protocol vulnerabilities, security policy compliance, and secure code testing. This section focuses on the test strategy required to supplement a typical functional test plan.

The test plans can be written by using the Bell Labs Security Framework layers – infrastructure, services, and applications, as applicable. For each layer asset, the testing can be further narrowed by management, control, or end user plane. Thus, if a new application is introduced, and assuming that the infrastructure/services are the same, the new test plan can focus on the application layer while running regression tests on the infrastructure and services layers.

It should be noted that the value of the framework is to assist in a systematic, modular development of test scenarios instead of using an ad hoc process. Also, depending on the resource availability, it is possible to combine infrastructure and services perspective into one group (such as router port and service). The important goal is to ensure that router port and service-related management are considered when the test plan details are developed.

In the firewall example, for the infrastructure layer asset, the checklist detailed in Table A.9 can be developed for each of the Bell Labs Security Framework dimensions.

Although Table IX lists only some sample test activities, the framework can be used by test experts to identify the scope of the test plan and relevant tools to support the verification process. If there are specific legal/policy requirements, then they would be addressed as well. Configuration and protocol vulnerabilities will also be included per the relevant layer/plane perspective. Even if the Bell Labs Security Framework is not used to drive test plan development, it provides a reference framework to verify that all security aspects are systematically addressed.

Table A.9 Checklist for each of the Bell Labs Security Framework Dimensions

Dimension	Testing Activity
Access control	Verify that the management user interface for the firewall has adequate access control mechanism in place.
	Verify that it is not possible to gain access to the operating system on which the firewall is built.
Authentication	Verify that none of the administrative logins or the operating system account has an easy-to-crack password.
	Verify that each firewall performs mutual authentication to the management system.
Non-repudiation	Verify that all activities of all firewall administrators are logged.
	Verify that all firewalls and the management system use certificates for authentication.
Data confidentiality	Verify that all traffic between the firewall and the management system is encrypted.
Communications security	Verify that it is not possible for a rogue management system to divert all management traffic to itself.
Data integrity	Verify that all firewall policies have appropriate integrity protection mechanisms (MD5 hash) to ensure that no unauthorized modification has been made.
Availability	Verify that the firewall can sustain the SYN flood DoS attack.
	Verify that the firewall's management interface is responding even while it is being attacked.
Data privacy	Verify that the firewall has adequate protection for port scanning that could be used to deduce the firewall policies.

Integrating Security in the Product Management

Product management processes and support from senior management play a crucial role in ensuring that the organization develops secure products. The organization must incorporate security guidance into its general products and project management processes. Senior management must support and endorse security initiatives and continuously stress the importance of security to the development teams. Project management processes need to consider communication requirements and linkage among development lifecycle phases as these areas relate to the security of the developed product. Key areas involving security that project management staff needs to be concerned with during the lifecycle are discussed in the following sections.

Policy for secure product development

Security policy is critical to the product lifecycle as it echoes senior management's view of security and its importance to product lifecycle. The security policy translates management's expectations into business, organizational, process, and high-level technical security goals. The security policy drives the security lifecycle and the implementation of security across the product/solution lifecycle.

The policy should summarize management's expectations of security for products and solutions. The security policy should govern:

1. How products should operate, i.e., product functionality in the realm of security, covering basic and potential revenue-generating features.

2. How products are developed and supported, i.e., staff expertise expectations, development, and test expectations.

3. How security is organized to support the new and existing products and associated process needs, i.e., incident response, training needs.

4. How products will comply with customer operational requirements and applicable regulatory requirements, as well as procedures for communicating with customers.

When defining a security policy for product development organization, the Bell Labs Security Framework can facilitate identifying management goals and disposition for key security areas (security dimensions) for critical assets such as access control, authentication, non-repudiation, availability, data confidentiality, and how technical risks should be assessed, so that the policy can appropriately reflect these goals. The high-level technical aspects of a security policy can be based on the Bell Labs Security Framework with specific focus on the needs of the particular product unit's goals and processes.

Management oversight

During the entire product/solution lifecycle, management should actively support security through clear direction, demonstrated commitment, dedicated resources, explicit assignment of team members, approval of roles and responsibilities, and acknowledgment of security responsibilities overall. The project manager is responsible for making sure management commitment is in place and understood throughout the organization.

Upper management can impart a strong statement regarding commitment by including the Bell Labs Security Framework in corporate security policy and organization objectives, and by providing the necessary resources to apply the Bell Labs Security Framework during the product lifecycle.

Risk assessment and management

Risk assessment and management should be a thread through the entire product/solution lifecycle. The Bell Labs Security Framework threat analysis can be used during the risk assessment phase to provide a thorough assessment of threat exposures/scenarios, levels of risks, and mitigations for the assets identified in the analysis. The Bell Labs Security Framework provides a systematic implementation of the various controls to meet risk treatment objectives. All activities and deliverables must be tracked through project management.

Measurement and feedback

During the product lifecycle, measurement techniques of controls/functional requirements developed during the risk assessment and management phase need to be agreed on and implemented. Measuring the effectiveness of the controls allows managers (1) to determine how effective the controls are and (2) to converge on necessary improvements. The Bell Labs Security Framework can be used to provide a comprehensive justification of the defined measures and would be consistent with the threat and vulnerability analysis done during risk assessment.

Resources and training

For an effective product/solution lifecycle, it is essential that resources are provided and security-related roles are defined. In addition, the entire organization should be aware of the assigned team and their security responsibilities. The Bell Labs Security Framework provides a vehicle for an organization to understand what is relevant in security from an accountability perspective. For example, is there a person responsible and/or the subject matter expert assigned for technical privacy-related challenges?

Security awareness, education, and training activities should be suitable and applicable to each person's defined role, responsibilities, and skills. In addition, training must be provided on the Bell Labs Security Framework for those involved with the framework during the product lifecycle. As part of overall project management, training activities must be scheduled, tracked, and recorded.

Project planning and tracking

During the entire lifecycle of a product, all deliverables and sequencing of deliverables must be recorded and tracked by the program manager. As stated previously, project management should reflect the necessary communications and linkages among lifecycle activities and multiple development and requirements teams, as well as the eventual implementation of the product.

Relationship to other standards

The Bell Labs Security Framework should be used in conjunction with other industry standards (e.g., ISO/IEC 27001, ISO/IEC 17799, ITU, Internet Engineering Task Force [IETF], Institute of Electrical and Electronics Engineers [IEEE], 3rd Generation Partnership Project [3GPP*], and 3rd Generation Partnership Project 2 [3GPP2]) to support security from both an information and a network perspective. For example, business continuity and disaster recovery (BCDR) plans and the related security aspects are essential to ensure on-time delivery of the product. To create this BCDR plan, all critical assets need to be known. For IT- and network-related activities, the Bell Labs Security Framework will identify these critical assets and define the associated risks.

Conclusion

The Bell Labs Security Framework, the foundation for the ITU-T X.805 and ISO 18028-2 standards, was developed to help network operators, government agencies, enterprises, and product developers understand in a systematic way the appropriate level of security to be incorporated in their products or solution from concept to requirements, design, architecture, implementation, testing, deployment, and ongoing operations.

Bell Labs Security Framework concepts can be effectively applied to the product/solution/service development lifecycle to:

- Perform security requirements analysis,

- Identify and prioritize the vulnerabilities that need to be addressed,

- Identify security controls required,

- Develop customized tools such as checklists for secure development by applying a common security framework to a specific product and its deployment environment,

- Reduce the additional vulnerabilities introduced in the implementation phase,

- Streamline the test process to ensure that all aspects of security are tested, and

- Help design various security policies, checklists, and other tools used during the development lifecycle.

Though the deployment and end-of-life phases have not been discussed in this paper, it is important to follow secure practices for tasks such as secure configuration, patch management, secure disposal, and secret removal during these phases; otherwise security controls implemented in the development phase may be compromised, leaving the overall solution vulnerable.

ISO/IEC 18028-2 and ITU-T X.805 are important to security because they help uncover vulnerabilities in existing products, networks, and solutions, and they offer a framework that can be used as a basis for developing a common methodology for defining robust security deployment programs for converged, multivendor next-generation networks.

Acknowledgments

The authors would like to thank Rao Vasireddy of the Bell Labs Security Technology and Application Research group and Bob Thornberry of the Alcatel-Lucent Chief Technology Officer (CTO) organization for reviewing the paper and providing valuable feedback.

*Trademarks

3GPP is a trademark of the European Telecommunications Standards Institute.
  CWSP is a service mark of Planet3 Wireless, Inc.

References

[1] E. Barker, W. Barker, W. Burr, W. Polk, and M. Smid, "Recommendation for Key Management – Part 1: General," National Institute of Standards and Technology, Computer Security Division, NIST SP800–57, Mar. 2007, <http://csrc.nist.gov/publications/nistpubs/>.

[2] CERT, "TCP SYN Flooding and IP Spoofing Attacks," Advisory CA-1996–21, Nov. 29, 2000, <http://www.cert.org/advisories/CA-1996-21.html>.

[3] International Organization for Standardization and International Electrotechnical Commission, "Information Technology – Security Techniques – IT Network Security – Part 2: Network Security Architecture," ISO/IEC 18028–2, Feb. 2006, <http://www.iso.org>.

[4] International Telecommunication Union, Telecommunication Standardization Sector, "Security Architecture for Open Systems Interconnection (OSI) for CCITT Applications," ITU-T Rec. X.800, 1991, <http://www.itu.int>.

[5] International Telecommunication Union, Telecommunication Standardization Sector, "Security Architecture for Systems Providing End-to-End Communications," ITU-T Rec. X.805, Oct. 2003, <http://www.itu.int>.

[6] International Telecommunication Union, Telecommunication Standardization Sector, "Security for the Management Plane: Security Mechanism," ITU-T Rec. M.3016.3, Apr. 2005, <http://www.itu.int>.

[7] A. R. McGee, S. R. Vasireddy, C. Xie, D. D. Picklesimer, U. Chandrashekhar, and S. H. Richman,"A Framework for Ensuring Network Security, "Bell Labs Tech. J., 8: 4 (2004),–.

[8] Network Reliability and Interoperability Council, NRIC Best Practices, <http://www.nric.org>.

[9] M. Souppaya, K. Kent, and P. M. Johnson, "Guidance for Securing Microsoft Windows XP Systems for IT Professionals: A NIST Security Configuration Checklist," National Institute of Standards and Technology, Computer Security Division, NIST SP 800-68, Oct. 2005, <http://csrc.nist.gov/publications/nistpubs/>.

[10] M. Souppaya, J. P. Wack, and K. Kent, "Security Configuration Checklists Program for IT Products – Guidance for Checklists Users and Developers," National Institute of Standards and Technology, Computer Security Division, NIST SP800–70, May 2005, <http://csrc.nist.gov/publications/nistpubs/>.

[11] G. Stoneburner, A. Goguen, and A. Feringa, "Risk Management Guide for Information Technology Systems," National Institute of Standards and Technology, Computer Security Division, NIST SP 800-30, July 2002, <http://csrc.nist.gov/publications/nistpubs/>.

[12] J. Wack, K. Cutler, and J. Pole, "Guidelines on Firewalls and Firewall Policy," National Institute of Standards and Technology, Computer Security Division, NIST SP800–41, Jan. 2002, <http://csrc. nist.gov/publications/nistpubs/>.

[13] J. Wack, M. Tracy, and M. Souppaya, "Guideline on Network Security Testing," National Institute of Standards and Technology, Computer Security Division, NIST SP800–42, Oct. 2003, <http://csrc.nist.gov/publications/nistpubs/>.

[14] A. Woodie,"IBM X-Force Says for-Profit Cyber Attacks to Increase in 2007," Linux Beacon,4: 6 (Feb. 13, 2007), <http://www.itjungle.com/tlb/tlb021307-story 10.html>.

O Security stds and Best practices

ASHOK K. GUPTA *is a distinguished member of technical staff in the Security Standards & Application Research Department at Bell Labs in Murray Hill, New Jersey. He has over 20 years of diverse experience in the fields of security, enterprise IT infrastructure, wireless networking, content delivery, and management-information system applications. His current areas of interest include end point policy enforcement and security of mobile devices and wireless networks. He holds the following certifications: Certified Information Systems Security Professional (CISSP), Global Information Assurance Certification (GIAC, Security Essentials Certification (GSEC), Certified Wireless Security Professional (CWSP*), and Project Management Professional (PMP).*

UMA CHANDRASHEKHAR *leads the Security Technology Application Research Team in the Security Solutions organization at Bell Labs in Murray Hill, New Jersey. Ms. Chandrashekhar's experience covers the areas of security program lifecycle from concept to systems engineering, secure data communications, operations planning, network management, and deployment. Her experience also includes leading the Interoperability Industry Test Plan (IITP) phases to support the reliability of the Signaling System 7 (SS7) network, which included major industry players as part of the National Reliability Interoperability*

Council (NRIC) recommendations on the reliability of the nation's infrastructure. She led her team to the development of the Bell Labs Security Model that is now the basis of the global ITU-T X.805 standard. She has a master's degree in electrical engineering and is certified as a project manager (PMP), as well as a certified security professional (CISSP). Prior to joining Bell Labs, her work experience included postings with network operators, vendors, and research organizations. Ms. Chandrashekhar served as the guest editor for the special issue on Network Security (v8-4) of the Bell Labs Technical Journal. She is currently the coeditor of ISO/IEC 27003.

 SUHASINI V. SABNIS is a distinguished member of technical staff in the Security Technology and Applications Research group at Bell Labs in Murray Hill, New Jersey. She has over 19 years of experience in the area of telecommunications network systems engineering/operations, services development, services management, next-generation network security, security standards, audits, and compliance. Her current research interests include technical security realization and verification in next-generation networks. Ms. Sabnis received a B.S. degree in mathematics from the Indian Institute of Technology in Mumbai and M.S. degrees in statistics/operations research and computer science from Penn State University and Virginia Tech, respectively.

 FRANK A. BASTRY is a member of technical staff in the Security Solutions Organization at Bell Labs in Murray Hill, New Jersey. He has over 28 years of experience and in-depth expertise in information security management, security architecture analysis, systems engineering, business continuity planning, and wireline and wireless network planning and has led and managed large product systems engineering configurator teams. His research interests include network security architectures and critical infrastructure analysis. Mr. Bastry received a B.S. degree in computer sciences from Monmouth University in West Long Branch, New Jersey, and an M.S. degree in management of technology from the Stevens Institute of Technology in Hoboken, New Jersey.

Appendix B

Using the Bell Labs Security Framework to Enhance the ISO 17799/27001 Information Security Management System

Andrew R. McGee, Frank A. Bastry, Uma Chandrashekhar, S. Rao Vasireddy and Lori A. Flynn

The global information technology (IT) industry recognizes the need for standards to improve the quality and consistency of security for IT products and services. As such, the International Organization for Standardization/International Electrotechnical Commission (ISO/IEC) 27000 series is focusing on the requirements, security controls, and implementation guidance for an organization's information security management system (ISMS). This guidance establishes general principles that can be used in various industries and government; however, standardized techniques are also needed to identify, implement, and operate security controls as part of the ISMS life cycle. The Bell Labs Security Framework identifies both the minimal and differentiating security controls by decomposing an IT product or service into a layered

Bell Labs Technical Journal 12(3), 39–54(2007) © 2007 Alcatel-Lucent. Published by Wiley Periodicals, Inc. Published online in Wiley InterScience (www.interscience. wiley.com). • DOI: 10.1002/bltj.20248 *hierarchy of equipment and facilities groupings and examining the types of activities that occur at each layer in a standardized manner. Furthermore, the Bell Labs Security Framework security dimensions provide the necessary mechanisms to implement and operate the selected controls. The Bell Labs Security Framework enhances the ISO/IEC 27000 series by providing a comprehensive end-to-end approach to implementing IT security. © 2007 Alcatel-Lucent.*

Introduction

The global information technology (IT) industry recognizes the need for standards to improve the quality and consistency of security for IT products and services. As such, the International Organization for Standardization/International Electrotechnical Commission (ISO/IEC) 27000 series is focusing on the requirements, security controls, and implementation guidance for an organization's information security management system (ISMS). This guidance establishes general principles. In addition, standardized techniques are needed to identify, implement, and operate security controls as part of the ISMS life cycle.

The Bell Labs Security Framework [10] can be used to complement ISO/IEC 27001 [4] by providing specific guidance for the establishment, implementation, and operation of an ISMS. This paper describes a standardized, systematic, methodical approach utilizing the Bell Labs Security Framework in enterprise and government networks to: (1) identify risks, (2) select and set technical control objectives, (3) determine controls to mitigate risks, (4) design controls to meet control objectives and/or risk tolerance levels, and (5) implement procedures to enable prompt detection of security events and response to security incidents. A case study is also provided to demonstrate how the Bell Labs Security Framework can be used in conjunction with ISO/IEC 27001 to establish, implement, and operate an ISMS that provides a comprehensive, end-to-end approach to IT security.

Augmenting ISO/IEC 27001 with the Bell Labs Security Framework

ISO/IEC 27001 provides a model for establishing, implementing, operating, monitoring, reviewing, maintaining, and improving an information security management system within the context of an organization's overall business goals and the risks that it faces.

The Bell Labs Security Framework partitions a telecommunications or IT network into a three-layered hierarchy of equipment and facilities groupings: (1) the infrastructure security layer, (2) the services security layer, and (3) the applications security layer. These security layers build on one another to provide network-based solutions. As such, they are a series of enablers for secure network solutions: the infrastructure security layer enables the services security layer, and the services security layer enables the applications security layer. The Bell Labs Security Framework addresses the fact that all layers have different security vulnerabilities and offers the flexibility of countering potential threats in a manner most suited for the particular security layer. The Bell Labs Security Framework security layers represent a different category than the Open System Interconnection (OSI) reference model [2] layers; all three security layers can be applied to each layer of the OSI reference model. **Panel 2** provides a detailed description of the Bell Labs Security Framework security layers.

Panel 1. Abbreviations, Acronyms, and Terms

3GPP – 3rd Generation Partnership Project

3GPP2 – 3rd Generation Partnership Project 2

ACL – Access control list

AH – Authentication header

DISA – Defense Information Systems Agency

ESP – Encapsulated Security Protocol

ETSI – European Telecommunications Standards Institute

IEC – International Electrotechnical Commission

IETF – Internet Engineering Task Force

IP – Internet Protocol

IPsec – IP security

ISMS – Information Security Management System

ISO – International Organization for Standardization

IT – Information technology

ITU-T – International Telecommunication Union, Telecommunication Standardization Sector

NIST – National Institute of Standards and Technology

NRIC – Network Reliability and Interoperability Council

NSA – National Security Agency

OSI – Open System Interconnection

VPN – Virtual private network

Panel 2. Bell Labs Security Framework Security Layers

The Bell Labs Security Framework partitions a telecommunications or IT network into a three-layered hierarchy of equipment and facilities groupings: (1) the infrastructure security layer, (2) the services security layer, and (3) the applications security layer. These security layers build on one another to provide network-based solutions.

The *infrastructure security layer* consists of individual network elements and hardware platforms, including the hardware and software composing them, as well as network transmission facilities. The infrastructure security layer represents the fundamental building blocks of networks, and their services or applications. Examples of components that belong to the infrastructure security layer are individual routers, switches, and servers as well as the communications links among them.

The *services security layer* consists of services that customers receive from service providers or network operators. These services range from basic transport and basic IP connectivity (e.g., Internet access); IP service enablers such as authentication, authorization, and accounting services; dynamic host configuration and domain name services; to value-added services such as Voice over IP, quality of service, virtual private networks, location services, and 800 services.

The *applications security layer* focuses on network-based applications accessed by IT network end users or customers of the service provider or network operator. These applications are enabled by network services and are characterized by human-to-machine interaction. Examples of these types of applications include basic applications such as file transport (e.g., File Transport Protocol) and Web browsing applications; fundamental applications such as directory assistance (e.g., 411 service), network-based voice messaging, and email; as well as high-end applications such as customer relationship management, human resource systems, electronic/mobile commerce, network-based training, and video collaboration.

In addition, the Bell Labs Security Framework defines the three types of activities that can occur at every layer as security planes. The three security planes present at every layer are the management security plane, control/signaling security plane, and end user security plane.

The eight Bell Labs Security Framework security dimensions are sets of security measures that address a particular aspect of network security. These eight security dimensions are applied to each layer/plane combination to protect against all major security threats. The Bell Labs Security Framework security dimensions are:

1. Access control,

2. Authentication,

3. Non-repudiation,

4. Data confidentiality,

5. Communication security,   *info flows only betwr authorized End pts*

6. Data integrity,

7. Availability, and

8. Privacy.

Properly designed and implemented security dimensions support security policy and facilitate the rules set by security management. **Panel 3** provides a detailed description of the Bell Labs Security Framework security dimensions. The relationships among the security layers, planes, and dimensions are depicted in Figure B.1.

ISO/IEC 27001 applies the "Plan–Do–Check–Act" model to structure the process of establishing, implementing, operating, monitoring, reviewing, maintaining, and improving an ISMS in the following phases:

- *Plan:* Establish the ISMS.

- *Do:* Implement and operate the ISMS.

- *Check:* Monitor and review the ISMS.

- *Act:* Maintain and improve the ISMS.

Panel 3. Bell Labs Security Framework Security Dimensions

The Bell Labs Security Framework utilizes standard security services and mechanisms, such as those found in ITU-T Recommendation X.800 [6] to define eight basic dimensions of security that must be addressed to thwart attempts to exploit network vulnerabilities. These dimensions are not limited to the network but extend to applications as well. The security dimensions are as follows:

- *Access control*, which protects against unauthorized use of network resources. Access control ensures that only authorized personnel or devices are allowed access to network elements, stored information, information flows, services, and applications.

- *Authentication*, which confirms the identities of communicating entities. Authentication ensures the validity of the claimed identities of the entities (e.g., person, device, service, or application) participating in communication and provides assurance that an entity is not attempting a masquerade or unauthorized replay of a previous communication.

- *Non-repudiation*, which provides proof of the origin of data or the cause of an event or action. It ensures the existence of evidence that can be used to prove that some type of event or action has taken place so that the cause of the event or action cannot be repudiated later. † entity that initiated event or action?

- *Data confidentiality*, which protects data from unauthorized disclosure. Data confidentiality ensures that data are protected against unauthorized access or viewing.

- *Communication security*, which ensures that information only flows between authorized end points. The information flow is not diverted or intercepted as it flows between these end points.

- *Data integrity*, which ensures the correctness or accuracy of data against unauthorized modification, deletion, creation, and replication. Data integrity provides an indication of unauthorized activities in these areas.

- *Availability*, which ensures that there is no denial of authorized access to network elements, stored information, information flows, services, or applications due to events impacting the network.

- *Privacy*, which protects information that might be derived from the observation of network activities. This dimension includes information associated with individual users, service providers, enterprises, or the network infrastructure that might be obtained by either direct or covert means.

ISO/IEC 27001 provides a list of steps that must be performed in order to accomplish each of the phases. However, technical guidance on the specific actions that need to be performed for each step is needed. This paper focuses on how the Bell Labs Security Framework can be used to provide specificity for the actions required in the plan and do phases; the check and act phases will be addressed in future papers.

For the plan phase, to establish the ISMS, one needs to:

- Understand the business objectives and establish the high-level management policy covering security considerations,

- Identify the risks, and

- Select control objectives and controls for the treatment of risks.

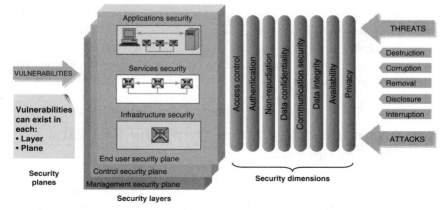

Figure B.1 The Bell Labs Security Framework.

For the do phase, to implement and operate the ISMS, one needs to:

- Implement controls selected previously to meet the control objectives, and

- Implement procedures and other controls capable of enabling prompt detection of security events and response to security incidents.

ISO/IEC 27001 is intended to serve as a single reference point for identifying the range of controls needed to align information systems with business objectives, and it addresses organizational, administrative, and procedural aspects of security. The specific controls needed for industry-centric applications (e.g., in financial, health, or telecommunications businesses) will be addressed in future documents within the ISO/IEC 27000 series. The Bell Labs Security Framework provides a structure that covers the technical aspects of the critical security mechanisms that must be considered from an operations viewpoint, an end user perspective, as well as the signaling aspects of transactions. The technical aspects are relevant to all industries, since they relate to the IT infrastructure needed to support the industry-specific applications. For example, when a security policy is being defined, the Bell Labs Security Framework can help identify management goals and disposition for key security areas such as access control, non-repudiation, privacy, availability, and communications security as well as how technical risks should be assessed, so that the policy can appropriately reflect these goals.

A Bell Labs Security Framework threat analysis can also be used during the ISMS risk assessment phase to provide a thorough assessment of threat exposures/scenarios, levels of risks, and mitigations for the assets identified in the analysis and defined by the ISMS scope. The Bell Labs Security Framework augments ISO/IEC 27001 to provide a more systematic implementation of the various controls to meet risk treatment objectives.

Implementation Guidance Using the Bell Labs Security Framework

ISO/IEC 27001 focuses mainly on an organization's security program. It provides high-level technical controls and high-level process controls. Typically, follow-on standards are created to provide implementation guidance for these high-level, direction-setting standards. The Bell Labs Security Framework can be used to provide implementation guidance on where to apply the process and technical controls contained in ISO/IEC 27001 as well as provide the next level of detail for these controls to satisfy the security design and implementation requirements of the ISMS plan and do phases discussed here.

Bell Labs Security Framework security implementation guidance provides the following capabilities to ensure that the end-to-end security requirements are satisfied. It allows users to:

- Verify that there are no critical gaps between security requirements, design and architecture plans,

- Evolve network level security by leveraging existing product-level security,

- Provide an assurance that the ISMS Plan and Do phases comply with industry standards and recommendations,

- Validate that critical, must-have security features are incorporated during ISMS implementation to minimize security incidents, and

- Evaluate ISMS implementation by ensuring the completeness of the results of analytical and testing methods.

Technology and protocol level specifications for network security are developed by various global standards organizations such as Internet Engineering Task Force (IETF), ISO/IEC, European Telecommunications Standards Institute (ETSI), International Telecommunication Union, Telecommunication Standardization Sector (ITU-T), 3rd Generation Partnership Project (3GPP*), and 3rd Generation Partnership Project 2 (3GPP2). Other organizations such as CERT*, the National Institute of Standards and Technology (NIST), and the Network Reliability and Interoperability Council (NRIC) develop security and reliability best practices. The Bell Labs Security Framework provides a common thread that ties these specifications and best practices together into a cohesive framework when implementing an Information Security Management System. (ISMS)

Methodology for Applying the Bell Labs Security Framework to ISO/IEC 27001

In this paper, the Bell Labs Security Framework's security layers, planes, and dimensions will be used in the following manner to provide specificity to each of the following steps.

Establish the ISMS:

- Identify the risks. The security scope (layers and planes) will be systematically analyzed to identify assets, threats to those assets, and vulnerabilities in those assets that might be exploited by threats or attackers.

- Select technical control objectives and controls for the treatment of risks. Control objectives and controls are selected for the relevant security layer and plane of each asset at risk.

Implement and operate the ISMS:

- Implement controls selected previously to meet the control objectives. The security dimensions, or attributes, will be used to provide the mechanisms required to implement and operate the selected controls. The security dimensions also address control objectives and controls that are not listed in ISO/IEC 27001 Annex A that may be selected as well.

- Implement procedures and other controls capable of enabling prompt detection of security events and response to security incidents. The security layers and planes will be utilized to determine the type and probable location of security events. Procedures and controls will be selected for application to the identified security layer and plane. The security dimensions contain mechanisms required to implement and operate the selected procedures and controls.

Examples of Applying the Bell Labs Security Framework to ISO/IEC 27001 Controls

ISO/IEC 27001:2005 Annex A contains control objectives and security controls. These control requirements were derived from ISO/IEC

17799:2005 [3], clauses 5 to 15. The 11 clauses or major sections include:

- Security policy,

- Organizing information security,

- Asset management,

- Human resources security,

- Physical and environmental security,

- Communications and operations management,

- Access control,

- Information systems acquisition, development, and maintenance,

- Information security incident management,

- Business continuity management, and

- Compliance.

The control objectives and security controls in Annex A can be selected as part of the Information Security Management System established and managed by an organization. These controls provide a blueprint of what the ISMS should address. ISO/IEC 17799:2005 provides implementation advice and guidance on best practices in support of the controls. The implementation advice and guidance found in ISO/IEC 17799:2005 will be updated and renamed as ISO/IEC 27002, which is currently in the process of ratification. This section examines typical ISO/IEC 27001 controls found in Annex A and demonstrates how the Bell Labs Security Framework can be used to augment them.

ISO/IEC 27001 control 5.1.1, entitled "Information security policy document," is a typical administrative control provided in Annex A. This control states, "An information security policy document should be approved by management, and published and communicated to all employees and relevant external parties." The implementation guidance for the information security policy document states that the policy must set out the organization's approach to managing information security. In the policy, management would state the use and benefits of the Bell Labs Security Framework in the approach. The applicability and implementation of the controls supported by the Bell Labs Security Framework layers/planes/dimensions would be dependent on the ISMS scope.

ISO/IEC 27001 control 10.9.2, entitled "On-line transactions," is a typical technical control provided in Annex A. This control states, "Information involved in on-line transactions should be protected to prevent incomplete transmission, misrouting, unauthorized message alteration, unauthorized disclosure, unauthorized message duplication, or replay." In order to protect information involved in online transactions, the Bell Labs Security Framework layers and planes are used to determine the necessary controls (in this case, control 10.9.2), and where they need to be applied, for online transactions. The Bell Labs Security Framework dimensions specify measures required to implement and operate the control, for example,: implementing Internet Protocol security authentication headers (i.e., IPsec AH) [8] of the data integrity dimension to prevent unauthorized message alteration in the services security layer and IPsec Encapsulated Security Protocol (ESP) [9] of the data confidentiality dimension to prevent unauthorized disclosure in the services security layer.

A similar analysis has been performed for all the controls contained in ISO/IEC 27001 to determine whether applying the Bell Labs Security Framework can augment them. Table B.I provides the results that were obtained for the controls contained in section A.7, "Asset management."

Case Study: Using the Bell Labs Security Framework to Establish, Implement, and Operate an ISMS

The purpose of this case study is to demonstrate, by way of example, how the Bell Labs Security Framework is used to enhance ISO/IEC 27001. A case study using the Bell Labs Security Framework in conjunction with ISO/IEC 27001 to establish, implement, and operate an Information Security Management System is presented. As this case study will show, the Bell Labs Security Framework can be used to identify where ISO/IEC 27001 controls need to be applied in an end-to-end network, as well as to provide specificity for their implementation and operation at various network locations, thus augmenting ISO/IEC 27001 to create an ISMS that provides a comprehensive end-to-end approach to IT security.

Table B.1 Applicability of Bell Labs Security Framework to ISO/IEC 27001 Controls

ISO 27001 Section	Control Name	Subcontrol Name	Control Description	Bell Labs Security Framework Applicable?
A.7	Asset management			
A.7.1	Responsibility for assets			
A.7.1.1	Responsibility for assets	Inventory of assets	All assets shall be clearly identified and an inventory of all important assets drawn up and maintained.	Yes
A.7.1.2	Responsibility for assets	Ownership of assets	All information and assets associated with information processing facilities shall be owned by a designated part of the organization.	Yes
A.7.1.3	Responsibility for assets	Acceptable use of assets	Rules for acceptable use of information and assets associated with information processing facilities shall be identified, documented, and implemented.	Yes
A.7.2	Information classification			
A.7.2.1	Information classification	Classification guidelines	Information shall be classified in terms of its value, legal requirements, sensitivity, and criticality to the organization.	Yes
A.7.2.2	Information classification	Information labeling and handling	An appropriate set of procedures for information labeling and handling shall be developed and implemented in accordance with the classification scheme adopted by the organization.	N/A

IEC—International Electrotechnical Commission
ISO—International Organization for Standardization

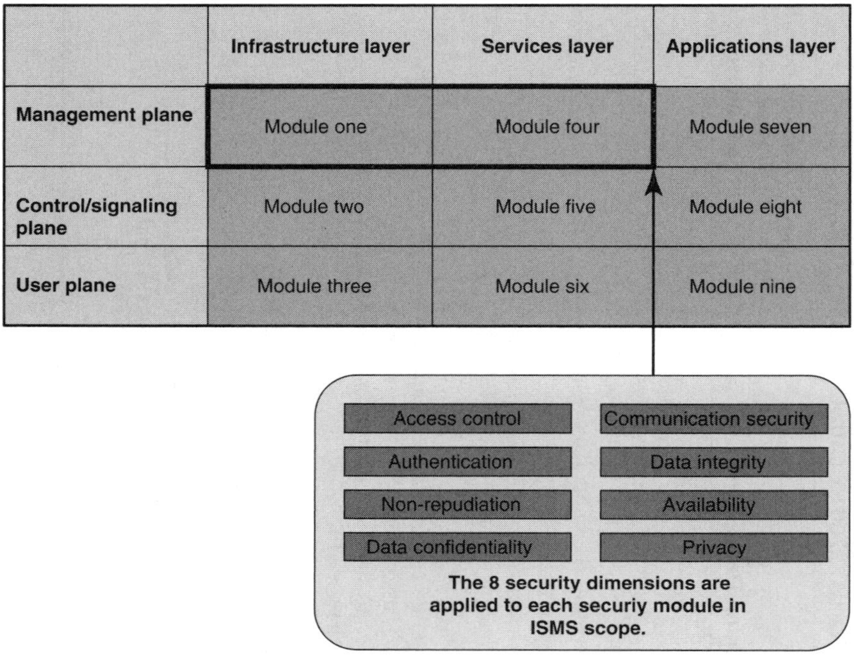

	Infrastructure layer	Services layer	Applications layer
Management plane	Module one	Module four	Module seven
Control/signaling plane	Module two	Module five	Module eight
User plane	Module three	Module six	Module nine

Access control   Communication security

Authentication   Data integrity

Non-repudiation   Availability

Data confidentiality   Privacy

The 8 security dimensions are applied to each securiy module in ISMS scope.

ISMS – Information security management system

Figure B.2 Tabular form of the Bell Labs Security Framework.

Figure B.2 depicts the tabular form of the Bell Labs Security Framework that highlights its modular nature. The intersection of a security plane and layer represents a security module that can be included or excluded, depending on the scope of the ISMS being established. From the figure, one can see that if the ISMS is being established for the management of information infrastructure and information services, then Bell Labs Security Framework modules one and four are in scope.

For the purposes of this case study, we consider establishing, implementing, and operating an ISMS for the management of the information infrastructure and services of a large enterprise that stores its employee information in a data center. The Bell Labs Security Framework scope is therefore as depicted in Figure B.2. This scope does not represent everything that is required for the implementation of an enterprise wide ISMS but is broad enough to demonstrate how the Bell Labs Security Framework can be used in conjunction with ISO/IEC

27001 to establish, implement, and operate an Information Security Management System. The same types of activities are performed if the applications security layer, signaling plane, and end user plane are also included in the ISMS scope.

The employee information stored in the data center also includes personal information that should be restricted to authorized users only. Protecting this employee information is defined to be within the scope and boundaries of this ISMS and has been identified through the ISMS asset identification and valuation process as an essential asset that needs protection. The employee information is accessed by several support organizations employed by the enterprise, one of which is the help desk; in addition, the data center and systems contained therein are maintained by the corporate IT organization. As seen in Figure B.3, the help desk accesses employee information for a number of operations including handling complaints, supporting orders for new IT services, and resolving problems employees are having with IT services (e.g., remote access). In addition, the corporate IT organization accesses employee information as part of its maintenance activities, e.g., file system maintenance, system updates, and patch management.

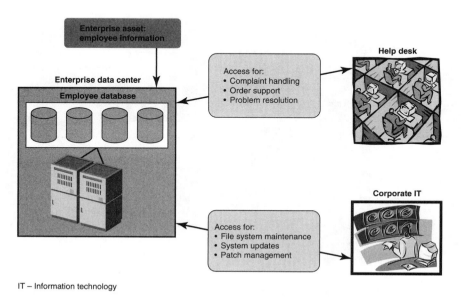

IT – Information technology

Figure B.3 Access scenario for enterprise asset.

As part of establishing, implementing, and operating an ISMS for the management of information infrastructure and services, the Bell Labs Security Framework's concepts of management plane, infrastructure security layer, and services security layer are utilized to analyze the employee information database as part of a risk assessment. This analysis reveals that the employee information is accessed by the enterprise's help desk as part of service management (e.g., managing employee remote access service), as well as by the enterprise's corporate IT organization as part of infrastructure management (e.g., performing backups). At this point, a Bell Labs Security Framework analysis is performed in concert with the ISMS risk assessment to identify threats and vulnerabilities in the management plane of the employee information database infrastructure and services security layers. In this example, the analysis reveals that members of the corporate IT organization can view and modify employee information, thereby making it vulnerable to disclosure and corruption in the infrastructure security layer. In addition, as part of performing problem resolution, employee information is transmitted in the clear between the data center and the help desk, thereby making it vulnerable to disclosure, corruption, and interception in the services security layer as depicted in Figure B.4.

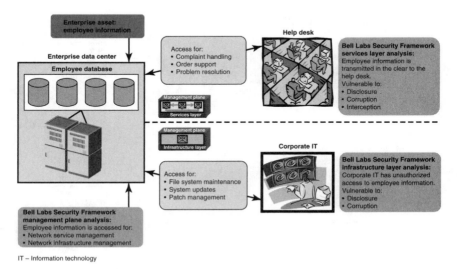

IT – Information technology

Figure B.4 Bell Labs Security Framework threat and vulnerability analysis for enterprise asset.

Continuing with the process used to establish an ISMS, at this point a risk analysis is performed that assesses the business impacts upon the organization that might result from security failures in the employee information as well as the realistic likelihood that these security failures would occur in light of the prevailing threats, vulnerabilities, and controls currently implemented by the enterprise. This analysis culminates in a decision by the organization to apply controls, accept the risk, reject the risk, or transfer the risk. The Bell Labs Security Framework adds more intelligence to the risk analysis. The Bell Labs Security Framework is used to identify controls currently implemented by the enterprise and their applicability to protecting employee information by recognizing that controls implemented in one layer or plane can mitigate threats and vulnerabilities present in other layers or planes.

For the purposes of this case study, a conclusion of the risk analysis is that controls need to be applied to protect employee information from the previously identified threats and vulnerabilities. Hence, as part of establishing the ISMS, control objectives and controls must be identified and selected to protect employee information against threats and vulnerabilities in the management plane of its infrastructure and services security layers.

Continuing with the example, ISO/IEC 27001 control A. 10.9.2 is one of the controls identified and selected as being required to protect the management of employee information in the services and infrastructure security layers because of the vulnerabilities and threats identified there by the Bell Labs Security Framework analysis. This is depicted in Figure B.5. ISO/IEC 27001 control A. 10.9.2 states that "information involved in on-line transactions shall be protected to prevent incomplete transmission, misrouting, unauthorized message alteration, unauthorized disclosure, unauthorized message duplication or replay."

Management approval of the residual risks and management authorization to implement and operate the ISMS is then obtained and a statement of applicability is prepared to provide a summary of decisions concerning risk treatment as the remaining steps of establishing an ISMS.

As part of implementing and operating the enterprise's ISMS, the Bell Labs Security Framework's dimensions provide explicit implementation and operation guidance for control A. 10.9.2 in the services and infrastructure security layers for the employee information asset.

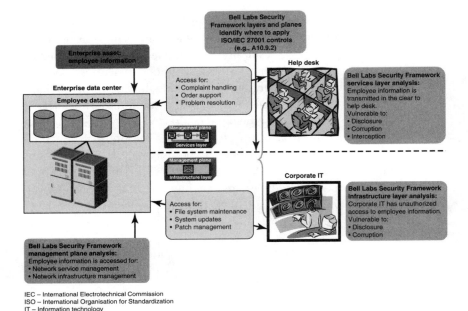

Figure B.5 The Bell Labs Security Framework identifies where to apply ISO/IEC 27001 controls.

Figure B.6 depicts how the Bell Labs Security Framework dimensions provide for the implementation and operation of control A. 10.9.2 to protect the employee information asset.

In the services security layer, the Bell Labs Security Framework's communication flow security dimension ensures that information flows only between authorized end points (i.e., that the information is not diverted or intercepted as it flows between these end points), and it therefore provides for the use of virtual private networks (VPNs) to prevent misrouting.

The Bell Labs Security Framework's data integrity dimension ensures the correctness or accuracy of data – that the data are protected against unauthorized modification, deletion, creation, and replication – and provides an indication of these unauthorized activities. The data integrity dimension thus provides for the use of IPsec AH in the services security layer to prevent incomplete transmission, and unauthorized message alteration and duplication, as well as to prevent message replay. In the infrastructure security layer, the data integrity dimension provides for the use of file checksums to detect unauthorized alteration.

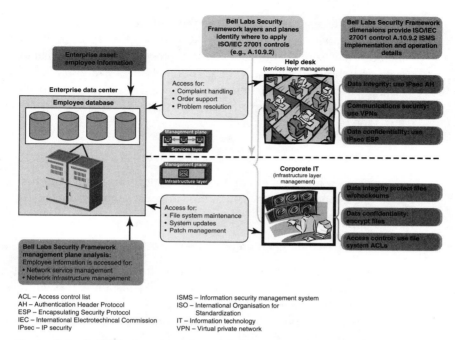

Figure B.6 Bell Labs Security Framework dimensions provide implementation and operation details for ISO/IEC 27001 controls.

The Bell Labs Security Framework's data confidentiality dimension protects data from unauthorized disclosure and provides for the use of IPsec ESP in the services security layer to prevent unauthorized disclosure. In the infrastructure security layer, the data confidentiality dimension provides for the use of file encryption.

In the infrastructure security layer, the Bell Labs Security Framework's access control dimension provides authorization for the use of the network resources. Access control ensures that only authorized personnel or devices are allowed access to network elements, stored information, information flows, services, and applications. The access control dimension thus provides for the use of file system access control lists (ACLs) to prevent unauthorized duplication.

Therefore, as a result of using the Bell Labs Security Framework to enhance ISO/IEC 27001 to establish, implement, and operate an ISMS, the enterprise decides to deploy IPsec VPNs with authentication headers and Encapsulated Security Protocol enabled to protect the transmission of employee information between the data center and

Access Control Lists ?

help desk. The enterprise also decides to protect the employee identification database with file system ACLs as well as to encrypt and
include checksums in the database to protect employee information
from unauthorized access by the corporate IT organization.

Finally, to complete the implementation and begin operation of the
ISMS, the enterprise performs the following activities contained in ISO/
IEC 27001:

- Formulates and implements a risk treatment plan,

- Defines how to measure the effectiveness of controls and how
  these measurements are to be used to assess control effectiveness,

- Implements training and awareness programs,

- Manages the operation of and resources for the ISMS,

- Implements procedures and other controls capable of enabling
  prompt detection of security events in response to security
  incidents (the Bell Labs Security Framework is used to identify
  where these procedures and other controls are to be placed in a
  manner similar to what has been described above).

Using the Bell Labs Security Framework to Implement an ISMS for Government Networks

Today there are numerous international government standards and
guidelines in the area of information security, and they provide specific
security recommendations for numerous systems, applications, and
processes. These guidelines are developed by various organizations
specific to civilian government agencies. In the United States, organizations such as the National Institute of Standards and Technology
(NIST), the Defense Information Systems Agency (DISA), and the
National Security Agency (NSA) provide detailed standards for internal
agency use as well as for industry use.

The Bell Labs Security Framework provides a unified and comprehensive view by marrying global industry (e.g., ISO/IEC, ITU-T, IETF,
3GPP, 3GPP2) and government standards/guidelines (e.g., in the
United States, those of NIST, NSA, DISA, and other agencies). In
addition to helping decipher the importance of a specific standard
and categorically analyze what it addresses, the Bell Labs Security

will this still exist after Janet Oreg's NIST std comes out? Need to check!

Conclusion **201**

Framework will help identify areas where further focus is needed. For example, NIST 800-53 [1] can work in conjunction with ISO/IEC 17799 or ISO/IEC 27002 when it becomes finalized. These two documents can be further enhanced with additional focus on the Bell Labs Security Framework's privacy and non-repudiation security dimensions.

The Bell Labs Security Framework was developed to help service providers, government agencies, and enterprises understand in a modular way how to incorporate the right level of security in their solutions throughout the solution's life cycle. This is critical in order to have a successful implementation of an ISMS.

Conclusion

The global movement to improve security controls is undeniable and has stimulated a growing acceptance of business and IT models that define internal controls for managing risks. As a global model for best practices in information security, ISO/IEC 27001 has become the optimal choice for managing information security needs in many organizations. Yet, while some of the controls described in ISO/IEC 27001 provide very specific guidance on their implementation and operation, most of them do not. Organizations undertaking the implementation of an ISO/IEC 27001 ISMS can leverage the Bell Labs Security Framework for a granular technical perspective of the various ISO/IEC 27001 controls.

This paper has described a standardized, systematic, methodical approach utilizing the Bell Labs Security Framework to identify risks, select control objectives and controls for the mitigation of risks, implement controls to meet control objectives, and implement procedures capable of enabling prompt detection of security events and response to security incidents. The case study demonstrated how the Bell Labs Security Framework can be used in conjunction with ISO/IEC 27001 to establish, implement, and operate ISMS controls in IT and government networks.

The Bell Labs Security Framework is used to identify where the necessary ISO/IEC 27001 controls need to be applied by systematically analyzing the juxtaposition of a given asset with the Bell Labs Security Framework layers and planes in a standardized manner to identify threats and vulnerabilities to that asset comprehensively as part of an organization's risk assessment. The Bell Labs Security Framework identifies the necessary ISO/IEC 27001 controls and incorporates granularity in terms of which security layer and plane they should be applied to, thereby ensuring that the right controls are applied at the right location to thoroughly secure assets at risk. The Bell Labs Security Framework dimensions provide guidance for the implementation and operation of ISO/IEC 27001 controls to different layers and planes. In addition, the Bell Labs Security Framework security dimensions provide a basis for additional control objectives and controls that are not included in ISO/IEC 27001 that may be selected, implemented, and operated as part of an organization's ISMS. The framework also supports the creation of new controls needed for specific industry verticals (e.g., finance, health, telecommunications). The synergistic use of the Bell Labs Security Framework with ISO/IEC 27001 creates an ISMS that provides comprehensive end-to-end security by applying, implementing, and operating security controls in a holistic, standardized manner.

Further Reading

The Bell Labs Security Framework has been instantiated by the International Telecommunication Union Telecommunication Standardization Sector as ITU-T Recommendation X.805 "Security Architecture for Systems Providing End-to-End Communications" [7]]. It has also been instantiated by the International Organization for Standardization/International Electro-technical Commission as ISO/IEC standard 18028-2, "Information Technology – Security Techniques – IT Network Security – Part 2: Network Security Architecture" [5]]. The interested reader is referred to these references for additional information about the Bell Labs Security Framework.

This paper has focused on the ISO/IEC 27001 standard, which provides requirements for security controls and implementation guidance for an organization's Information Security Management System. ISO/IEC 27001 is interdependent with a number of other security standards and standards organizations. An earlier *Bell Labs Technical Journal* paper, entitled "Overview of Data and Telecommunications Security Standardization Efforts in ISO, IEC, ITU, and IETF" [1], provides an overview and description of the inter-dependencies of the various security standards and standards bodies.

*Trademarks

3GPP is a trademark of the European Telecommunications Standards Institute.
CERT is a registered trademark of Carnegie Mellon University.

References

[1] H. Bertine, I. Faynberg, and H.-L. Lu, "Overview of Data and Telecommunications Security Standardization Efforts in ISO, IEC, ITU, and IETF,"Bell Labs Tech. J., 8: 4 (2004), 203–229.

[2] International Organization for Standardization and International Electrotechnical Commission, "Information Technology – Open Systems Interconnection – Basic Reference Model: The Basic Model," ISO/IEC 7498–1:1994, Nov. 15, 1994, <http://www.iso.org>.

[3] International Organization for Standardization and International Electrotechnical Commission, "Information Technology – Security Techniques – Code of Practice for Information Security Management," ISO/IEC 17799:2005, June 15, 2005, <http://www.iso.org>.

[4] International Organization for Standardization and International Electrotechnical Commission, "Information Technology – Security Techniques – Information Security Management Systems – Requirements," ISO/IEC 27001:2005, Oct. 15, 2005, <http://www.iso.org>.

[5] International Organization for Standardization and International Electrotechnical Commission, "Information Technology – Security Techniques – IT Network Security – Part 2: Network Security Architecture," ISO/IEC 18028-2:2006, Feb. 1, 2006, <http://www. iso.org>.

[6] International Telecommunication Union, Telecommunication Standardization Sector, "Security Architecture for Open Systems Interconnection for CCITT Applications," ITU-T Rec. X.800, 1991, <http://www. itu.int>.

[7] International Telecommunication Union, Telecommunication Standardization Sector, "Security Architecture for Systems Providing End-to-End Communications," ITU-T Rec. X.805, Oct. 2003, <http://www.itu. int>.

[8] S. Kent, "IP Authentication Header," IETF RFC 4302, Dec. 2005, <http://www.ietf.org/rfc/rfc4302.txt>.

[9] S. Kent, "IP Encapsulating Security Payload (ESP)," IETF RFC 4303, Dec. 2005, <http://www.ietf.org/rfc/rfc4303.txt>.

[10] A. R. McGee, S. R. Vasireddy, C. Xie, D. D. Picklesimer, U. Chandrashekhar, and S. H. Richman, "A Framework for Ensuring Network Security," Bell Labs Tech. J.,8: 4 (2004)7–27.

[11] R. Ross, S. Katzke, A. Johnson, M. Swanson, G. Stoneburner, G. Rogers, and A. Lee, "Recommended Security Controls for Federal Information Systems," National Institute of Standards and Technology, Computer Security Division, NIST SP 800-53, Feb. 2005, <http://csrc.nist.gov/publications/nistpubs/800–53/SP800-53.pdf>.

ANDREW R. MCGEE is a distinguished member of technical staff in the Security Technology Application Research Group at Bell Labs in Murray Hill, New Jersey. Mr. McGee has over 20 years of data communications experience and is currently responsible for the development and analysis of advanced security architectures and security services for next-generation networks. His research interests include data network architectures and virtual private networking technologies, and he holds a patent in the area of data networking. Mr. McGee received a B.S. degree from Michigan State University in East Lansing and an M.S. degree from Rutgers University in New Jersey, both in computer science.

FRANK A. BASTRY is a member of technical staff in the Security Solutions Organization at Bell Labs in Murray Hill, New Jersey. He has over 28 years of experience and in-depth expertise in information security management, security architecture analysis, systems engineering, business continuity planning, and wireline and wireless network planning and has led and managed large product systems engineering configurator teams. His research interests include network security architectures and critical infrastructure analysis. Mr. Bastry received a B.S. degree in computer sciences from Monmouth University in West Long Branch, New Jersey, and an M.S. degree in management of technology from the Stevens Institute of Technology in Hoboken, New Jersey.

UMA CHANDRASHEKHAR leads the Security Technology Applications Research Team in the Security Solutions organization at Bell Labs in Murray Hill, New Jersey. Her team has responsibility for developing innovative solutions addressing security challenges in both wireless and wireline technology.Ms. Chandrashekhar's experience covers the areas of security program life cycle from concept to systems engineering, secure data communications, operations planning, network management, and deployment. Her experience also includes leading the Interoperability Industry Test Plan (IITP) phases to support the

reliability of the Signaling System 7 (SS7) network, which included major industry players as part of the National Reliability Interoperability Council (NRIC) recommendations on reliability of the nation's infrastructure. She has led and project-managed strategic projects from inception to market in the areas of network operations, reliability, security enablers, network monitoring systems, and network management. She led her team to the development of the Bell Labs Security Model that is now the basis of the global ITU-T X.805 standard. She has a master's degree in electrical engineering and is certified as a project manager (PMP), as well as a certified security professional (CISSP). Prior to joining Bell Labs, her work experience included postings with network operators, vendors, and research organizations. Ms. Chandrashekhar served as the guest editor for the Bell Labs Technical Journal's special issue on Network Security (v8-4). She is currently the coeditor for working drafts of ISO/IEC 27003.

S. RAO VASIREDDY is a member of technical staff in the Security Technology Application Research organization at Bell Labs in Murray Hill, New Jersey. He has 19 years of experience in the research and development of data and voice communications services, and in network security, quality, and reliability assessment. Mr. Vasireddy has led projects in the areas of design and development of IP service architectures, security architecture frameworks, and security strategy development for 3G wireless networks. He participates in ITU-T, ISO/IEC, and ATIS standards organizations, contributing in the area of network security. He has a master's degree in computer sciences from the University of Louisville, Kentucky, and a master's degree in electrical engineering from Regional Engineering College, India.

LORI A. FLYNN is a member of technical staff at LGS Bell Labs in Whippany, New Jersey. Her responsibilities include network security research and network routing research on subjects including quality of service (QoS), ad hoc systems, multiple input-multiple output (MIMO)-based systems, and multicast. She works with IETF, ISO, and ITU network standards. She holds a B.S. in molecular biology from the University of Wisconsin at Parkside and a Ph.D. in computer science from the University of California at Santa Cruz. Her research interests include network security, ad hoc routing, international standards, and secure voting systems.

Appendix C

Ch 2, Ref 1

The key to understanding the financial risks as well as costs of cyber security is to fully embrace its multidisciplinary nature. Cyber risk is not just a technical problem to be solved by the company's chief technology officer. Nor is it just a "legal problem" to be handed over to the company's chief legal counsel; a "customer relationship problem" to be solved by the company's communications director; a "compliance issue" for the regulatory guru; or a "crisis management" problem. Rather, it is all of these and more.

Calculating the financial impact of cyber risk

The first step in understanding a true risk management approach to network security is to understand how risk management professionals understand net financial risk. Net financial risk can be expressed as in Figure C.1.

To successfully analyze and manage financial risk requires a dialogue, sparked by a series of pointed questions directed at the major stakeholders in all corporate domains: the chief legal counsel, chief technology officer and chief risk officer; plus, heads of corporate communications, investor relations, human resources and customer service. Each of these individuals should be "in the room" and the CFO may be surprised to find that individuals with different positions in the company will give very different, sometimes contrary, responses to the

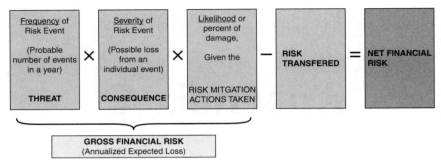

Appendix C.1   The financial risk of cyber impact

same question. Each stakeholder has a different mission and thus their advice will reflect their respective priorities. The challenge is for an organization to address each of these priorities and create an approach that reflects the needs of the entire enterprise.

To date, there are very few publications on applying a multidisciplined risk management approach to cyber security. One of those works was recently published by the American National Standards Institute (ANSI) and the Internet Security Alliance (ISA) called, "The Financial Impact of Cyber Risk, 50 Questions Every CFO Should Ask" (available as a free download at http://webstore.ansi.org/cybersecurity.aspx).

Once the right people are "in the room," each can review a particular risk mitigation action and determine the impact of that action on potential financial loss within its department. Examples of risk mitigation actions are numerous and can include such varied expenses as buying more technology, buying more risk transfer insurance, modifying legal agreements, hiring a crisis management consultant, organizing a customer call center, creating an inventory of applicable laws and regulations and creating an inventory of regulated data.

From the work of ANSI/ISA one can develop an action plan based on the financial ROI discussed above. The model provides a simple method to look at current and expected probabilities of financial risk. By estimating the financial improvement if certain risk mitigating actions are taken, a chief financial officer can better determine the company's ROI arising from suggested steps to mitigate the company's overall Net Financial Risk.

Risk Mitigation Actions (RMAs) vary based on the business of the company. However, typical RMAs might include introducing additional technology, staff increases, insurance, change in contract language in vendor or customer agreements, change in business activity, change in business continuity plan, or change or implementation of crisis management plan.

Ch 2, Ref 2: A Transaction Based Network Valuation Model

To specify the model, the future benefits of transactions must be discounted to net present value terms. It is also important to recognize that transactions are not always simple and paired as an online book purchase, where you deliver money and receive a book. Some transactions, such as licensing anti-virus software, occur annually, but most benefits are derived on a usage basis over that period of time. Over a year you may send thousands of emails. Each of these is a transaction that has value, or you would presumably not engage in it. But these transactions are not paired. They are part of a bundle of transactions you conduct within the context of your relationship with a network. Put in economic terms, the net present value (*V*) of any network (*j*) to any individual (i) is equal to the sum of the net present value of the benefit of all transactions less the net present value of the costs of all transactions on the network over any given period of time (*t*), as shown in the following equation.

$$V_{i,j} = \sum_{k=1}^{n} \frac{B_{i,k}}{(1+r)^{t_k}} - \sum_{l=1}^{n} \frac{C_{i,l}}{(1+r_l)^{t_l}}$$

Where

$V_{i,j}$ = net present value of all transactions of k = 1 through n to individual $_i$ with respect to network $_j$

$_i$ = one user of the network

$_j$ = identifies one network or network system

$B_{i,k}$ = the benefit value of transaction $_k$ to individual $_i$

$C_{i,l}$ = the cost of transaction $_l$ to individual $_i$

r_k and r_l = the discount rate of interest to the time of transaction $_k$ or $_l$

t_k or t_l = the elapsed time in years to transaction $_k$ or $_1$

To simplify subsequent derivations of the equation, the net present value benefit and cost terms will be simplified without the discount function and be italicized as simply $B_{i,k}$ and $C_{i,l}$. Other terms italicized will also express net present values of those terms, and a simple sigma will represent the relevant series of transactions over any defined time period.

Thus the equation is simplified to:

$$V_{i,j} = \sum B_{i,k} - \sum C_{i,l}$$

Valuing an Entire Network

The above equation represents the value of the Internet to one user. The value of the entire Internet or any network Nj is the summation of the value of that network to all individuals or entities, i through n, engaged in transactions on that network. Thus a summation term is now added before $V_{i,j}$.

$$\sum_{i=1}^{n} V_{i,j} = \sum B_{i,k} - \sum C_{i,l}$$

The Sum Value of All Networks

Similarly, to value all networks to all users in the world simply requires a summation of all networks $j = 1$ through n.

$$\sum_{j=1}^{n} \sum_{i=1}^{n} V_{i,j} = \sum B_{i,k} - \sum C_{i,l}$$

The total net value of all networks in the world is equal to the total value of net benefit of all networks to all users.

This total value is presumably less than total Gross Domestic Product (GDP) and greater than zero. Global GDP for 2008 is estimated to be **45 trillion dollars**. Worldwide telecom revenues are estimated to be $1.7 trillion for 2008, including both wire-line and wireless communications. They are forecast to reach $2.7 trillion by 2013. This represents approximately 3% of global GDP, and $4.6 billion per day in telecom gross revenues.

These figures on the estimated size of the global telecom industry represent a significant underestimate of the value of networks enabled by telecom capabilities. Due to advanced technologies and economies of scale, telecom service capabilities continue to expand while the real cost of service continues to fall. The value added by network access and usage yields a vastly larger economic impact. Moreover, there are many other networks whose value is not reflected in these telecom revenues, including television networks and social networks, among others. The global net value added of all networks may well be somewhere between 1 and 10% of global GDP, or $450 billion to $4.5 trillion per annum. Just think of how much the internet is worth to you and remember that 1.3 billion other humans use it too, and this is but one network.

How does one begin to determine the value generated through network transactions. As a starting point, consider the different forms of value that are provided through transactions among networks enabled by electronic media. Transactions in this context can be defined as interactions that provide value to participants. Initially, one can consider dividing participants into two groups – individuals and organizations.

Ch 3, Ref 1

3rd Generation Partnership Project, "IP Multimedia Subsystem (IMS); (Stage 2)," Rel. 5, 3GPP TS 23.228, Dec. 2004, <http://www.3gpp.org/ftp/specs/archive/23_series/23.228>, <http://www.3gpp.org/ftp/specs/ html-info/23228.htm>.

Ch 3, Ref 2

IMS Architecture – Potential Vulnerabilities

- – Signaling replay attacks whereby the dialog between an end-user and IMS is captured and replayed in order to get the IMS network to admit the attacker.

- – Media session hijacking consists of sending a spoofed SIP REDIRECT message to an endpoint that redirects the call's bearer channel to another endpoint.

- – Uncorrelated billing and media usage. This occurs because the signaling messages (SIP) and bearer packets (RTP/RTCP) take completely diverse paths through the converged network. Once IMS directs the network elements on the bearer path to set up a call between the two endpoints, the service provider keeps track of the time until a SIP BYE message is received for billing purposes. It is then up to the endpoints to disconnect from the network. If the endpoints have a specialized SIP stack that issues BYE messages without disconnecting from the network, the endpoints can continue to communicate over the bearer path free of charge.

– Theft of service due to hijacked or misrouted SIP REGISTER or INVITE messages. These are the SIP messages that an endpoint issues to IMS in order to attach to the network (REGISTER) and make a call (INVITE).

– Invasion of privacy due to sniffed SIP messages. Even though SIP messages do not contain bearer traffic, they contain caller and called information which can be used to perform call pattern tracking to discover identity, affiliation, presence and usage.

– Service interruption by forging BYE messages that tear down calls prematurely.

Ch3, Ref 3: Protecting the domain name service (DNS)

The central role of DNS in the current converged IP network is well known. It may not be known that DNS plays an even larger role in Web 2.0 networks. The DNSSEC protocol consists of security enhancements added onto the basic protocol after the fact though it is currently not widely deployed. Recently publicized vulnerabilities in the DNS messages used to update and maintain the domain name to IP address mappings in the DNS servers illustrates the need to secure the DNS protocol. As users interact with a wide range of network-based services and applications, DNS name resolution activity will be almost constant. Then there are the behind-the-scenes DNS references performed by the applications and services themselves. The opportunities for fraud due to DNS cache poisoning because of insecurities in the DNS protocol remain significant.

Ch3, Ref 4

The Femto Base Station Router (BSR) provides a perfect example of this phenomenon. A Femto BSR moves the telecommunications access network into the environment of subscriber residences and enterprises (an environment that must be considered hostile from the perspective of security) so tamper proofing becomes a key design consideration.

Ch 3, Ref 5

One might think that securing devices in the IMS core (CSCF, BGCF, MGCF, MGW) might just consist of securing their management interfaces. However, closer examination of the IMS core reveals that the Proxy-CSCF (P-CSCF) interfaces with end-users via SIP, so that interface must also be secure. Likewise, the Interrogating-CSCF (I-CSCF) interfaces with external IMS networks, so that interface must be secure as well. Since the purpose of the I-CSCF is to hide the internal network details from external service providers, it is an imperative to secure that interface.

Ch 3, Ref 6

In the SaaS model, the customer relinquishes control over software versions or changing requirements; the costs to use the service become a continuous expense, rather than a single expense with its associated infrastructure at time of purchase. The burden of securing application software and the content now shifts to the SaaS service provider. The customer relinquishes control over the software and the protection of the content – a situation where all the eggs really are in one basket and under the control of a SaaS service provider.

Ch 3, Ref 7

An example of this transmutation is SPAM to SPIT (SPIT defined as SPAM in IP telephony). Spammers deliver unwanted e-mail messages flooding e-mail traffic nodes and in-boxes. SPIT works in the same context. The primary cause for SPAM is the lack of authentication capabilities in the protocols used to deliver e-mail messages. This lack of authentication capabilities is leveraged by botnets, including thousands of zombie computers under the control of criminals that contain e-mailer software and are leased out to spammers. These botnets are therefore able to forge e-mail messages that are not flagged as being forged and are ultimately delivered to unlucky recipients. The issue of authenticating e-mail messages has been under study for years now with no resolution in site.

It is nowhere near as prevalent as SPAM, but with the increasing adoption of IP telephones SPIT may also become a problem in the future. IMS authentication via SIP Digest and IMS AKA is an attempt to address this issue of forged SIP messages used for call control. However, these authentication mechanisms are optional. Therefore, potential exists for botnets to be formed using SIP emulators to set up calls with random IP addresses and prerecorded messages that are played for the person on the other end of the call. An interesting aspect of this configuration would be that these calls would bypass the official IMS systems and their billing capabilities, resulting in no expense for the SPIT generator.

First there was SPAM; then there was SPIT; now there is the potential for SPIV (SPAM in IPTV), not to be confused with television advertisements. This is futuristic (no evidence seen as yet), but it takes no great leap of imagination that fraud can find an opportunity to create bogus video content and inject it onto the IP connection that delivers IPTV into homes. There are actually devices that are being used to do this type of injection legitimately today, by overwriting advertisements broadcast by the national feed with local advertisements. This is how advertisements for a local vendor can appear during a nationally broadcast sporting event such as Monday Night Football in the United States.

Ch 3, Ref 8

Keeping medical records with a content service provider is a good example where there are significant benefits and where there are significant security concerns. A person needing medical attention while traveling outside of access to their health provider could simply make their records available to the attending practitioner online and potentially avoid a misdiagnosis or costly lab work – the records, including current medications, allergies and so forth would be readily available to them. The health industry can also benefit from improvements in the efficiency of information flow and ultimately improvements in overall business efficiency. In the wrong hands, the most personal information about an individual can be compromised – the kind of information that can be used to determine insurability or even limitations for jobs. There is probably no more contentious issue than this one; the potential for misuse is almost without limit.

Ch 3, Ref 9

An aspect of maintaining the integrity of information stored in the cloud is related to SaaS. Malware infection of application software violates the integrity of the software; can the Saas provider distributing to customers assure that the software is free of malware? Also, what about uninterested third parties – parties that are infected by enterprises who were infected by the SaaS application provider? These are issues that need to be worked before SaaS goes mainstream in Web 2.0.

Glossary

3G	3G is the third generation of tele standards and technology for mobile networking, superseding 2.5G. It is based on the International Telecommunication Union (ITU) family of standards under the IMT-2000. www.wikipedia.org
4G	4G an abbreviation for Fourth-Generation, is a term used to describe the next complete evolution in wireless communications. A 4G system will be able to provide a comprehensive IP solution where voice, data and streamed multimedia can be given to users on an "Anytime, Anywhere" basis, and at higher data rates than previous generations. www.wikipedia.org
Access control	From the ITU-T X.805 Recommendation http://www.itu.int/rec/T-REC-X.805/en
Aftermarket Security	A term representing the idea that security is purchased as an add-on – as in anti-virus protection purchased to protect the operation of a computer.
Assets	In reference to the Bell Labs Security Framework, the identification of all the components and interface points in a particular network element, network subsystem, or network system to be considered in determining vulnerabilities and appropriate mitigations.
Authentication	From the ITU-T X.805 Recommendation http://www.itu.int/rec/T-REC-X.805/en
Availability	From the ITU-T X.805 Recommendation http://www.itu.int/rec/T-REC-X.805/en

BASEL II

An international standard for banking with recommendations for applicable laws and regulations
http://www.bis.org/publ/bcbsca.htm

Bell Labs Security Framework

A security model first developed at Bell Laboratories that became the basis for the ITU-T X.805 Recommendation. The model was used inside of Alcatel-Lucent to develop guidelines for how security should be considered for the design of networks and network elements.

California Senate Bill 1386 (SB 1386)

Existing law regulates the maintenance and dissemination of personal information by state agencies, as defined, and requires each agency to keep an accurate account of disclosures made pursuant to specified provisions. Existing law also requires a business, as defined, to take all reasonable steps to destroy a customer's records that contain personal information when the business will no longer retain those records. Existing law provides civil remedies for violations of these provisions.
http://info.sen.ca.gov/pub/01-02/bill/sen/sb_1351-1400/sb_1386_bill_20020926_chaptered.html

Certification

Used in reference to a set of confirmations applied to establish a certain degree of security hardening. There are many forms of certification, in this case, the use is made to the ISO 27001 certification.
http://en.wikipedia.org/wiki/Cyber_security_certification

Cloud Computing

In reference to Internet computing – where the service is provided through the Internet as in Software as a Service (SaaS).
http://en.wikipedia.org/wiki/Cloud_Computing

CoBIT

Internationally recognized IT governance guidelines
http://www.isaca.org/Template.cfm?Section=COBIT6&Template=/TaggedPage/TaggedPageDisplay.cfm&TPLID=55&ContentID=7981

Communications Security

From the ITU-T X.805 Recommendation
http://www.itu.int/rec/T-REC-X.805/en

Compliance

In reference to regulatory compliance, particularly those that require some form of cyber security standard practice.
http://en.wikipedia.org/wiki/Compliance_(regulation)

Convergence

The move from separate infrastructures and technologies for voice, video and data to one technology platform – Internet

Protocol (IP) – and toward a unified infrastructure, not separate plants.
www.wikipedia.org

CSIS

Center for Strategic and International Studies
www.csis.org

Cyber-Value

Denotes the idea that value is primarily determined by a brand and the online service that the company provides as opposed to the physical assets.

Data Confidentiality

From the ITU-T X.805 Recommendation
http://www.itu.int/rec/T-REC-X.805/en

Denial of service (DoS) attacks

A denial-of-service attack (DoS attack) or distributed denial-of-service attack (DDoS attack) is an attempt to make a computer resource unavailable to its intended users. Although the means to carry out, motives for, and targets of a DoS attack may vary, it generally consists of the concerted, malevolent efforts of a person or persons to prevent an Internet site or service from functioning efficiently or at all, temporarily or indefinitely. Perpetrators of DoS attacks typically target sites or services hosted on high-profile web servers such as banks, credit card payment gateways.
www.wikipedia.org

Digital Rights Management

Is a generic term that refers to access control technologies used by hardware manufacturers, publishers, and copyright holders to limit usage of digital media or devices. The term is used to describe any technology which makes the unauthorized use of media or devices technically formidable and generally doesn't include other forms of copy protection which can be circumvented without modifying the media or device, such as serial numbers or key-files. It can also refer to restrictions associated with specific instances of digital works or devices.
www.wikipedia.org

DoS

A denial-of-service attack (DoS attack) or distributed denial-of-service attack (DDoS attack) is an attempt to make a computer resource unavailable to its intended users. Although the means to carry out, motives for, and targets of a DoS attack may vary, it generally consists of the concerted efforts of a person or persons to prevent an Internet site or service from functioning efficiently or at

all, temporarily or indefinitely. Perpetrators of DoS attacks typically target sites or services hosted on high-profile web servers such as banks, credit card payment gateways, and even root nameservers.
http://en.wikipedia.org/wiki/Denial-of-service_attack

Enterprise Risk Management

In reference to the management of risk by an enterprise to meet organizational objectives. Involves treating risk in the whole, not as separate activities.
http://en.wikipedia.org/wiki/Enterprise_risk_management

Facebook

Facebook, formerly The Facebook, is a free-access social networking website that is operated and privately owned by Facebook, Inc.[1] Users can join networks organized by city, workplace, school, and region to connect and interact with other people. People can also add friends and send them messages, and update their personal profiles to notify friends about themselves. The website's name refers to the paper facebooks depicting members of a campus community that some US colleges and preparatory schools give to incoming students, faculty, and staff as a way to get to know other people on campus.
http://en.wikipedia.org/wiki/Facebook

Factor Analysis of Information Risk

Framework for understanding, analyzing, and measuring information risk
http://fairwiki.riskmanagementinsight.com/

Family Educational Rights and Privacy Act (FERPA)

The Family Educational Rights and Privacy Act of 1974 (FERPA or the Buckley Amendment) is a United States federal law codified at 20 U.S.C. § 1232g, with implementing regulations in title 34, part 99 of the Code of Federal Regulations. The regulations provide that educational agencies and institutions that receive funding under a program administered by the U. S. Department of Education must provide students with access to their education records, an opportunity to seek to have the records amended, and some control over the disclosure of information from the records. With several exceptions, schools must have a student's consent prior to the disclosure of education records. Examples of situations affected by FERPA include school employees divulging information to someone other than the child's parents about a child's grades or behavior, and school work posted on a bulletin board with a grade.

http://en.wikipedia.org/wiki/Family_Educational_Rights_ and_Privacy_Act

Federal Information Systems Management Act (FISMA)

A United States federal law enacted in 2002 as Title III of the E-Government Act of 2002 (Pub.L. 107-347, 116 Stat. 2899). The act was meant to bolster computer and network security within the Federal Government and affiliated parties (such as government contractors) by mandating yearly audits.
www.wikipedia.org

Femto Base Station Router (BSR)

A small cellular base station (for the home or small business) connecting cell phones to a service provider typically through a DSL line
http://en.wikipedia.org/wiki/Femtocell

FFIEC

The Council is a formal interagency body empowered to prescribe uniform principles, standards, and report forms for the federal examination of financial institutions by the Board of Governors of the Federal Reserve System (FRB), the Federal Deposit Insurance Corporation (FDIC), the National Credit Union Administration (NCUA), the Office of the Comptroller of the Currency (OCC), and the Office of Thrift Supervision (OTS), and to make recommendations to promote uniformity in the supervision of financial institutions.
www.ffiec.gov

Gramm-Leach-Bliley Act (GLBA)

Also known as the Gramm-Leach-Bliley Financial Services Modernization Act, Pub.L. 106-102, 113 Stat. 1338, enacted November 12, 1999, is an Act of the United States Congress which repealed part of the Glass-Steagall Act of 1933, opening up competition among banks, securities companies and insurance companies. The Glass-Steagall Act prohibited a bank from offering investment, commercial banking, and insurance services.
http://banking.senate.gov/conf/

Health Insurance Portability and Accountability Act (HIPAA).

Was enacted by the U.S. Congress in 1996. According to the Centers for Medicare and Medicaid Services (CMS) website, Title I of HIPAA protects health insurance coverage for workers and their families when they change or lose their jobs. Title II of HIPAA, known as the Administrative Simplification (AS) provisions, requires the estab-

lishment of national standards for electronic health care transactions and national identifiers for providers, health insurance plans, and employers.
www.wikipedia.org

IDS

Intrusion Detection System is software and/or hardware designed to detect unwanted attempts at accessing, manipulating, and/or disabling of computer systems, mainly through a network, such as the Internet. These attempts may take the form of attacks, as examples, by crackers, malware and/or disgruntled employees. An IDS cannot directly detect attacks within properly encrypted traffic.
www.wikipedia.org

IFRAME

IFrame (from Inline Frame) is an HTML element which makes it possible to embed an HTML document inside another HTML document
http://en.wikipedia.org/wiki/IFrame

Information Communications Technology (ICT) Systems

As defined by the Information Technology Association of America (ITAA), is "the study, design, development, implementation, support or management of computer-based information systems, particularly software applications and computer hardware." IT deals with the use of electronic computers and computer software to convert, store, protect, process, transmit, and securely retrieve information.
www.wikipedia.org

Information Security Management System (ISMS)

Policy related guidelines in the ISO/IEC 27001 standard.
http://en.wikipedia.org/wiki/ISMS

IP Multimedia Susbsystem (IMS)

An architectural framework for delivering IP multimedia services.
http://en.wikipedia.org/wiki/IP_Multimedia_Subsystem

IP Telephony

Internet (packet switched) based voice communications - also called Voice over IP
http://en.wikipedia.org/wiki/IP_Telephony

IPS

Intrusion Prevention System

IPTV

IPTV is a system where a digital television service is delivered using Internet Protocol over a network infrastructure, which may include delivery by a broadband connection.
www.wikipedia.org

ISO	International Standards Organization
ISO 27000	Is part of a growing family of ISO/IEC ISMS standards, the 'ISO/IEC 27000 series'. ISO/IEC 27000 will be a new international standard entitled: "Information technology - Security techniques - Information security management systems - Overview and vocabulary". http://www.27000.org/
ITIL	Internationally recognized IT governance guidelines http://www.itil-officialsite.com/home/home.asp
ITU	International Telecommunications Union
ITU-T X.805 Recommendations	The International Telecommunications Union (ITU) Sector T coordinates telecommunications standards. X.805 is the specific recommendation. http://www.itu.int/rec/T-REC-X.805/en
Kiviat Chart	Also known as a Kiviat Diagram with three or more quantifiable variables in this case to array security vectors used in the X.805 standard. http://en.wikipedia.org/wiki/Kiviat_diagram
LAN	Local Area Network
Managed Security Service Provider (MSSP).	Is an Internet service provider (ISP) that provides an organization with some amount of network security management, which may include virus blocking, spam blocking, intrusion detection, firewalls, and virtual private network (VPN) management. An MSSP can also handle system changes, modifications, and upgrades. http://searchitchannel.techtarget.com/sDefinition/0,sid96_gci912633,00.html
Mashup	In web development, a mashup is a web application that combines data from more than one source into a single integrated tool. The term Mashup implies easy, fast integration, frequently done by access to open APIs and data sources to produce results that were not the original goal of the data owners. An example is the use of cartographic data from Google Maps to add location information to real-estate data, thereby creating a new and distinct web service that was not originally provided by either source. http://en.wikipedia.org/wiki/Mashup_(web_application_hybrid)

Meta-Data	Meta-data examples: "data about other data" - MP3, cookies, visited web sites, etc. www.wikipedia.org
NERC	North American Electric Reliability Corporation is a non-profit corporation based in Princeton, NJ, was formed on March 28, 2006 as the successor to the North American Electric Reliability Council (also known as NERC). The original NERC was formed on June 1, 1968 by the electric utility industry to promote the reliability and adequacy of bulk power transmission in the electric utility systems of North America. NERC's mission states that it is to "ensure that the bulk power system in North America is reliable." www.wikipedia.org
NIST	National Institute of Standards and Technology is a measurement standards laboratory which is a non-regulatory agency of the United States Department of Commerce. The institute's mission is to promote U.S. innovation and industrial competitiveness by advancing measurement science, standards, and technology in ways that enhance economic security and improve quality of life. www.wikipedia.org
NIST 800-53	Special Publications in the 800 series present documents of general interest to the computer security community. The Special Publication 800 series was established in 1990 to provide a separate identity for information technology security publications. This Special Publication 800 series reports on ITL's research, guidelines, and outreach efforts in computer security, and its collaborative activities with industry, government, and academic organizations. http://csrc.nist.gov/publications/PubsSPs.html
Non-Repudiation	From the ITU-T X.805 Recommendation http://www.itu.int/rec/T-REC-X.805/en
Non-Wall Gardened	Non-wall Gardened – where the network operator can act as a channel. With this model, smaller service providers, enterprises and developers can now use more advanced mobile services in a simple way to provide specific end-user services. www.ericsson.com/mobilityworld/sub/open/ technologies/parlayx/index.html

Payment Card Industry (PCI)	In reference to the Payment Card Industry Data Security Standard (PCI-DSS) providing minimum security standards required of companies that process - transmit cardholder information http://en.wikipedia.org/wiki/PCI_DSS
Perimeter-based security	A term representing the idea that security is applied at the entry-exit points of a network as with firewalls. www.wikipedia.org
Personally Identifiable Information	Data of a personal nature that can be used to uniquely identify a person. http://en.wikipedia.org/wiki/Personally_identifiable_information
Privacy	From the ITU-T X.805 Recommendation http://www.itu.int/rec/T-REC-X.805/en
Public Key Infrastructure	Is a set of hardware, software, people, policies, and procedures needed to create, manage, store, distribute, and revoke digital certificates. www.wikipedia.org
RAN	Radio Access Network
SaaS	Software as a Service (SaaS, typically pronounced 'sass') is a model of software deployment where an application is licensed for use as a service provided to customers on demand. On demand licensing and use alleviates the customer's burden of equipping a device with every application. It also reduces traditional End User Licensing Agreement (EULA) software maintenance, ongoing operation patches, and patch support complexity in an organization. http://en.wikipedia.org/wiki/Software_as_a_service
Sarbanes-Oxley	The legislation came into force in 2002 and introduced major changes to the regulation of financial practice and corporate governance. Named after Senator Paul Sarbanes and Representative Michael Oxley, who were its main architects, it also set a number of deadlines for compliance. The Sarbanes-Oxley Act is arranged into eleven titles. As far as compliance is concerned, the most important sections within these are often considered to be 302, 401, 404, 409, 802 and 906. www.soxlaw.com
Second Life	A Virtual World developed by Linden Lab that launched on June 23, 2003 and is accessible via the Internet. A free

client program called the Second Life Viewer enables its users, called Residents, to interact with each other through avatars. Residents can explore, meet other residents, socialize, participate in individual and group activities, and create and trade virtual property and services with one another, or travel throughout the world, which residents refer to as the grid. Second Life caters for users aged over eighteen, while its sister site Teen Second Life is restricted to users aged between thirteen and eighteen. www.wikipedia.org

Security Defense In-Depth

Is an Information Assurance (IA) strategy in which multiple layers of defense are placed throughout an Information Technology (IT) system. It addresses security vulnerabilities in personnel, technology and operations for the duration of the system's lifecycle. http://www.nsa.gov/snac/support/defenseindepth.pdf

SOA

In computing, service-oriented architecture (SOA) provides methods for systems development and integration where systems group functionality around business processes and package these as interoperable services. An SOA infrastructure allows different applications to exchange data with one another as they participate in business processes. Service-orientation aims at a loose coupling of services with operating systems, programming languages and other technologies which underlie applications.[1] SOA separates functions into distinct units, or services[2], which developers make accessible over a network in order that users can combine and reuse them in the production of business applications.[3] These services communicate with each other by passing data from one service to another, or by coordinating an activity between two or more services. Many commentators see SOA concepts as built upon and evolving from older concepts of distributed computing[3][2] and modular programming. http://en.wikipedia.org/wiki/Service-oriented_architecture

Software as a Service (SaaS)

A model of software deployment where an application is licensed for use as a service provided to customers on demand. On demand licensing and use alleviates the customer's burden of equipping a device with every application. It also reduces traditional end user licensing agreement (EULA) software maintenance, ongoing oper-

ation patches, and patch support complexity in an organization. On demand licensing enables software to become a variable expense, rather than a fixed cost at the time of purchase. It also enables licensing only the amount of software needed versus traditional licenses per device. SaaS also enables the buyer to share licenses across their organization and between organizations, to reduce the cost of acquiring End User License Agreement (EULA) for every device in the firm.
www.wikipedia.org

Statement on Auditing Standards (SAS) 70

In reference to an auditing statement
http://en.wikipedia.org/wiki/SAS_70

STEPS

Security Tool for Evaluating Products and Solutions is a tool developed to aid in design and assessment of security using the ITU-T X.805 Recommendation

System and Data Integrity

From the ITU-T X.805 Recommendation
http://www.itu.int/rec/T-REC-X.805/en

the X.805 standard

Security architecture for systems providing end-to-end communications
http://www.itu.int/rec/T-REC-X.805-200310-I/en

Transmutation

Transmutation used to describe the phenomenon where as an example, a virus delivered by email to compromise computers is now re-crafted for telephony.
www.wikipedia.org

Triple Play

In telecommunications, the triple play service is a marketing term for the provisioning of the two broadband services, high-speed Internet access and television, and one narrowband service, telephone, over a single broadband connection. Triple play focuses on a combined business model rather than solving technical issues or a common standard.
www.wikipedia.org

Voice Over IP (VoIP)

Voice over Internet Protocol (VoIP, IPA:/vəɪp/) is a general term for a family of transmission technologies for delivery of voice communications over IP networks such as the Internet or other packet-switched networks. Other terms frequently encountered and synonymous with VoIP are IP telephony, Internet telephony, voice over broadband (VoBB), broadband telephony, and broadband phone.
http://en.wikipedia.org/wiki/Voice_over_IP

WAN	Wide Area Network
Web 2.0	Web 2.0 describes the changing trends in the use of World Wide Web technology and web design that aim to enhance creativity, communications, secure information sharing, collaboration and functionality of the web. www.wikipedia.org
Web 3.0	Web. 3.0 is one of the terms used to describe the evolutionary stage of the Web that follows Web 2.0. Also called the semantic web. www.wikipedia.org
World Wide Web	World Wide Web is a system of interlinked hypertext documents accessed via the Internet www.wikipedia.org
Zero-Day or Zero Second Attack	Is defined as a timed attack that takes place within a short time span, usually less than one day (hence the term "zero day"). Zero day attacks are carefully orchestrated to do the maximum damage in one day because traditional anti-virus tools (software patches, Norton antivirus) do not have enough time to react. A Zero Second attack is a derivation from Zero day to communicate the idea that there may not even be 24 hours, the attack could occur without warning as the vector remains hidden from detection until the moment of the attack. Detection at this point occurs as the attack has already created its intended impact. http://www.dba-oracle.com/t_zero_day_attack_definition.htm

Index